FORENSIC ARCHAEOLOGY: ADVANCES IN THEORY AND PRACTICE

John Hunter
and
Margaret Cox

Routledge
Taylor & Francis Group

LONDON AND NEW YORK

First published 2005
by Routledge
2 Park Square, Milton Park, Abingdon, Oxon OX14 4RN

Simultaneously published in the USA and Canada
by Routledge
270 Madison Ave, New York, NY 10016

Routledge is an imprint of the Taylor & Francis Group

© 2005 John Hunter and Margaret Cox.
Individual contributions © 2005 individual contributors

Typeset in Sabon by
Keystroke, Jacaranda Lodge, Wolverhampton
Printed and bound in Great Britain by
TJ International Ltd, Padstow, Cornwall

British Library Cataloguing in Publication Data
A catalogue record for this book is available from the British Library

Library of Congress Cataloging in Publication Data

ISBN 0–415–27311–0 (hbk)
ISBN 0–415–27312–9 (pbk)

CONTENTS

FIGURES

TABLES

CONTRIBUTORS

Paul Cheetham is Senior Lecturer at the University of Bournemouth. He has an extensive background in field archaeology, archaeological computing and geophysics, as well as being an experienced forensic practitioner in the UK and he has also worked internationally. He has undertaken archaeological geophysical work on the World Heritage sites of Fountains Abbey, Jarlshof and Pompeii, and through his teaching and research continues to explore areas of interface between archaeological and forensic sciences.

Margaret Cox is Head of the Forensic and Bioarchaeological Sciences Group at Bournemouth University where she is Professor of Forensic Archaeology and Anthropology and Director of Forensic Programmes. She is an experienced forensic archaeologist and anthropologist who has worked in the UK, who has also worked in Cyprus, Rwanda, Kosovo and Iraq. She is also an experienced biological anthropologist assessing archaeological remains and has published extensively in both the archaeological and forensic spheres. Since 1999 she has been the UK Government Ministry of Defence's Forensic Anthropologist and regularly examines the remains of British service personnel from previous conflicts. Margaret is also the Chief Executive Officer and Founder of the Inforce Foundation (International Forensic Centre of Excellence for the Investigation of Genocide).

Robert Dilley qualified as solicitor in 1974 and worked in local government and private practice specialising in Civil and Criminal Law. He was a Senior Lecturer at Bournemouth University where he taught in the School of Finance and Law. He had particular interests in forensic skills, human rights, criminal litigation and expert evidence. Robert died in June 2005.

William D. Haglund is Director of the International Forensic Program for Physicians for Human Rights, Washington, DC. His previous experience includes: Chief Medical Investigator of the King County Medical Examiner's Office; and United Nations' Senior Forensic Advisor for the International Criminal Tribunals for Rwanda and the Former Yugoslavia. He has organised and directed forensic missions including those in Guatemala, Honduras, Rwanda, Somaliland, Georgia/Abkhazia, the former Yugoslavia, Cyprus, Sri Lanka, Indonesia and Afghanistan.

Ian Hanson is an archaeologist and forensic consultant who has worked as a professional rescue and research archaeologist since 1994 on excavations in Europe, Africa and the Middle East. Since 1997 he has undertaken forensic work for the United Nations, the International Criminal Tribunal for the Former Yugoslavia (UN ICTY), Fundación de Antropología Forense de Guatemala (FAFG), Kenyon International Emergency Services, the Inforce Foundation and the UK Police; he has spent over 24 months in the field in Bosnia, Croatia, Guatemala, DR Congo, Cyprus and Iraq investigating genocide, war crimes and human rights.

John Hunter is Professor of Ancient History and Archaeology at the University of Birmingham, UK, where he specialises in forensic archaeology, the archaeology of Scotland, and cultural resource management. He has published widely on all three, and this is his second co-authored textbook on forensic archaeology. He helped found the Forensic Search Advisory Group and lectures widely to police forces and other law enforcement agencies throughout the UK as well as working operationally in the field or acting as a consultant in forensic cases. He has experience working in the Balkans and in Iraq, and is a registered forensic archaeologist and lead assessor in forensic archaeology for the Council for the Registration of Forensic Practitioners.

Tal Simmons lectures in the Department of Forensic and Investigative Sciences, University of Central Lancashire, UK, with interests in humanitarian forensic anthropology, taphonomy, population variation in techniques of age estimation, and trauma. Her past appointments include: Director, Forensic Monitoring Project (Bosnia), Physicians for Human Rights; Senior Forensic Consultant (Kosova), Organization for Security and Cooperation in Europe; Lab Director for PHR (Cyprus); consultant to PHR (Sri Lanka), FAFG and CAFCA (Guatemala).

Jon Sterenberg is an experienced field archaeologist who has worked on the archaeological investigation of mass graves since 1997. He has interests in geophysics and GIS and been employed by the International Criminal Tribunal for former Yugoslavia (ICTY), the United Nations in Sierra Leone (UNAMSIL) and the International Commission on Missing Persons (ICMP). He has worked in Iraq on behalf of the Coalition Provisional Authority (CPA) and is now Director of Exhumation and Examination for ICMP in Sarajevo.

Richard Wright is Emeritus Professor of Anthropology at the University of Sydney with a wide archaeological experience in Australia as well as interests in human osteology. He worked for the Australian government on mass graves in the Ukraine in 1990–91 and was pre-eminent in demonstrating the value of archaeological methodology. He was appointed Chief Archaeologist for the UN's International Criminal Tribunal for the Former Yugoslavia 1997–2000 and has special interests in the events following the fall of Srebrenica in July 1995.

ACKNOWLEDGEMENTS

Many professional colleagues and friends have provided advice and encouragement in the preparation and writing of this volume. In particular, the authors would like to thank Barrie Simpson, Paul Cheetham, Mick Swindells and Gerry Cronin for helpful comments on the text. Much of the photographic and graphic work was carried out by Graham Norrie and Henry Buglass respectively, and the authors would also like to acknowledge the support of the University of Birmingham (JH) and Bournemouth University (MC), as well as the Arts and Humanities Research Board. The authors are also indebted to the many police forces who kindly gave permission to use material: Durham Constabulary; Greater Manchester Police; Gwent Police; Hertfordshire Constabulary; Leicestershire Constabulary; The Metropolitan Police; Nottinghamshire Constabulary; the Police Force of Northern Ireland; The Royal Falklands Police; West Mercia Police; West Midlands Police; West Yorkshire Police; and Wiltshire Constabulary. Individual illustrations are acknowledged, as appropriate, in the captions.

Every effort has been made to acknowledge the copyright holders, but in a few cases this has not been possible. Any omissions brought to our attention will be remedied in future editions.

1

INTRODUCTION

1.1 Background

Most people have heard of archaeology, and many people have now met an archaeologist. Media portrayal of archaeology has been much improved and the images presented by the *Time Team* or similar programmes are far removed from erstwhile barrow robbers, esoteric professors or Indiana Jones figures. Archaeology has moved on, bolstered by public awareness of 'the past' in its various forms, and strengthened by a raft of legislative measures and planning directives dealing with archaeological sites and monuments as part of a wider concern with matters of heritage. Changes in attitude have recognised archaeology's social value, and the impact of development in both town and countryside has highlighted its practical importance. Both have provided the archaeologist with a more respectable public profile.

At the beginning of the twenty-first century there were probably some 4,500 archaeologists working in the UK (Aitchison 1999: 6) compared with mere hundreds 30 years ago. Many of these posts are based in local government, especially within planning departments, but many others have sprung up as private consultancies or within engineering or environmental companies to support the wider position of heritage in development work. There is a co-ordinating professional organisation – the Institute of Field Archaeologists (IFA) – to which many belong, and there are a variety of published works which attest to the archaeologists' role in the wider context of the construction industry, in landscape management, and in the general development arena (e.g. DoE 1990; Hunter and Ralston 1993; Hey and Lacey 2001; Darvill and Russell 2002). Archaeological sites are assessed and evaluated in advance of threats; some become excavated as an integral part of the development process. Archaeology has become sanitised, part of a larger corporate activity and, although it intrinsically maintains a research dimension as *raison d'être*, its practitioners cut fairly mundane figures in comparison to earlier perceptions.

However, the evolution to professionalism has an important corollary. The archaeologist's role is now formalised and established, and is contained within the processes of the work of other professional groups. Archaeologists function within a commercial market place where costing and ability to conform to agreed procedures and time-scales are understood. What may have been lost in the free spirit of thirst for knowledge and understanding has been balanced out by professional recognition. This itself has made it easier to support archaeology's credibility in the transition to a forensic context – a complete shift of paradigm into the working environment of other forensic professionals.

1.2 Archaeology in a forensic environment

The potential application of archaeological theory to scenes of crime, either in search or recovery scenarios is now well attested, and the following chapters contain a number of case studies in illustration. Since 1988 when archaeological endeavours began to be absorbed seriously by police forces in the UK, and with the first review published some six years later (Hunter 1994), the relationship between archaeology and criminal investigation has slowly developed and been moulded through experience and better understanding. Academic respectability has largely followed in its wake, but not without suspicion from academic purists, and with the attendant difficulty of not knowing whether its publication niche lay in either archaeological or forensic literature. It has not been a prolific area of publication partly for this reason, and partly because the discipline is developing rapidly and still finding its feet in a context which is substantially *sub judice*. Its emergence has been flagged by textbooks (in the USA, Morse *et al.* 1983; in the UK, Hunter *et al.* 1996), critical reviews (e.g. Hunter 1999, 2001; Cox 2001a), papers offering technical guidance (e.g. Dirkmaat and Adovasio 1997) important new avenues of interest such as taphonomy (e.g. Haglund and Sorg 1997; 2002), and the advent of mass grave investigation (e.g. Schmitt 2002; Haglund 2002; Haglund *et al.* 2001). The growth of forensic archaeology in mass graves has merited an additional chapter in this volume (Chapter 5). In the USA, growth of interest is reflected in a complete volume of the *Journal of Historical Archaeology* dedicated to exploring the parameters of the new field in an attempt to 'define the role of archaeology and archaeologists in forensic work' (Scott and Connor 2001: 101).

This evolution of forensic archaeology has been far from smooth and tends to mirror the earlier US experience where similar nascent problems were also encountered (see Jackson 2002), but aggravated by confusion between the respective roles of anthropologists and archaeologists (Haglund 2001: 27). However, much of the problem is one of external perception. Difficulties encountered at professional level inevitably reflect a more fundamental public misunderstanding of the nature of archaeology and its forensic application. Unfortunately, the term 'forensic archaeology' is popularly used in TV archaeology in relation to investigation of, for example, the diseases and traumas of Egyptian mummies, the food consumed by ancient bog victims, battlefield sites, or the fate of the famous iceman, the Neolithic 'Otzi' in the higher reaches of the Austrian/Italian Alps. Here there is confusion between the words 'science' and 'forensic'. While these archaeological problems employ investigative science into the fate of human remains, they are not in themselves 'forensic' in that the issues concerned are unrelated to legal matters or courts of law. A cartoon published in *The Guardian* (Figure 1.1) which shows two 'forensic archaeologists' examining an elderly refrigerator, and endeavouring to determine whether it was male or female, typifies the misconception. It is, nevertheless, satisfying, if ironic, that the same cartoon now places the newly-coined term 'forensic archaeologist' firmly within popular culture.

'Forensic' is a word with a peculiar attraction which media companies deliberately exploit in order to boost circulation or viewing figures, and this explains the plethora of TV drama series focusing on pathology, criminology, and investigative science (see also Chapter 8, Section 8.1.2). The word has a perceived glamour status, quite different from reality, largely through being substantially misunderstood as a term. Its inherent attraction is also exploited by a number of UK universities offering vocational degree

Figure 1.1 Part of cartoon
published in *The Guardian*
11 November 2000

Source: courtesy of Steven Appleby.

programmes which focus on forensic science, usually with a biochemistry base. Forensic archaeology is a very minor discipline by comparison: there are currently only three UK universities which offer the subject as a component or module of their undergraduate Archaeology programmes (Birmingham, Bradford and Bournemouth) with a total throughput of some 80–90 students annually since the mid-1990s. These are modules which provide awareness, intellectual breadth and technical understanding, as opposed to vocational opportunity. Such modules are popular, but students learn quickly the fictitious nature of TV drama and the artificiality of sedate village murders in the Home Counties. Instead, the reality is with social sub-cultures – prostitution, drugs dealing, and paedophilia – contexts in which the value of human life has little meaning, where torture, abuse and corruption are standard, and where sexual depravity and perversion are high profile. Much of the investigation concerns children and the sexual abuse of children. It entails the practitioner coming to terms with him/her self, becoming detached from the emotional issues involved, and expressing views objectively in court. This is not a pleasant arena, but is one where archaeology has an important role to play, and a context of which all archaeology students should at least have some awareness. Archaeology's new social and political role in the excavation of mass graves resulting from alleged genocides in Central and South America and in the former Yugoslavia (Chapter 5) makes this awareness all the more pertinent (e.g. Stover and Peress 1998; Stover and Ryan 2001).

Forensic archaeology is not simply the definition of an area of overlapping disciplines, nor the application of techniques from one discipline to another. It involves the transference of theory and underlying principles into an unusual context. Apart from judicial constraints and investigation processes, it requires knowledge of other scene professionals (the pathologist, forensic scientist, etc.) in the same way that the developer archaeologist has familiarity with the requirements and language of relevant professional groups working within the construction industry (e.g. engineers, surveyors, architects and plant contractors). *Gravitas* apart, perhaps there is little real difference, except that the point of contact is more acute and the various skill bases require a greater degree of active integration. For example, a major incident draws in, at short notice, a range of individuals (Figure 1.2) representing a host of different operational roles and an equally diverse range of technical and academic backgrounds. None of these individuals can work effectively without understanding the evidential requirements or function of others in the group. The archaeological sector, therefore, has some responsibility to ensure that the nature of its own contribution is understood within this wider community. Some of the new disciplines will be familiar to the archaeologist, although their development will have followed a forensic trajectory, such as in ecology (e.g. Hall 1997; Brown *et al.* 2002), geophysics (e.g. Davis *et al.* 2000), conservation (Janaway 2002) or spatial patterning (e.g. Scott 2001) where both the aims and the context will be unusual. Others may almost certainly be more alien such as ballistics, entomology, biochemistry and a range of forensic sciences. Furthermore, an ostensibly simple exercise of mission poses a number of problems, partly in accessing the different professional groups in collective situations, and partly in having to target some 43 different police forces in the UK.

The number of homicides in the UK is recorded annually by Home Office statistics (typically 700–800 each year), but probably less than some 15 per cent of the total will ideally require an archaeological approach, either through burial or surface scatter. According to word of mouth and anecdote, probably half this 15 per cent is recovered archaeologically in circumstances where there has been a briefing for all concerned, the disposal site has been identified, and an archaeologist has been properly integrated into the search and recovery process. In those burials where archaeologists are not utilised (also from word of mouth and anecdote), the victims are presumably dug up without awareness or full understanding of the evidential importance of contextual integrity and contamination. This may be through necessity of speed following from an enforced custody timetable (see Chapter 7, Section 7.2), possibly because the victim may have already been recovered during an existing operation, or as a result of the perceived costs. In some instances, the location of the body may be known, the offender may have made a full confession, and the idea of introducing specialists when a case was ostensibly already sewn up may seem an unnecessary luxury to a pressured Senior Investigating Officer (SIO) working within financial constraints.

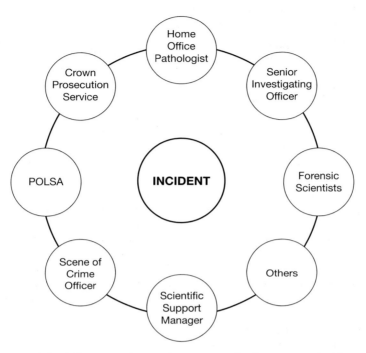

Figure 1.2 Some of the different professional groups involved in a major incident

Many police forces now happily accept archaeological support, recognise its value, and invite archaeologists in as soon as the occasion demands. This stems from years of 'mission' through presentations, conference papers, publications and case involvement. Moreover, Crown Court homicide verdicts have used archaeological evidence on several occasions – a fact which itself lays non-archaeological victim recovery open to more exacting cross-examination. It may also have necessitated a higher element of back-covering in the field, but at least this ensures that both prosecution and defence agencies are becoming more primed as to the nature and value of archaeological evidence and the importance of archaeological input. Case experience has now developed a clear line of thinking that is slowly being adopted: namely, that successful conviction can depend on effective archaeological recovery, and that proper recovery in its turn can depend on prudent and considered searching. There is no real division of archaeological process between search and recovery; and that to create such a division may have the effect of reducing the amount of evidence that can be recovered.

1.3 The forensic process in the UK

In a typical incident involving buried human remains the archaeologist will be responsible to the *Senior Investigating Officer* (SIO) who has absolute responsibility for outcome. The SIO will have progressed through police ranks to a senior position, the current role being one for which management skills are paramount. While not necessarily possessing specialist forensic science knowledge or awareness themselves, they have access to such advice which they are then at liberty to reject or accept as they see fit. Training at this level is management-based, and undertaken at a number of regional centres where archaeological content, other than as part of a case study, is unlikely to feature. However, there has been persistent and successful archaeological input at a number of centres, notably at the National Crime and Operations Faculty (CENTREX), and at the Scottish Police College at Tulliallan, the latter providing a central catchment for all police training in Scotland. Experience has shown that when SIOs decide to use archaeological expertise, this occurs most frequently from open-mindedness in taking advice. Less frequently, it results from additional awareness training or from personal interest.

This advice can come from many quarters, notably from the *Scientific Support Manager* (SSM), whose scene role will be to advise the SIO on any areas of expertise, specialism, or equipment that a particular incident may require. SSMs are key personnel in any major incident and some targeting has been successful at the regular conferences on scientific support which take place under the auspices of the Association of Chief Police Officers (ACPO). Similarly, in search scenarios, key figures will be the Police Search Advisors (POLSAs) who are specially trained in search techniques, and who can advise accordingly on necessary equipment and skills. The majority of police search operations are directed towards the recovery of arms, drugs or stolen goods, but a significant number are concerned with missing persons and dedicated courses in which archaeology is integrated are offered at a central training facility in Kent.

Scene of Crime Officers (SOCOs), now increasingly referred to as *Crime Scene Examiners* (CSEs) or *Forensic Investigators* (FIs), are the most likely personnel with whom the archaeologist will have working contact at an incident. The similarity between scene of crime work and archaeological excavation is considerable (Hunter *et al.* 1996, 47f), and there are an increasing number of SOCOs with formal qualifications in archaeology. Both are front line and essentially 'hands on' involving recording, photography, sampling and recovery of material. SOCO training is provided through a small number of training centres, notably the National Training Centre at Harperley Hall, Durham, which also runs an intensive forensic archaeology course with the University of Birmingham. Archaeologists also have regular input into forensic courses run through the Metropolitan Police Force.

Most major incidents will be attended by the *Forensic Scientists*. The Forensic Science Service, now effectively privatised, and supplemented by private commercial organisations, consists of specialists in a range of fields most notably fibres, biochemistry (blood, DNA) and toxicology. Access to the FSS is through individual laboratories, although many committed forensic scientists attend conferences, especially regular meetings of the Forensic Science Society where new issues or awareness can be targeted. The same venues may also allow contact with other, less frequently used experts (e.g. entomologists, geologists or ecologists).

Any incident involving human remains will require the attentions of a Coroner, and an appointed *Home Office Pathologist*, usually based at one of the recognised regional medico-legal centres. The archaeologist will often work with the pathologist in order to recover the victim and maximise the available evidence. Some pathologists have been less sympathetic than others in this situation, perhaps justifiably, bearing in mind that their forensic opinions are usually crucial factors in subsequent court proceedings. This is probably the key area of mission, partly through the need to exercise collaboration in the recovery process, and partly through the growing presence and interests of forensic anthropologists in both the recovery and post-mortem analysis (see Chapter 6). Given the relatively small number of forensic pathologists, targeting is straightforward, and mutual understanding has been boosted by the close working relationships between archaeologists, anthropologists and pathologists in mass grave situations during recent years (see also Chapter 5).

Once the physical investigation of the case is complete and the various supporting agencies have left, the *Crown Prosecution Service* (CPS) will be presented with the case data and begin to sift through the evidence and evaluate the various contributions. If lawyers have little or no understanding of archaeological evidence, the data may be undervalued or even unrecognised. Equally, defence counsel may need priming in order to seize an opportunity to exploit archaeological shortcomings in the prosecution. All cases are different: in some, obvious archaeological benefits are put to one side because the case can be addressed more effectively without further 'confusion'; in others, the archaeological evidence is drawn in to create a more complete picture, even although the archaeological evidence on its own is neither strong nor convincing. Each case will be addressed on its own merits and the value of the prosecution evidence weighted according to strategy. This does not, of course, mean that the defence counsel will adopt a similar weighting, nor that it will view the archaeological evidence in the same light. Archaeologists who have worked with barristers will know that awareness of archaeological principles is best attained on a 'per case' basis delivered in a jargon-free, readily understandable and logical manner that can be easily consumed by a jury. The jury's awareness and perception, however, are another matter altogether, but it is behoven upon the witness to ensure that the jury understands the evidence presented if justice is to be achieved.

Straightforward awareness training among these different professional groups is not a solution in itself because the process is two-way: the archaeologist needs to be able to understand the evidential requirements of other personnel, the methods that are used, scene etiquette, the protocols that apply, and the legal parameters within which the incident is investigated (Chapter 7). There are now calls to extend this to include knowledge of human rights, ballistics, weaponry, as well as a greater understanding of modern artefacts from buried environments (e.g. Stover and Ryan 2001, 24), and the US literature contains much useful guidance based on first-hand experience (e.g. Haglund 2001). Furthermore, although the searching for buried human remains can utilise the essential principles of desktop landscape analysis (Chapter 2), experience has also shown a wider picture of involvement. Successful location of remains may often entail psychological understanding of the likely suspect – 'offender profiling' as it has become known (e.g. Britton 1997; Stevens 1997) – and the archaeologist is drawn into the realm of behaviour psychology not only in the generality of crime patterning, but also in the specific profile of the individual in question. It is now clear that offenders tend to dispose of their victims according to predictable patterns based on a range of complex factors including gender, age and personal relationship, location, geographical awareness, and vehicle involvement (e.g. Boudreaux *et al.* 1999; Morton and Lord 2002). While this equation may not provide empirical answers to search problems, it does at least provide a starting point, for example, using the central statistics derived from previous cases and held by the Centralised Analytical Team Collating Homicide Expertise and Management (CATCHEM) at Derbyshire Constabulary. The

Figure 1.3 Students excavating and recording a half-sectioned grave containing buried (plastic) human remains

forensic archaeologist needs to understand a wide range of issues, and needs to be able to incorporate other disciplines within an already burgeoning framework of potential evidence.

While there is no substitute for a field background, a number of courses have been run to support archaeologists in this venture: Bournemouth University commenced an MSc in *Forensic Archaeology* (1996) and Bradford University an MSc in *Forensic Archaeology and Crime Scene Management* (2003), both endeavouring to recruit graduates in archaeology, law, and biological subject areas as well as law enforcement professionals in order to resolve this two-way problem in awareness and training; Birmingham, Bradford and Bournemouth Universities have also run short courses intended for both archaeologists and law enforcement officers; and the University of Durham now hosts an the annual American Armed Forces course on forensic archaeology and anthropology which draws in tutors from a range of British and US institutions.

1.4 Growing pains

The experiences of archaeology's hesitant steps into the UK forensic arena chime well with those in the USA where Jackson's narrative (2002) of the evolution of NecroSearch International (a voluntary group set up to provide assistance in the locating and recovery of homicide victims) provides remarkably close parallels – the occasional embarrassment of getting the protocols wrong, the suspicion viewed by other professionals unfamiliar with archaeological evidence, the feeling of complete loneliness and overwhelming responsibility at a scene of crime, even the uncertainty of how much to charge. These are genuine difficulties when a new discipline (archaeology) enters an existing environment of established procedures (criminal investigation).

1.4.1 General working arrangements

Experience has shown that as much time is often spent waiting around as in being active at a scene of a crime. The nature of some investigations is such as to require a range of scene personnel arriving from different places and working to unpredictable schedules. The Home Office pathologist is a notable example and investigation or recovery of human remains usually has to tread water until his/her arrival and opinion, often a matter of hours. Other common delays may be caused through ensuring the scene is appropriately recorded before work commences, ensuring that necessary health and safety factors are covered, and that everything is in place for the due collection of evidence for legal purpose. There have been frustrating occasions when archaeologists have arrived at the appropriate rendezvous police station at the agreed time of 8.00 a.m., found themselves waiting for an hour drinking coffee until other personnel gather, then escorted to the scene, started work at 10 a.m., only to discover that the whole exercise shut down for lunch at 12.30. Technical difficulties, finding the right equipment or personnel, obtaining a decision from an absentee SIO, or awaiting results of a witness interview have all posed delays. Work only commences when everything is in place. The archaeologist, like any other specialist, is there to be switched on and off.

Archaeological participation is not a God-given right – it depends on the awareness, intuition and caution of the SIO or other appropriate authorities (see also Sonderman 2001, for a US analogy). There have been a small number of occasions when the archaeological conviction of the SIO has not been fully shared by others at the scene, whose perception of the archaeologist has been limited to comments about buried treasure and the inevitable snigger. There have been a substantial number of scenes in which the archaeologist has played a major role (below); there are those where it is clear that archaeologists could have been of value but have not been used, and there have also been a number of false alarms, notably those involving the buried remains of animals (e.g. Chapter 4, case 22).

Operations run at various speeds. In some instances there has been a relatively slow process of events through briefings, field visits, and investigations. This often reflects the fact that the incident was several years old, or that preparations needed to be handled sensitively. Others go faster, particularly if a potential offender was in custody, a warrant was needed, or a grave located in unexpected circumstances. If specialist (e.g. archaeological) input was necessary, all courtesies, facilities and tolerance were available to achieve the desired outcome. No support was too much, no problem too difficult to resolve, all associated personnel could be immediately contactable on a range of telephone numbers day and night to give support, and the archaeologist was made to feel appropriately important. However, once the work was completed and the statement produced, the same personnel moved on to the next scene of investigation and it became remarkably difficult to make contact or sustain enthusiasm. An event which may have been of mind-blowing interest and importance to the archaeologist was just one of many similar jobs that a scene of crime officer or detective experienced that month. Only when preparations were made to bring the case to court were the archaeologists again brought back into the system, hounded into preparing evidence, made to stand in the witness box and again feel the focus of attention. And when the exercise was complete, they were reconsigned to forensic nothingness as the world moved on and other (non-archaeological) cases absorbed the time and efforts of the other forensic personnel. It is as well for the archaeologist to appreciate the transient nature of forensic involvement from the outset. Nevertheless, the need to avoid 'dabbling' in forensic archaeology in order to maintain professional integrity (Crist 2001: 45) is inevitably in conflict with the small case load available.

It may also be important to recognise that the archaeologist, like all other specialists, may not be privy to the full data available on an investigation. SIOs tend to retain certain elements of information which reflect significant features of the offender's *modus operandi* or facts which may be known only to the offender. This withholding of information is standard practice. It allows the SIO to share exclusively a specific aspect of a case with the offender to ensure rightful conviction. Inevitably, this may affect the interests of a specialist involved in the enquiry, making it all the more important that each SIO should be familiar with the nature of archaeological evidence and of methods used to retrieve such evidence. Equally, there will be cases where previous avenues of enquiry have proved fruitless, where location and recovery of the body are paramount and where the SIO will rely heavily on newly developed skills (or skills not used in the previous enquiry) in cold case review. In such circumstances there may be a greater degree of openness, for example, in the search for a missing young marine (Chapter 2, case 1), or two missing children (Chapter 2, case 2). In both, the archaeologists were integrated fully into the enquiry rather than being introduced and discharged at specific points which the SIO felt appropriate. Moreover, as archaeological case experience grows, SIOs have increasingly relied on the archaeologist for information on previous incidents, for example, how the situations differed, what the main problems were, and how the various complexities were satisfactorily resolved. Some forces/units maintain their own preferred archaeologist – a person they commissioned through recommendation on an earlier occasion, one with whom they have established a successful working relationship, and one in whom they have confidence. The key to all successful scene operations is teamwork and the ability of the individual parties to find the situation mutually acceptable.

It has been especially important for an archaeologist in these situations to remember the importance of scientific impartiality, that the work is not necessarily a quest to support the SIO's case. The same degree of neutrality also occurs in advising defence or appeal clients, for example, in a scenario where a child had been discovered partially buried in woodland, where a conviction had been obtained, but where there was subsequent doubt as to whether the body had been moved in the interval between murder and discovery (Chapter 2, case 11). The exercise was not to find evidence that might support an appeal process, but to review the evidence objectively and to pass opinion (see Chapter 7). The need for impartiality is even more apparent in court where the archaeologist takes the role of expert witness and carries responsibility not just for the case in question but for the profession as a whole.

1.4.2 The search process

Searches have involved the elimination of land as much as finding the remains in question. Not finding remains is not a measure of failure, but a reminder that forensic archaeology is as much about negative evidence and of elimination, as it is of discovery. A substantial number of cases have involved disproving allegations of burial, these allegations normally adhering to a particular pattern (see Chapter 2). Technical aids, notably aerial photography and geophysical surveying, also bring their own problems. These can unfortunately be viewed as 'black box' solutions without much understanding of their effectiveness or limitations by police authorities or, in some instances, even by their operators when transferred from a civilian to a forensic environment (also Chapter 2). The fact that one method may not register any anomalies does not necessarily mean that the area can be eliminated. All methods work on different principles and are of varying forensic value (see Killam 1990; Davenport 2001; France *et al.* 1997: 500f; Buck 2003). Anomalous features seen from the air or through geophysical techniques involve a commitment: they will all need to be investigated by intervention, perhaps even if they are of the wrong size or character, or located in an inappropriate place. Once these techniques have been applied, the enquiry has no option but to follow them through and eliminate each one, irrespective of their perceived value.

Awareness of the range of techniques and their developments has been startlingly narrow among some police forces and, on the misunderstanding that all techniques do much the same, choice seems to have been made according to price. The Forensic Search Advisory Group (FSAG) was established precisely to counter this, and with much success (below). Through the FSAG, police forces and their Scientific Support Managers (SSMs) have increasingly introduced the archaeologist at an early stage into the search process, one typical case in the West Midlands eventually drawing on specialists in archaeology, archaeozoology, anthropology and cremations (Chapter 2, case 5). Search work has often been undertaken in tandem with specialist Police Search Advisors (POLSAs) and their teams whose role in investigations of missing persons has increased considerably during the last decade. However, their protocols and techniques have evolved from counter-terrorist origins, as well as searching for drugs, firearms, stolen goods, etc. and can be at variance with those of the archaeologist. The two have to work as an integrated team; experience has shown that each can learn much from the other.

A substantial number of archaeological sites, particularly those in rural areas, consist of open ground in the form of fields or hillsides which lends itself well to geophysical survey. It provides the opportunity for large-scale survey within which individual anomalies can be identified against a larger background, and these landscapes generally possess a low background 'noise' which enables such anomalies to stand out. On urban sites both the size and background tend to make geophysical survey untenable (although radar is sometimes utilised). In forensic situations, the environment has tended to retain the disadvantages of the urban model. Many scenarios have occurred in back gardens (see Chapter 2, case 4) where the survey area is relatively small, the ground surface

11

variable, and the background disturbance significant. But on the positive side, many gardens have contained grassy areas which provide for easier survey, although open spaces have tended not to feature as disposal locations (for an exception, see Erzinclioglu 2000, 170). Experience has also shown that the majority of gardens investigated required initial clearance of rubbish, overgrowth, rotting household material, dog excrement and general squalor before work could commence – a process which itself could have the effect of disturbing surface evidence.

Even in completely rural areas the environment can be unaccommodating. On Saddleworth Moor, for example (see Chapter 2, case 8), which provided an image of open landscape amenable to geophysics, there is a substantial difference between what is possible in *theory* and what is possible in *practice*. Considered clinically, the landscape lent itself well to radar, resistivity and magnetometry, but the practical difficulties of surface terrain, geomorphology, and waterlogging made for a much less comfortable application (Figure 1.4). The learning experience has been simply that successful geophysical survey requires the landscape, substrate, hydrological regime and environment to be seen at first hand before techniques or sequences of techniques are chosen.

Unfortunately, this is not always possible and often the information supplied in advance of an operation has been less than desirable, usually through necessity in order to prevent any suspicion. It may simply not have been possible to view a person's garden or an area of landscape in any detail before a warrant was issued or before a search could commence. While this may have little bearing on the overall investigation, it can have considerable impact on the use of geophysical survey: in one case, a small modern estate dwelling appeared to have a grassy rear garden according to aerial photography and neither the present nor previous tenant had been contacted regarding this history of the garden in case it aroused unnecessary interest. The archaeologists had attended to undertake resistivity survey on the basis of the grass cover but, on entry, discovered that the previous tenant had concreted the entire area. The present tenant, in turn, had broken it with a sledge hammer, covered it with topsoil and turfed it over. The presence of the (hidden) concrete completely invalidated the resistance equipment. In another case, archaeologists had prepared to undertake a sensitive magnetometer survey in a defined area of a churchyard. However, in order to keep the activity discreet, the investigating officers had erected a large screen supported by iron scaffolding around the area and effectively made the instrument useless. This was the fault of the archaeologists in not making the appropriate preparations and enquiries. Aerial photographs taken from a single helicopter run are often useful in providing intelligence (see Chapter 2, case 6), but sometimes the topography is obscure, and the scale of important ground disturbances difficult to interpret. In one instance, a briefing defined the search area on the basis of an aerial photograph as being 'about the size of a tennis court', while in reality it was almost the size of a football pitch. Unfortunately the equipment and resources had already been organised on the basis of the former.

1.4.3 The recovery process

Fundamental to archaeological theory is stratigraphy which has an important role to play, not only in the excavation of graves but also in the evaluation of disturbed ground. In a number of instances, murder enquiries have targeted a specific garden or defined area (see Chapter 2) where surface disturbance required investigation. In a typical

Figure 1.4 Practical difficulties during geophysical survey caused by topography and vegetation in a moorland landscape

case in north-east England an individual had been missing and a number of areas of newly dug soil had been identified by police in the individual's garden. These needed checking and the garden eliminating. The archaeological response was to excavate narrow trenches across each disturbance, or to half-section them in order to identify the depth of natural deposits and the nature of the infill/disturbance in section. The methodology was of great interest to the scene of crime personnel who immediately grasped the concept of stratigraphic investigation and the efficiency with which it could be done to eliminate the individual disturbances. The SIO, however, was unable to grasp the concept, was unconvinced and insisted on all the investigated areas being excavated totally to a depth well into natural undisturbed deposits. Perhaps, more charitably, he needed to satisfy himself in his own mind as the person ultimately responsible, that the garden could be fully eliminated.

Stratigraphy has also been a frequent issue in the unexpected discovery of human remains usually occurring in building construction, development work generally, or by members of the public walking their dogs. Increasingly these remains are now being left *in situ* where they can be contextually examined, but there have been many instances when they have been removed before any record could be made. In one, the remains were removed but a marker stake 'helpfully' placed on the ground surface above an exposed section rather than in the section itself where it would have been of some use. These stray bone scenarios continue to be especially awkward: the task usually lies in demonstrating either that there is an articulated burial adjacent, or that there is not – an interpretation which might be severely hindered by post-depositional factors such as ploughing (e.g. Haglund *et al.* 2002). In the case of the former, progress is straight-forward and the burial may even be relatively easy to date, but in the latter the remains have to be explained as a product of redeposition from another place, or as resulting from scavenging or disturbance, and this is less easy to demonstrate. Some ambiguities have been resolved by radiocarbon dating, by using the phenomenon of high weapon radiation in the atmosphere in the 1950–1963 period (e.g. Ubelaker 2001), but this only provides a coarse definition for elimination purposes.

Scavenging can produce awkward circumstances, particularly if the disposal of the body is on the present ground surface (Chapter 2, case 10). Individual elements of skeletal disarticulation then have to be identified, often in varied vegetation where they can become partly concealed by leaves and organic matter, and where there is no clear definition of search boundary. The issue is inevitably aggravated, as in one particular case where a small boy was dumped and scavenged in woodland (Chapter 4, case 26), if animals such as badgers remove elements of the body to underground locations. There have been other instances where the remains resulted from accidental or suicidal rather than criminal activity, the problems being in establishing whether the human remains have been deliberately buried (i.e. by human and probably criminal action) and partly eroded out or, alternatively, have become buried (i.e. by natural formation processes, hill wash, etc., Figure 1.5). This is a distinction which archaeologists are well equipped to resolve (Chapter 4, case 25).

Experience has shown, however, in all instances of 'stray' or ambiguous disposals, that the single most frequent problem encountered has been that caused by human activity, by trampling or other actions, usually in all innocence by investigating authorities. In some scenarios, particularly in enclosed spaces such as gardens, the number of personnel can have significant implications in detecting vegetation or topographical anomalies, or even in operating effectively. Equally, there have been occasions when trenches have been dug, either by hand or machine, and where only the archaeologist has been competent to clean or examine the base or sections. The remaining personnel, often numbering over 20, spent much of the day watching. Work at a scene is role based, but it requires certain personnel to be on hand even if they are not immediately active. It is also helpful to know when shifts occur and the points at which overtime kicks in. For the former there is always a potential hiatus and possible retraining process; for the latter, a noticeable enthusiasm by staff in being retained operationally.

Naturally enough, in matters of recovery, SIOs and pathologists have varied considerably in their acceptance and treatment of archaeologists. In most of the instances where an archaeologist has been involved, this has been through full co-operation and teamwork and through carefully briefing of all concerned. Mutual understanding of evidential values is critical in confined or difficult circumstances where logistics alone necessitate detailed co-operation and awareness. A particular example here was the

Figure 1.5 The partly exposed rib cage of articulated skeletal remains. In this instance the problem was in determining whether the remains had been deliberately buried, or whether they had become buried by natural processes.

Source: courtesy of Barrie Simpson

recovery of a young girl in a cellar which was so narrow that only a small number of people could enter the room, and only one person could be involved in the excavation of the grave at any one time (Chapter 4, case 20). SIOs and pathologists often have great faith in scene managers and the specialists they introduce. In some cases the main burden of excavating and exposing the body and evidential recording was carried out in advance of the pathologist's attendance, but with their support and recognition of the archaeologist's role. Final lifting of the remains has, in every case experienced, been a team effort.

1.5 Qualities and competence of a forensic archaeologist

The need for UK forensic archaeologists to be recognised as 'competent', whether by law enforcement groups or by peers, has become more sharply focused with the creation of the Council for the Registration of Forensic Practitioners (CRFP) in 2000. This is a government-supported regulatory council for forensic evidence, stemming from well-publicised flaws in 'expert' evidence highlighted by a Royal Commission of Justice report (1993). The CRFP's purpose is intended to ensure adequacy of professional standards across the full range of forensic disciplines under the three main headings of *science*, *medicine* and *incident investigation*, embracing every skill and specialist area likely to be drawn in (Kershaw 2001), including forensic archaeology and forensic anthropology. The CRFP maintains an overarching role in this process (see Ebsworth 2000), including representatives of the public, the courts, those who employ forensic practitioners or contract for their services, and practitioners themselves. It holds responsibility for strategy, sets the overall policy framework, and oversees the detailed registration process.

The register has a direct function. The SIO or scene manager has the reassurance that any person listed, whether for fingerprinting, toxicology or document analysis, has competence fit for purpose; they will therefore know what to expect of an archaeologist working at a scene of crime and have confidence in the archaeologist's ability and expertise to do what is required. Registration therefore ensures that those persons who operate as forensic archaeologists at scenes of crime, whether in a search or recovery capacity, or who offer advice, or who act as experts either for prosecution or defence purposes, are competent to do so, are able to offer independent scientific opinion of high quality, and, in doing so, have the backing and confidence of their professional community. In the USA, practising forensic anthropologists already conform to a registration process (certification) through the American Board of Forensic Anthropology, and a similar process is already being voiced for forensic archaeologists (Crist 2001). Conversely, of course, individuals *not* on any register may thus by definition not be recognised as competent and may therefore be perceived as vulnerable in court, irrespective of their work quality, experience and expertise.

Registration is also time limited: individuals are also subject to re-assessment at regular intervals to ensure continuing competence. Archaeologists currently work within the aegis of the Institute of Field Archaeologists (IFA), a self-regulatory body which has established working codes of practice in field archaeology, which operates a disciplinary process for its members, and which ranks levels of validated membership according to proven experience, peer review, competence and ability under a range of specialisms. To date, forensic archaeology has not featured as a specific area of competence within the terms of the IFA, partly through relatively recent evolution, and partly in view of the small number of operatives. Many of these operatives, however, are full members of the IFA with validation under appropriate areas (e.g. excavation, survey, etc.). Like forensic registration, membership of the IFA is not obligatory (in fact, fewer than half of all active professional archaeologists in the UK are members) but the desirability of joining is becoming increasingly necessary, if only for commercial reasons. Here too it seems likely that membership will eventually become the norm, heightened no doubt by the content of the Malta Convention which requires archaeological work to be carried out 'by qualified, specially authorised persons' (ECPAH 1992, Article 3). In many other parts of Europe, and further afield, archaeology is more highly controlled, often requiring licences (e.g. Ireland and Russia) or specific qualifications (Niquette 2001), and is often more strictly regulated than forensic science in the UK before the creation of the CRFP. Ironically, through registration, and despite their small numbers, British forensic archaeologists are finding themselves spearheading a new phase of professionalism in archaeology generally.

Those few forensic archaeologists who are operationally active tend to be mutually supportive, communicate frequently, and pass work round according to geographical proximity and personal expertise. The total number of archaeologists called upon to assist at a scene of crime is probably not more than around 30. Perhaps less than

10 are regularly attendants at scenes. Even fewer give evidence in court. Given these low numbers and the infrequency of scene involvement, participation in the registration process has to be seen as recognition of the subject's credibility in a forensic environment – a position which would have been unimaginable a decade ago.

Although the number of archaeologists who work in a forensic capacity is relatively small, a larger number are occasionally consulted by the police on buried matters and, more commonly, on material, usually bones, recovered during building work or found casually by members of the public exercising their dogs. Each of these 'archaeologists' has a relevant level of competence, irrespective as to whether they work in universities, museums, local authorities, archaeological units, or are self-employed. Equally relevant is the increasing number of scene of crime personnel (mostly ex-archaeologists and SOCOs with relevant course qualifications under their belts) who have shown both motivation and interest in forensic archaeology and who already work inside the law enforcement system. In theory, the registration process is relevant to anyone involved with archaeological evidence that may be used in court. Questions which are now being raised concern the point at which the line should be drawn. Exactly how should a forensic archaeologist (or a forensic anthropologist) be defined, and which criteria should be adopted to denote competency in this new discipline?

The nature of forensic archaeology and the definition of competency are clearly critical. They reflect the character of the work undertaken and also define those attributes of skill, knowledge and personal qualities which serve to distinguish the forensic archaeologist from other archaeologists, as well as identifying those qualities which all archaeologists may hold in common. Key differences, for example, will be a broad knowledge of police structure (including criminal investigation and scene of crime organisation), an understanding of legal frameworks (including court systems, disclosure and chain of evidence), and a basic familiarity with physical anthropology. However, the fundamental aspect of forensic archaeology is undoubtedly field expertise which can only stem from long experience in both excavation and survey – experience that enables the practitioner to evaluate field problems rapidly, solve stratigraphic problems confidently, record quickly as second nature, and generally fly by the seat of their pants in a difficult or novel environment. This ability is one 'acquired over years of field experience' (Owsley 2001: 38) and is not one gained in the classroom. In many countries, those working on archaeological material are guided by theory, rules and regulations, codes of conduct and protocols adopted and adapted over many decades of practice as set out by their professional body. While adaptation and even innovation are acceptable in unusual contexts (e.g. wetlands or underwater), generally there is little divergence from accepted procedures. However, the key to successful integration of archaeology into a forensic context is to retain the tool-kit of options normally available, but to modify an existing approach, or devise a new one, as the need demands. Lateral thought is crucial, as is the confidence to apply it.

Hoshower (1998) sensibly advocates the abandonment of a rigid adherence to textbook investigation, which has evolved to maximise the potential of archaeological sites. She advocates the adoption of flexible, common-sense, streamlined approaches as the norm in forensic cases. Her context, however, is very different. It concerns the recovery of (very shattered) remains of USAF individuals in modern war zones. Although the context is both 'forensic' and 'archaeological', it bears little similarity to the purist study of archaeological remains, but both successful location and recovery possess their own set of exacting methodologies, even if they necessitate eliminating 'irrelevant and time-consuming archaeological procedures' in the process (ibid.: 56). Irrespective of context, the challenge for the archaeologist is to devise the most appropriate method of meeting the legal (or, in the case of mass graves, also the humanitarian, see Haglund *et al.* 2001: 66) requirements of individual cases, methods that will not sacrifice the integrity of data, or the ability to offer confident interpretation. The archaeologist often has to devise such a strategy very quickly, under the scrutiny of other investigators, with little or no time for reflection, and in a way which reflects the aims and the mandate of the investigating authority. These factors will inevitably have to take into account such factors as terrain, time constraints, health and safety issues, and emotionally charged environments. Moreover, in the excavation of mass graves, cultural dictates, fear, the presence of military rule, local politics and even malpractice may also arise and inevitably influence procedures and practice (see Cox 2001b).

1.6 Comparisons

Archaeology is about asking questions, is destructive and non-repeatable, and thus invasive action is only undertaken when specific problems need to be resolved. These problems are not always clear in a forensic environment, in fact, most of the complaints voiced by forensic scientists are that investigating authorities do not always ask specific questions when handing over items or samples for analysis (e.g. Erzinclioglu 2000: 39f). Analysis for its own sake is worthless, but at least can often be replicated. Excavation is not replicable; there is no point in excavating unless there are specific questions to answer. The nature of this questioning has been discussed previously and the perceived divergence between forensic archaeology and 'normal' research-driven archaeology detailed (Hunter 1999).

There are significant differences: forensic questioning regarding identity and cause/ manner of death are rarely relevant factors in purely archaeological scenarios, and determining the interval since death is required to be much more specific in a forensic investigation than it would in more traditional archaeology. In the excavation of clandestine burials the questioning may be more refined and consider, for example, the nature of the implement used to create the grave; the extent to which the grave may have been carefully prepared or hurriedly dug out; the presence of material (e.g. fibres) transferred from offender to grave fill, and the nature of any unusual or foreign material within the grave deposits (see Hochrein 2001). Furthermore, taphonomic factors – differentiating between peri- and post-mortem change and other complex post-depositional effects – take on a more critical role than in the typical developer-led excavation of an ancient cemetery (Haglund 2001: 28). In this regard, comparisons of forensic and archaeological data have already established the importance of a fuller understanding of both diagenesis and recovery factors (Cox and Bell 1999). Equally fundamental, the forensic questioning is ultimately geared towards identifying the perpetrator. Interrogation of the data is targeted accordingly and is quite distinct from the interrogation of ancient archaeological remains simply because the objectives of the respective excavations are fundamentally different. Put succinctly, in forensic archaeology 'evidence is not gathered to uncover the broad patterns of human behaviour, but rather to reconstruct the specifics of a single event' (Connor and Scott 2001: 3).

While the questioning themes will be essentially the same from one forensic grave to another, there may inevitably be subtle differences according to the weight of the evidence required. In the context of mass graves, for example, the questioning may be somewhat simpler and expressed only in terms of 'How were these victims killed?', 'Is there evidence of coercion?', and 'When were these victims killed?' There might, in addition, be a more careful interrogation of the excavated data in order to assess human rights abuse and exposure of atrocities (see Haglund *et al.* 2001: 57), and this has since been identified as a key element in minimum standards of recovery from mass burials (Hunter *et al.* 2001). By contrast, the level of individuality may be much harder to come to terms with, partly through commingling, partly through deliberate confusion and mixing of clothes and identifying elements by perpetrators, through lack of comparative medical and dental records and, less comfortably, through sheer logistic difficulties and volume of remains. Adding to such complexities as are apparent above, must be the definition of the crime. Mass graves may contain the remains of victims of alleged mass-murder, genocide, war crimes, or crimes against humanity.

The nature of the questioning will always govern the character of the investigation. If the interrogation is primarily to tie a particular military individual or group of individuals to a specific act of mass murder for which there are witnesses, then the excavation may only need to be concerned with proving that the particular crime and human rights abuse have occurred. Factors of individualisation may not enter the equation. Whether this is satisfactory or not from ethical or humanitarian standpoints is another issue entirely (see Chapter 8, Section 8.2). Equally debatable, but perhaps more sympathetically acceptable given the global and humanitarian extent of the crime and the need for closure, is the recovery of buried victims primarily for identification purposes, with only secondary attention afforded to other issues.

Successful (indeed competent) forensic archaeology depends on fieldwork ability. No matter how great the scene of crime experience, or knowledge from books, or classes attended, there is no substitute for an extensive fieldwork background. There are, for example, a range of university qualifications at sub-degree, degree and postgraduate levels which contain elements of forensic archaeology, but although these programmes contain content which is relevant, they do not in themselves necessarily mutate students into forensic archaeologists, nor give them a mandate to operate in the field.

1.6.1 *'Traditional' archaeology*

Under most non-forensic conditions a supervisor of an excavation will be in charge of a team of archaeologists, be in a position to take total control, to make executive decisions and to take ultimate responsibility for the result of the findings. On a developer-led project the exercise will be carefully controlled and monitored, for example, according to MAP2 principles, for a specific period of time and at a specific cost. The programme will be planned in advance, manpower and equipment identified, the site previously evaluated with both the natural and human histories of the landscape known in general. During the course of the investigation, the archaeologist will be able to call upon equally experienced colleagues on the site for second opinions, for discussion regarding change of strategy, and to assist in day-to-day decision-making. Excavation will normally take place under natural light during the standard working day, and no other professionals will be involved other than the developer and other construction agencies whose requirements have already been laid down in advance of the excavation. In rarer instances of excavation undertaken purely for research purposes, there will be even greater flexibility of time, discussion, retreat due to weather, or even the option of returning for another season at a later date.

In both, however, the ultimate findings will be summarised by selection of appropriate data and argument, and probably emerge in an academic journal or similar organ some years later written for peers who will pass judgement accordingly. In the meantime, however, discussion of progress may take place more widely and more publicly, and in some instances with media involvement.

1.6.2 Forensic archaeology

At a scene of a crime, however, much of this will be different. In the majority of cases the incident will have arisen with little notice, although perhaps less so in many mass-grave investigations. Even in those cases which follow an extensive series of briefings, information may only be limited and available through covert means to avoid suspicion, for example, by aerial photography. In many instances access will be made at a specific time in early morning through a magistrate's search warrant and involve a highly organised process of entry and search originally set out according to *The Police and Criminal Evidence Act 1984* (see Chapter 7). It may also involve taking a suspect into custody allowing a limited time (in England, 36 hours with possible extension, in Scotland, 6 hours only) for any search to be undertaken. The sensitive nature of the timing is one to which the archaeologist must conform and become actively integrated despite any inconvenience. This is neither an occasion for playing the *prima donna*, nor for finding flat batteries in the magnetometer.

There will be instances where the archaeologist will be requested to attend a scene which has already been secured, taped, and provisionally recorded. In dubious or preliminary scenarios, time may be sufficiently flexible to allow the scene to be made secure overnight while appropriate arrangements are made, but in more positive situations this may not be possible. There may already be a cordon manned by uniformed officers, an incident van containing an SIO, other detectives and a press officer, a scene of crime team who have already erected a tent and are awaiting further instructions, and there may be a large van containing a team of support unit officers dedicated to the operation. And, unless the situation has been kept very quiet, the media will also have arrived. The entire scenario will be managed by the SIO who will have total control of the scene population, the individual components of the main enquiry, and the operational command of all those who participate. The cost in terms of manpower and public funds is considerable and, as far as the archaeologist is concerned, the cost is probably even greater in terms of professional credibility. The archaeologist's preliminary investigations, advice or opinions may influence the next stage of the enquiry. They may necessitate standing down the whole operation, or conversely they may move it up a gear, introducing a search team or other specialist support personnel such as a forensic scientist and pathologist. Furthermore, any work involving human remains necessitates ethical responsibility on behalf of those involved, and all practitioners, registered or otherwise, need to be familiar with ethical standards (Chapter 8, Section 8.2).

In circumstances such as this, there is no opportunity to 'go away and think about it'. It requires rapid and considered thought, the ability to think quickly, evaluate, and show confidence in making a decision. Control is vested in the SIO (although in some mass grave contexts the archaeologist may be able to exercise a greater degree of control, depending on circumstances), there is no-one to provide a valued second opinion, no experienced help, and any assistants supporting the excavation will have to be trained on the spot. Sections and plans will have to be accomplished rapidly, records made on the understanding that all information will have to be disclosed, exhibits seized and a chain of custody maintained (see Melbye and Jimenez 1997), and the whole work undertaken in close collaboration with other specialists whose evidential requirements will need to be fully understood in case they are compromised. There is a point here when the archaeologist must have the conviction to recognise the points at which his or her expertise is no longer relevant, or when their work is strictly complementary (for example, when working with the pathologist).

When the work is done, the report is written as soon as possible as a formal statement and submitted as part of the overall evidence. Amplification of that statement occurs as an expert witness some time later in the Crown Court at the hands of a friendly Crown Prosecutor. The findings are not presented to archaeological peers, but instead to a lay jury. Interrogation of the same statement, supporting evidence and all site records follows immediately (see Chapter 7), but may be guided (and aggravated) by another source of archaeological expertise commissioned by the defence. Defence interrogation is not intended to be friendly. It is intentionally geared to minimise the value of the expert evidence, and diminish with it any professional credibility maintained by the witness. This is commonly understood practice in other disciplines (notably forensic pathology) but is still a disconcerting, unusual and adversarial arena for archaeologists.

Court is the ultimate test of the archaeologist's credibility. No matter who invites the archaeologist to participate in an investigation, their duty is to the court. Impartiality in investigation and interpretation of evidence is imperative, and is essential if justice is to be done. Credibility in court relies very much upon experience and qualifications as well as upon having the essential professional and interpersonal skills to ensure that evidence can be given with confidence and credibility. Complicated issues of method-ology and science need to be communicated clearly, concisely and in a manner which is not patronising. It is not enough to be proficient as an archaeologist or an anthro-pologist. An understanding of basic criminal law is essential and, for those who practise their skills abroad in the investigation of genocide, crimes against humanity and war crimes, some understanding of international legislation and protocols is a further basic necessity (e.g. Kittichaisaree 2001).

1.7 Forensic groups

The first group to develop specifically with a forensic archaeological interest or com-ponent was NecroSearch International (above) founded in Colorado in 1991 by a group of like-minded individuals who recognised the importance and relevance of utilising archaeological and anthropological techniques in search and recovery contexts. By then, however, an Argentine forensic team specialising in anthropology and recovery had already emerged in the early 1980s but was more concerned with issues of human rights, and excavations undertaken by Professor Richard Wright in the Ukraine in 1990 had set the scene for the systematic archaeological excavation of mass graves. The Colorado group was more concerned with individual homicide events and expanded to include the disciplines of geophysics, entomology and criminalistics, and its evolution has been well documented (Jackson 2002). NecroSearch has its own research and experimental site near Denver and maintains a high profile in police work throughout the USA and abroad. Its members now number over 20 and meet monthly to discuss case work, technical developments and research plans. Known as 'the pig people' as a result of their experimental work with buried pig carcasses (France *et al.* 1997), they support police work through invitation and reputation and have developed a deliberate scientific detachment from the emotional aspects of case involvement. One of their operatives described his case contribution as 'a scientist working on a problem, not a cause' (Jackson 2002: 221) – a comment which reflects much on an objective analysis of a situation and on operational maturity.

NecroSearch served as the model for the Forensic Search Advisory Group (FSAG) which was established in the UK in the mid-1990s to fulfil a similar role. A small number of forensic archaeologists working on a commissioned basis for police forces realised independently that general awareness of search techniques tended to be extremely limited, technological capabilities were often misunderstood, and that the concept of using sequences of search techniques was rarely appreciated. It was not always recognised that different scene contexts required different approaches, and that the various methods that could be deployed had significant limitations as well as positive advantages (Chapter 2). More crucially, there was no central point from which up-to-date advice or support could be gathered. Simple questions such as 'What are the range of suitable techniques available?' or 'Which are the best techniques for this particular scenario?' were unanswered simply because there was no-one to ask. Forces had their own lists of 'support' personnel but these were not always geared to forensic application and were often directed elsewhere. Typical support was often derived from military or engineering contexts whose motives were genuine enough but whose experience was vested in the detection of mines, fractures in reinforced concrete, or depth of landfill sites for contamination purposes. Their understanding of, and familiarity with, detection signals from decaying human remains were minimal, and forces ran the very real danger of eliminating sites on the basis of inexperience. A particular case in point was the use of radar which received high profile as a consequence of investigations in Cromwell Street, Gloucester, and which was avidly applied to a number of subsequent scenarios, irrespective of its value or feasibility in the physical environments in question.

Setting up the FSAG was a response to this situation. The original group included specialists in archaeology, aerial interpretation (military), crime detection (SIOs), physical anthropology, geophysics, scene of crime examination, cadaver dog handling, and decay biochemistry (taphonomy), but experience has since allowed the Group to expand to include specialists in pathology, ecology, entomology and POLSA Officers. Nevertheless, the purpose remains the same, namely, to provide a central service to police forces by means of a 24-hour facility which was originally set up in 1996 and which has been operative ever since. The small number of members provide a free advisory service to anyone who requires it, as well as being a point of contact for the National Crime and Operations Faculty (CENTREX) at the National Police Training College, Bramshill. The group promotes search methodologies, instigates research programmes, discusses case studies with a view to improving its services, and works to a specified Code of Conduct. 'Mission' is still a major feature of the work undertaken and although advice normally consists of identifying appropriate techniques for the search in question, it often has the aim of encouraging a more fundamental methodology. Since the foundation of the FSAG, other groups have been established with similar purpose, notably the Swedish *Arbetsgruppen for Forensic Arkeologi* (AFFA), and the Belgian *Disaster Victim Identification Unit* (DVI) which originally emerged as a result of the Zeebrugge disaster.

In the late 1990s individual expertise which had been applied in clandestine burials or disasters was adapted and put to good use in the excavation of mass graves, initially in Rwanda, and later in the Balkans as a result of civil war and associated alleged genocide (see Chapter 5). It built on work already carried out by Physicians for Human Rights (PHR) established in 1986. This generated further organisational arrangements in order to provide evidence for the International Criminal Court in The Hague and resulted directly in the formation of the International Criminal Tribunal for the Former Yugoslavia (ICTY) which arranged and undertook excavations. The number of buried victims runs into tens of thousands and, despite best intentions, and for reasons of sheer practicality, this total is unlikely ever to be exhumed purely for the purpose of convicting offenders. Resulting pressure on resources together with prevailing political conditions has inevitably resulted in exhumation undertaken locally with the prime intention of identifying individuals and returning remains to their families. This is now being co-ordinated by the International Commission on Missing Persons (ICMP) – an organisation established by former US President Clinton – which employs archaeologists to monitor the excavation work, and which has undertaken a massive programme of DNA analysis for identification purpose.

Conflict in the Balkans was also directly responsible for the establishment of two British-based groups concerned with the wider remit of the recovery and identification of mass graves: the *Centre for International Forensic Assistance* (CIFA); and the *International Forensic Centre of Excellence for the Investigation of Genocide* (INFORCE). CIFA has the aims of providing forensic science expertise in the investigation of war crimes, mass disasters, and individual cases of a criminal nature and of human rights abuse, world-wide at any time. Its database of personnel covers a wide range of expertise, including forensic archaeology and anthropology, and CIFA also seeks to promote training and dissemination of the relevant disciplines. INFORCE is an independent, charitable institution concerned with the location and recovery of victims of unlawful killing, particularly genocide, but with an emphasis on humanitarian needs, ethics and legislation. It also promotes an educational base for teaching and research in appropriate areas as well as capacity building in post-conflict areas. Like CIFA, it has access to a wide range of experts and case experience.

References

Aitchison, K. 1999. *A Survey on Archaeological Jobs in the UK*, Council for British Archaeology, English Heritage, Reading: Institute of Field Archaeologists.

Boudreaux, M.C., Lord, W.D. and Dutra, R.L. 1999. 'Child abduction: aged-based analyses of offender, victim, and offence characteristics in 550 cases of alleged child disappearance', *Journal of Forensic Sciences* 44:3, 539–553.

Britton, P. 1997. *The Jigsaw Man*, London: Bantam Press.

Brown, A.G., Smith, A. and Elmhirst, O. 2002. 'The combined use of pollen and soil analyses in a search and subsequent murder investigation', *Journal of Forensic Sciences* 47:3, 614–618.

Buck, S.C. 2003. 'Searching for graves using geophysical technology: field tests with ground penetrating radar, magnetometry, and electrical resistivity', *Journal of Forensic Sciences* 48:1, 5–11.

Connor, M. and Scott, D.D. 2001. 'Paradigms and perpetrators', *Journal of Historical Archaeology* 35:1, 1–6.

Cox, M. 2001a. 'Forensic archaeology: a United Kingdom perspective', in Godwin, M.G. (ed.) *Criminal Psychology and Forensic Technology*, New York: CRC Press, pp. 1–14.

Cox, M. 2001b. 'Forensic archaeology in the UK: questions of socio-intellectual context and socio-political responsibility', in Buchli, V. and Lucas, G. (eds) *Archaeologies of the Contemporary Past*, Cambridge: Cambridge University Press, pp. 145–157.

Cox, M. and Bell, L. 1999. 'Recovery of human skeletal elements from a recent UK murder enquiry: preservational signatures', *Journal of Forensic Sciences* 44:5, 945–950.

Crist, T.A.J. 2001. 'Bad to the bone? Historical archaeologists in the practice of forensic science', *Journal of Historical Archaeology* 35:1, 39–56.

Darvill, T. and Russell, B. 2002. *Archaeology after PPG16: Archaeological Investigations in England 1990–1999*, Bournemouth: Bournemouth University, School of Conservation Sciences Research Report 10, English Heritage and Bournemouth University.

Davenport, G.C. 2001. 'Remote sensing applications in forensic investigations', *Journal of Historical Archaeology*, 35:1, 87–100.

Davis, J.L., Heginbottom, J.A., Annan, A.P., Daniels, R.S., Berdal, B.P., Bergan, T., Duncan, K.E., Lewin, P.K., Oxford, J.S., Roberts, N., Skehel, J.J. and Smith C.R. 2000. 'Ground penetrating radar surveys to locate 1918 Spanish flu victims in permafrost', *Journal of Forensic Sciences* 45:1, 68–76.

Dirkmaat, D.C. and Adovasio, J.M. 1997. 'The role of archaeology in the recovery and interpretation of human remains from an outdoor forensic setting', in Haglund, W.D. and Sorg, M.H. (eds), *Forensic Taphonomy*, Boca Raton, FL: CRC Press, pp. 39–64.

DoE, 1990. *Planning Policy Guideline 16*, London: HMSO.

Ebsworth, E.A.V. 2000. 'The Council for the Registration of Forensic Practitioners', *Science and Justice* 40:2, 134–137.

ECPAH 1992. *European Convention on the Protection of the Archaeological Heritage*, Valetta.

Erzinclioglu, Z. 2000. *Maggots, Murder and Men*, Colchester: Harley Books.

France, D.L., Griffin, T.J., Swanburg, J.G., Lindemann, J.W., Davenport, G.C., Trammell, V., Travis, C.T., Kondratieff, B., Nelson, A., Castellano, K., Hopkins, D. and Adair, T. 1997. 'NecroSearch revisited: further multidisciplinary approaches to the detection of clandestine graves', in Haglund, W.D. and Sorg, M.H. (eds) *Forensic Taphonomy*, Boca Raton, FL: CRC Press, pp. 497–509.

Haglund, W.D. 2001. 'Archaeology and forensic death investigation', *Journal of Historical Archaeology* 35:1, 26–34.

Haglund, W.D. 2002. 'Recent mass graves, an introduction', in Haglund, W.D. and Sorg, M.H. (eds), *Advances in Forensic Taphonomy*, Boca Raton, FL: CRC Press, pp. 242–261.

Haglund, W.D., Connor, M. and Scott, D.D. 2001. 'The archaeology of contemporary mass graves', *Journal of Historical Archaeology* 35:1, 57–69.

Haglund, W. D., Connor, M. and Scott, D.D. 2002. 'The effect of cultivation on buried human remains', in Haglund, W.D. and Sorg, M.H (eds) *Advances in Forensic Taphonomy*, Boca Raton, FL: CRC Press, pp. 133–150.

Haglund, W.D. and Sorg, M.H. (eds) 1997. *Forensic Taphonomy: The Postmortem Fate of Human Remains*, Boca Raton, FL: CRC Press.

Haglund, W.D. and Sorg, M.H. (eds) 2002. *Advances in Forensic Taphonomy: Method, Theory and Archaeological Perspectives*, Boca Raton, FL: CRC Press.

Hall, D.W. 1997. 'Forensic botany', in Haglund, W.D. and Sorg, M.H. (eds) *Forensic Taphonomy*, Boca Raton, FL: CRC Press, pp. 353–363.

Hey, G. and Lacey, M. 2001. *Evaluation of Archaeological Decision Making Processes and Sampling Strategies*, Reading: English Heritage and the IFA.

Hochrein, M.J. 2001. 'An autopsy of the grave: recognising, collecting and preserving forensic geotaphonomic evidence', in Haglund, W.D. and Sorg, M.H (eds) *Advances in Forensic Taphonomy*, Boca Raton, FL: CRC Press, pp. 45–70.

Hoshower, L.M. 1998. 'Forensic archaeology and the need for flexible excavation strategies: a case study', *Journal of Forensic Science*, 43, 53–56.

Hunter, J.R. 1994. 'Forensic archaeology in Britain', *Antiquity* 68, 758–769.

Hunter, J.R. 1999. 'The excavation of modern murder', in Downes, J. and Pollard, T. *The Loved Body's Corruption*, Glasgow: Cruithne Press, 209–223.

Hunter, J.R. 2001. 'Foreword from Archaeology: A pilgim in forensic archaeology – a personal view', in Haglund, W.D. and Sorg, M.H (eds) *Advances in Forensic Taphonomy*, Boca Raton, FL: CRC Press, pp. xxv–xxxii.

Hunter, J.R. and Ralston, I.B.M. 1993. *Archaeological Resource Management in the UK: An Introduction*, Stroud: Alan Sutton.

Hunter, J.R., Brickley, M.B., Bourgeois, J., Bouts, W., Bourguignon, L., Hubrecht, F., De Winne, J., Van Haster, H., Hakbijl, T., De Jong, H., Smits, L., Van Wijngaarden, L. and Luschen, M. 2001. 'Forensic archaeology, forensic anthropology and human rights in Europe', *Science and Justice*, 41:3, 173–8.

Hunter, J.R, Roberts, C.A and Martin, A. 1996. *Studies in Crime: An Introduction to Forensic Archaeology*, London: Routledge.

Jackson, S. 2002. *No Stone Unturned*, New York: Kensington.

Janaway, R.C. 2002. 'Degradation of clothing and other dress materials associated with buried bodies of both archaeological and forensic interest', in Haglund, W.D. and Sorg, M.H. (eds) *Advances in Forensic Taphonomy*, Boca Raton, FL: CRC Press, pp. 379–402.

Kershaw, A. 2001. 'Expressing a standard', *Science and Justice* 41:3, 226–8.

Killam, E.W. 1990. *The Detection of Human Remains*, Springfield, IL: Charles C. Thomas.

Kittichaisaree, K. 2001. *International Criminal Law*, Oxford University Press, Oxford.

Melbye, J. and Jimenez, S.B. 1997. 'Chain of custody from the field to the courtroom', in Haglund, W.D. and Sorg, M.H. (eds) *Forensic Taphonomy*, Boca Raton, FL: CRC Press, pp. 65–75.

Morse, D., Duncan, J. and Stoutamire, J. 1983. *Handbook of Forensic Archaeology and Anthropology*, Tallahassee, FL: Rose Printing.

Morton, R.J. and Lord, W.D. 2002. 'Detection and recovery of abducted and murdered children: behavioral and taphonomic influences', in Haglund, W.D. and Sorg, M.H. (eds), *Advances in Forensic Taphonomy*, Boca Raton, FL: CRC Press, pp. 151–171.

Niquette, C.M. 2001. 'Europe, archaeology and professionalism: a transatlantic view', *The Archaeologist* 40, 14–16.

Owsley, D.W. 2001. 'Why the forensic anthropologist needs the archaeologist', *Journal of Historical Archaeology* 35:1, 35–38.

Royal Commission on Criminal Justice 1993. *Report* Cm 2263, London: HMSO.

Schmitt, S. 2002. 'Mass graves and the collection of forensic evidence: genocide, war crimes, and crimes against humanity', in Haglund, W.D. and Sorg, M.H. (eds) *Advances in Forensic Taphonomy*, Boca Raton, FL: CRC Press, pp. 277–292.

Scott, D.D. 2001. 'Firearms identification in support of identifying a mass execution at El Mozote, El Salvador', *Journal of Historical Archaeology* 35:1, 79–86.

Scott, D.D. and Connor, M. 2001. 'The role and future of archaeology in forensic science', *Journal of Historical Archaeology* 35:1, 101–104.

Sonderman, R.C. 2001. 'Looking for a needle in a haystack: developing closer relationships between law enforcement specialists and archaeology', *Journal of Historical Archaeology* 35:1, 70–78.

Stevens, J.A. 1997. 'Standard investigatory tools and offender profiling', in Jackson, J.L. and Beckerian, D.A. (eds) *Offender Profiling: Theory, Research and Practice*, Chichester: John Wiley, pp. 77–91.

Stover, E. and Peress, G. 1998. *The Graves: Srebrenica and Vukovar*, New York: Scala.

Stover, E. and Ryan, M. 2001. 'Breaking bread with the dead', *Journal of Historical Archaeology* 35:1, 7–25.

Ubelaker, D.H. 2001 'Artificial radiocarbon as an indicator of recent origin of organic remains in forensic cases', *Journal of Forensic Sciences* 46:6, 1285–1287.

2

SEARCH AND LOCATION

Case studies 1–13

2.1 Background

There is already quite a wide literature on search techniques for buried clandestine remains, notably Killam's *Detection of Human Remains* (1990), chapters in recent volumes (e.g. Hunter *et al.* 1996; Cox 2001), papers which evaluate methodologies in specific contexts (e.g. France *et al.* 1997) and a range of review works on specific methods (e.g. Komar 1999; Buck 2003). Locating burials falls within the wider remit of search *per se*, and hence within a wider methodological literature which embraces, for example, search and rescue, lost persons, mountain accidents, and runaway children (e.g. Stoffel 2001). However, there are significant differences in search for individuals who may still be alive and those who may have been disposed of and buried. Nevertheless, although the various subjects and contexts may differ, there are common underlying themes in terms of search theory, management and resourcing.

There are now numerous techniques available for identifying individual graves, and several of these are outlined below. Some are less widely used than others, but while all offer very specific advantages and limitations according to target, terrain and context of deployment, there is no single *perfect* method. Furthermore, the nature of any physical search may be influenced by other factors, for example, by health and safety considerations, intelligence from the offender or geographical profiling (e.g. Killam 1990: 15–18; Godwin and Canter 1997). The most frequently used search methods in the UK have been defined by the Forensic Search Advisory Group (FSAG) which was established in 1995 and these methods can be applied as part of a multidisciplinary search strategy. All searches, however, require a starting point either derived from 'last sighting', intelligence, offender profile, or the missing person's personal background. Without this key data, no matter how schematic, it is impossible to generate a search design. There is simply nowhere to start.

However, each individual design is bespoke and uses techniques weighted according to circumstance and value. For example, alleged burials within buildings, or below tarmac or flagging, will invariably require ground penetrating radar (GPR) simply through the method's unique ability to penetrate dense materials such as concrete floors within a defined area (e.g. cases 1 and 2). The search methods used for finding individual hand-dug burials can also be applied to mass graves, although some methods are shown to be especially valuable, notably a heavy reliance on witness accounts to narrow down a landscape into a more workable search area (see Haglund *et al.* 2001: 64; Schmitt 2002: 280). Mass graves also tend to reflect political activity and belong to a context of wider political history (Skinner *et al.* 2002). They show less concern for being either clandestine or requiring short passage from vehicle to burial site. But the differences in scale – the use of trucks for transport of victims and the presence of earth-moving machinery together with extensive effort of concealment can all provide their own imprints for detection in the same way as for the individual hand-dug grave. These differences in scale manifest themselves most obviously during excavation (see Chapter 5; also Skinner *et al.* 2002) and necessitate archaeological understanding of machine/plant types and tyres, complex human taphonomy, and differentiation of primary and secondary burials.

Search tends to follow a series of formalised stages (see Killam 1990: 11). Initial search methods tend to be those which can narrow down a larger search area into smaller defined units. These smaller units can then be examined more closely, usually using a different set of techniques. In both these large and small contexts a sequence of techniques is likely to be deployed in order to maximise the value of their respective capabilities (see below). However, sequencing has to be carefully designed in order to ensure that the use of one method does not negate the value or efficacy of a subsequent method. Archaeology is a destructive process, and therefore a preferred search sequence is one which moves from *non-invasive* through to *invasive* methods in order to minimise loss of information.

In ideal search scenarios, the archaeologist operates as part of a larger team containing other specialists, for example, a geophysicist, cadaver dog handler, image analyst, palynologist, anthropologists or police search officer (POLSA). All formal searches will be logged and recorded within the HOLMES system – a nationally recognised computer indexing system – and those under POLSA control will include a wider search report. All personnel in the search team have an obligation to ensure they document the area searched, the reasons for selection of area, the techniques used and any observations made, together with other pertinent information (weather, vegetation, etc.). This constitutes a record against which future search areas can be defined, other techniques applied, areas eliminated, or data re-evaluated. This record may be disclosable, for example, if remains were eventually discovered in an area which had already been searched.

Field searches can only be undertaken within defined boundaries. A search without a defined boundary is exposed to subjective analysis, is unsystematic and will leave itself open to criticism. Each case will define its own boundaries, usually based on physical landscape factors. These factors may have a *real* bearing on a search, for example, a specific area of woodland or a garden, or a taped area defining the broad location where a suspect was seen. Conversely the boundaries may have an *arbitrary* bearing, for example, an area of convenient size for a single day's search defined by roads, walls and hedges. In both cases, the boundaries identify a fixed area of land within which the appropriate choice, sequence and implementation of search techniques can be set against environmental contexts and probability of success (Stoffel 2001: Chapter 13). To move beyond these boundaries, or not to define boundaries at all, may be to negate the effectiveness of the same techniques. Thus, a defined area can be searched exhaustively and eliminated in a systematic way.

Often the most obvious defined boundary is the garden of a house from which a person went missing or which is the dwelling place of a suspect (Figure 2.1; there are many instances here, notably, cases 2–6). In many instances the garden is the least likely

Figure 2.1 A garden search being carried out by removal of topsoil and by looking for
disturbances in natural substrates

location of the victim, but an SIO will invariably have no option other than to search
it for a buried victim because (1) it represents the most obviously defined area in relation
to the context of the missing person (or of that the missing person's assailant);
(2) there is a public expectation that the garden should be searched; and (3) that under
the terms of the Human Rights Act (1998) not to do so might indicate lack of duty
to investigate 'properly'. In short, both public and press appear to expect a garden to
be excavated as standard. Large screens, taped areas, and SOCOs bearing wheelbarrows
are traditional components of this macabre image.

Burying human remains entails disturbance of the ground surface and this has
been well illustrated (e.g. Morse *et al.* 1983: Chapter 1; Hunter *et al.* 1996: 87). It is
the effects brought about by this disturbance that form the basis of many search
techniques (see below) but the process of body decomposition itself may produce a
dynamic which can have both direct and indirect effects on detection. Much has been
written on the processes and timescales involved, and on taphonomic factors in general
(Haglund and Sorg 1997, 2002). The key relevant elements are partly the decomposition
products which can influence not only surrounding vegetation, but also geophysical
effects (see Chapter 3), particularly the emission of heat which can reflect both decomposition and maggot activity during the decay process itself (see also case 7). Vegetation
change may be significant (see below) but will require knowledge of local ecology and
flora and the effects upon it of disturbance, changes in pH, nutrient enrichment,
increased moisture retention and changed water levels. In a mass grave, for example,
large numbers of victims are likely to affect all these processes at different times as the
decomposition process may occur differentially (see Chapter 5, Section 5.5.1).

Heat emission can either result as a consequence of either insect infestation of corpses, or putrefaction and autolysis (e.g. Scollar *et al.* 1990). However, the point at which decay occurs, and the time during which increased heat can be measured, depend on a range of local variables, notably climate, depth, oxidisation, soil bacteria, cause of death, clothing or wrapping, and pre-deposition insect infestation, as well as personal characteristics of the individual such as body fat, state of health, age, etc. (e.g. Janaway 1996, 2002). Depending on respective presence and interaction, these can have effects of impeding or advancing the decay process, hence affecting the time since burial at which heat is emitted. Only by having reasonable knowledge of these variables is it possible to predict when heat emission will occur, and for how long (see Chapter 3). This can be particularly complex in mass graves (although most mass graves are identified without recourse to heat detection methods) in view of the variable changes which can occur within compacted bodies (see Haglund 2002). Where bodies are heaped, usually as a result of being dumped into the grave by machine, those at the bottom and near the centre of each mass tend to remain better preserved or saponified than those nearer the top, or sides of the grave, which are more skeletonised or desiccated. Much, however, depends on the soil environment, hydrology, clothing, the extent to which any burning may have occurred, and also on whether the grave is primary or secondary. Secondary graves are those where the individuals have been moved from a primary burial location, usually by machine, often causing the integrity of individuals to become lost, body parts to become separated and the taphonomic processes to become accelerated.

2.2 Disturbance effects

Disturbing the ground creates a number of effects which can facilitate detection (Figure 2.2). These can be most conveniently grouped as *surface* characteristics (vegetation, topographical and soil), and *sub-surface characteristics* (geophysical). Sub-surface characteristics are only discussed in outline terms here and are covered in greater depth in Chapter 3.

2.2.1 *Surface characteristics*

Disturbance to the sub-surface inevitably affects the state and nature of the ground surface in terms of associated vegetation. When a grave is dug and filled in, the infill is inevitably looser, more aerated, and more prone to moisture infiltration than the surrounding undisturbed ground. This can have an effect on the surface immediately above the disturbance, and it may generate a growth environment which will provide increased nutritional support for vegetation, causing it to grow taller. This may be more pronounced when the body commences a decomposition process; it may alter the local flowering regime; or it may even result in the colonisation of different plant species due, for example, to the alkaline soils resulting from proteolysis (Janaway 1996), or to the access of dominant seeds to a more conducive growth medium. Nettles are notable examples, and in the Balkans, *Artemesia vulgaris* (wormwood) is often considered to be an effective marker of mass graves (see Chapter 5, Section 5.4). Dormant areas may also indicate where spoil was placed. Experimental work has demonstrated the speed at which new vegetational climax might occur (France *et al.* 1997: 504f). Conversely,

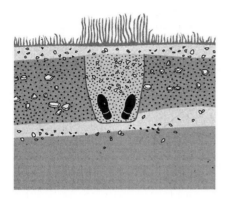

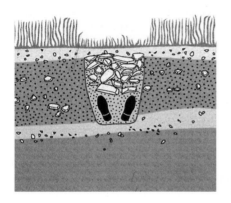

Figure 2.2 Illustration of theoretical effects caused by burial on vegetation

infilling the grave with solid materials or wrapping the body in polythene may inhibit growth effects but still create a species-specific or colonisation environment which is unusual. Further, simply disturbing dormant buried seeds can illicit a change. All these effects can be long-term, as witness prehistoric graves and other buried features which can still be identified from the air. It is rarely possible to create a grave and *not induce* a vegetation change of this type. Furthermore, the original digging of the grave will have compressed the vegetation surrounding the grave by both trampling and the heaping of spoil, providing additional markers to the grave location, albeit short-term.

Once a grave or pit has been dug in relatively consolidated ground and a body or other items introduced, it is almost impossible for the original spoil to be replaced within the grave. This is partly an issue of volume, and partly through the extracted soils being less consolidated than in their original state. If the victim or object is especially large, then this problem is compounded. In churchyards, the sexton will 'mound' the excess earth over a formal grave, effectively emphasising the shape, on the basis that during the subsequent period of consolidation, this mound will sink and the grave soils become consolidated in the general vicinity of the existing ground surface. Offenders may try and minimise this mounding phenomenon by flattening the surface over the grave, but this is a short-term solution: the soils will consolidate and sink causing a hollow over the grave. In fact, collapse of the abdominal cavity of the buried victim may even exacerbate this. Furthermore, dispersal of the excess soil in the immediate vicinity may be obvious to a trained eye and will, in any event, make its own short-term impact on the local vegetation. In summary, it is virtually impossible to infill a grave in a manner which will ensure topographical anonymity over both the shorter and longer term.

Clandestine graves have been found in a variety of different shapes, sizes and locations. Shallow graves might be argued as reflecting hurried disposal (see Chapter 4, Section 4.4), or the result of an offender trying ineptly to bury a victim in woodland and being (not unnaturally) thwarted by tree roots. Such shallow burials are often scavenged, bones or body elements being removed and brought to light by both wild and domestic animals, or sometimes by ploughing. Deeper graves are more secure but they create the effect of disturbing buried soil strata of different character and colour and creating a visually distinctive surface effect from the mixed backfill. This will be especially pronounced if the bedrock is of highly distinctive colour or character (e.g. yellow clay or chalk). The same surface effect, although of lesser impact, will be apparent if the grave is dug into stonier layers, gravel or similarly distinctive geological strata. Many of these bedrock strata lie relatively close to the surface, certainly within burial depth of approximately less than 1 metre, and their surface effects will be enhanced by the cleansing effects of rainfall or ploughing. Ploughing itself is not generally considered to have significant resurfacing and distribution effects on buried human remains (e.g. Haglund *et al.* 2002). However, case 14 has shown that it certainly has the potential to do so. In this case, a grave cut through by the plough 'pulled' bone and dentition into the plough cut, in the direction that the plough headed, for some metres from the grave. Clearly, had the farmer not noticed that his plough was snagged on fabric, and stopped, any subsequent ploughing would have exacerbated this. Clandestine burial during darkness may prevent the distinctiveness of subsoil inversion or ploughing being observed by the offender who would, in any event, probably be unaware of future land use or management which may emphasise any visible surface characteristics.

2.2.2 *Sub-surface characteristics*

Any disturbance in relatively undisturbed ground is likely to have the effect of creating a specific geophysical signature (see Chapter 3). The infill of a grave may differ from that of the surrounding ground in terms of colour, density, and general physical properties simply through being (1) disturbed, and (2) a consortium of the features of those individual layers through which it has been dug and of which it is constituted. There will be a contrast between the grave infill and the layers through which the grave has been dug. This contrast may be very small (for example, in terms of electrical or magnetic properties), and its clarity depends on the extent to which the characteristics of the grave fill, and those of the background into which it has been cut, are observable. The higher the background 'noise', the harder it is to identify the anomaly caused by the disturbance of the grave. This type of difference may be measured by a range of appropriate geophysical survey techniques (see below) undertaken systematically across the ground surface, typically taking measurements at 0.5m intervals across both planes, which can then be processed through appropriate software.

2.3 Search methods and design

Depending on circumstances, typical search methods might draw upon all or any of the following techniques in roughly the order listed. This list commences with non-invasive methods and moves gradually to those which involve disruption of the ground surface and potential loss of evidence:

- *cartographic analysis*: Ordnance Survey, geological, land use and historic map sources (including local sites and monuments records)
- *aerial photography*: vertical, oblique and satellite
- *field observation*: vegetation, topographical or geological features
- *geophysical survey*: typically resistivity, magnetometry and ground-penetrating radar
- *manual evaluation*: augering, probing (venting for dogs), trial trenching or stripping.

Increasing numbers of case studies have shown that search enquiries fall broadly into two distinct camps. In one, there is always a named victim, there is usually a suspect, the timescale of events is relatively well known, but the location of disposal is not well-defined (e.g. case 8). In the other, there is not necessarily a named victim, sometimes not even a missing person and rarely a suspect, but the information comes in the form of an allegation, usually a considerable time after the event and often clouded through poor memory, alcohol or drug abuse. Sometimes the allegation is made by an individual who has become obsessed with a well-known local missing person. They may genuinely believe that the victim is in a certain place and there is no intention to mislead. Usually, in these scenarios the location tends to be very specific, for example a particular garden or place in woodland (e.g. case 9).

From a police investigation point of view, there is an appreciable difference in objective between the two types. The former requires a positive search in order to find the victim, but in the latter the exercise is normally one of elimination and the method-ologies are thus not necessarily the same. The former scenario might initially be inclined towards feasibility, on what was possible, on the profiling of the suspect, and on defining broad target areas for attention using the general themes in the approximate order listed in a gradual focusing process. The latter would be more immediately invasive and aimed at providing thorough elimination. At the end of the day the specific location may need to be investigated by trial trench excavation and hence many of the pre-liminary procedures such as the introduction of sophisticated geophysics, dogs or other methods, may become superfluous other than for testing purposes, or for limiting reinstatement costs. The former scenario needs more careful handling, partly in order to target specific locations, and partly to ensure that areas which are *not* targeted can be eliminated for good reasons with confidence. In either case, the worst possible scenario is one in which the victim could be found within an area which had already been eliminated by searching.

2.3.1 Cartographic analysis

Maps are an essential search resource although in some developing world contexts, maps will not be particularly accurate or easily obtained. In the UK, however, mapping is provided by the Ordnance Survey service, whose maps are published in a range of scales and detail according to requirement. Many are available digitally. The 1:25,000 series is the minimum (1:10,000 is optimum) for analysing wider landscapes in terms of area, woodland, lakes and contours, as well as roads and footpaths which may have been used for access, but larger-scale maps provide a much greater level of detail if the search area can be narrowed down. Access points are significant as they can represent the furthest points to which a vehicle can travel for disposal purposes. From there cadavers need to be physically carried to a disposal point and this distance is limited by body weight and landscape. For more detailed analysis, the 1:1250 series is essential, but these are not always available for areas which are sparsely populated. Basic landscape knowledge will usefully inform any search strategy, and reference to successive maps of the same area will document changes in access and possible disposal sites over time. Earlier map editions, commencing with the Ordnance Survey first edition from the mid nineteenth century, may indicate certain useful features no longer evident on the present landscape, such as former mine shafts or drains, which may be of interest to the investigation. The location of ancient sites and monuments may also have a bearing on any remains found if they contain burial deposits which have become eroded.

Additional cartographic resources will include geological maps and those which relate to land use. The former will illustrate the bedrock geology and give some indication of those areas which can be eliminated through reason of geological outcropping and near-surface geology, for example, granite or limestone, which will inhibit any attempts at digging. Equally, deposits of drift geology such as clays, which tend to be waterlogged, can impede the use of certain investigative methods, and this need to be recognised before any search strategy is devised. Another important resource is land use maps which may illustrate how agricultural activity or geological exploitation will affect the likelihood of burial. Ploughed fields, for example, provide a more appropriate medium for burial than areas of pasture or root crop where recent disturbance is more readily detectable, whereas quarrying may pose a special need for investigation. Maps are not simply a primary resource, but a key tool in devising research strategies.

2.3.2 Aerial photography

Where available, conventional aerial photographs can provide an additional dimension to mapping, but this depends on the photographs being taken according to optimum angle, season, shadow, crop growth, and ploughing of soil in order to enhance the factors by which anomalies have been created on the ground. The disturbance created by a grave, although relatively insignificant in volumetric terms in the context of a wider landscape, can induce various strong visual effects and can be long term (Figure 2.3). These can include colour change (i.e. from stressed vegetation), enhanced or inhibited flowering, shadows from increased or stunted growth with the presence of a low sun (e.g. winter months or summer mornings or evenings), and spreads of subsurface material in plough soil according to the timing of the agricultural cycle. Furthermore, the use of infrared photography may, for example, pick up vegetation stress brought about by the proximity of decaying cadavers, and aerial thermal imaging can be used to detect the heat emitted during the relatively short period of decay itself (see Chapter 3). In the summer, it may also be possible to distinguish between disturbed and

Figure 2.3 Photograph showing how vegetation change above an Iron Age burial ground is still visible today on a seasonal basis

Source: courtesy of Jim Pickering.

undisturbed soils due to differential heat loss during the night (Scollar *et al.* 1990). Photographs need to be assessed in term of the factors they intend to optimise – lighting, seasonality, land use, and time since death – and these are factors which are unlikely to be captured together on any one occasion. A single photograph at one given point in time does not therefore represent a complete aerial analysis.

Aerial photographs also have an historic value in the UK in that both military, governmental, and local government authorities have commissioned systematic high altitude aerial photographic cover in order to monitor land use, agricultural development, landscape change and implementation of EC subsidies, as well as domestic and industrial development. This coverage commenced relatively soon after the Second World War and has been continued sporadically thereafter, with some local authorities taking a more systematic approach. The advantage of this cover is that the photographs can be used to monitor landscape change over the years. In instances where the victim has been missing for some time, perhaps for 10 or 20 years, this enables the state of former landscapes to be identified in relation to present surface features and land use. Such comparisons can be useful in highlighting areas of more recent change or disturbance. This is important as effective search requires knowledge of landscape history or, in smaller areas, land use. For example, in populated areas it is important to know when ancillary structures such as sheds, garages, swimming pools, or even patios, were constructed in order that they can be either targeted or eliminated from an enquiry. Equally, if land was once used for industrial or military purposes, it may

35

contain features or points of potential concealment known to a perpetrator. Alternatively, it may contain underlying strata of a depth or nature which might significantly hinder certain search techniques, or even support other techniques.

2.3.3 Field observation

The simple physical presence of searchers on the ground marks the first real point at which evidence can be damaged or even completely destroyed, and field observation requires the use of experienced personnel in evaluating vegetation or topographical change. These changes are often subtle and not necessarily recognisable by volunteers, especially in instances where they may be the result of sub-surface body decay as opposed to ground disturbance. In fact, untrained personnel are likely not only to overlook key evidence, but also run the risk of destroying it by simple foot action. Furthermore, in an instance of a missing child, a search design which assumes the child still to be alive, and one which assumes that the child is no longer alive, will not necessarily be the same. The former will almost certainly necessitate the controlled manipulation of large numbers of volunteers. SIOs will have numerous pressures to withstand (e.g. the media, parents and relatives, and local politics) and will almost certainly be deemed irresponsible by public acclaim if they fail to accept the offer of support from the local community. However, experience suggests that by the time the archaeologist is drawn in to a recent missing child case, not only is the child in all probability dead and the whereabouts of the body concealed, but at least part of the evidence for finding that child has also been destroyed in the process of preliminary search.

The search balance is a very delicate one for the SIO to maintain and requires a considered 'desktop' assessment before search commences. It seems to work best when volunteers are kept within manageable numbers in search areas which are peripheral rather than focal. This has the advantage of satisfying public demand and making the volunteers feel useful, but also allows the investigation to be conducted more carefully in key areas. The need for a major search to be matched by major deployment of unskilled manpower is no longer appropriate. A classic example is recorded in the archives of a major murder enquiry in the 1960s where lines of volunteers were used to search moorland (Figure 2.4). Not only would this effectively erase any subtlety of landscape change caused by burial, but the process of 'tamping' (probing sticks into the ground and then smelling the end for decomposition) would be largely wasted in view of the idiosyncratic properties of the peat. In cases such as this where unusual substrates are involved, the variables are numerous, complex and require expert advice.

Landscape search is best conducted by a relatively small number of skilled, suitably briefed, personnel who possess an appropriate level of knowledge of soil types (e.g. alluvial soils) which might hinder or facilitate digging, and who are familiar with local flora. This is essential if pollen studies are to be integrated into the search equation (e.g. Horrocks and Walsh 2001), or if particular pollen assemblages from wheel arches, or shoes can be referenced to specific locations (e.g. Brown *et al.* 2002). Searchers will also need to be able to differentiate between natural soil effects, and those resulting from anthropogenic origins, as well as possessing some understanding of the way soil types and local hydrology might affect the overall process of buried human remains

POLICE TAMPING THE MOORS AT SADDLEWORTH
Sniff for the telltale stench.

Figure 2.4 Volunteers searching for buried remains in the 1960s. The sticks were used to probe into the ground and then sniffed for the smell of decomposition.

(Gill-King 1997). It is also helpful if they possess some knowledge of scavenging, not only in recognising affected sites, but also having awareness of animal behaviour, in being able to recognise animal traces and understanding typical feeding and movement patterns of likely predators (e.g. foxes and badgers). Scavenging is a complex and largely underestimated phenomenon (e.g. Haglund 1997; Murad 1997; Turton 2004) which can be affected by a range of factors, notably season and environment (see case 10; also Chapter 4, case 26), sometimes with significant implications (case 11).

Although rarely defined as such, field craft is an integral part of the archaeologist's weaponry. The skills are seldom taught in any formal way, but tend to be developed by many archaeologists over time. Basic skills are covered in central POLSA courses and are also accrued by many dog handlers who recognise the importance of landscape change in the deployment of their dogs. Field craft is particularly apposite to those archaeologists concerned with fieldwalking or visiting landscapes in order to assess their archaeological value by non-invasive means. Most archaeologists will agree that understanding a landscape is not necessarily something that can be undertaken by a single visit. Landscape evaluation is best carried out through persistent walking of the field or fields, in various directions, taking into account slope and different lighting conditions, and can have a methodology in its own right (Killam 1990: Chapter 3). However, the process is not always compatible with the timescales of modern forensic enquiries. Perhaps more appropriate is 'winthroping' – the ability to travel from one landscape marker to another (e.g. significant shaped/sized trees, gates, rock outcrops or outbuildings) in a manner which is almost sub-conscious (e.g. Chapter 4, case 26).

Developed from counter-terrorist investigation, this enables the investigator to 'read' a landscape in the same way that it may originally have been followed by a perpetrator and thus to pursue a route which may lead to a grave. It assumes, as most search procedures assume, that burial is not a random phenomenon, but one which relies on fixed points, either for purposes of future recognition by the offender, or for rapid entry and exit during the period of disposal.

2.3.4 Geophysical survey techniques

A full appraisal of the use and value of geophysical survey techniques in forensic search is long overdue and follows in Chapter 3. This develops from earlier summaries of techniques and applications (e.g. Killam 1990; Hunter *et al*. 1996), and reflects an increasing number of papers devoted to the use of geophysical survey in detecting human remains (e.g. France *et al*. 1997; Davis *et al*. 2000; Nobes 2000; Davenport 2001; Buck 2003). However, some general points are worth summarising here within the broad context of search methodologies.

The two main methods used in traditional archaeological work in the UK tend to be resistivity and magnetometry, and both involve the systematic gridding of the area in question, usually into 20 × 20m units (see Gaffney and Gater 2003). The former involves passing an electrical current through the ground and measuring the resistance to that current at individual points, and the latter can detect minor magnetic change from disturbed soils or burning. Both depend on any 'anomalies' (as they are called) being observable within a wider geophysical background of undisturbed surrounding soils. In some circumstances ground-penetrating radar (GPR) has been deployed in archaeology, the technique having the peculiar ability to penetrate dense materials (e.g. concrete or tarmac) without the need to excavate or sample. The transference of this paradigm to forensic work is in theory relatively straightforward in that both traditional and forensic archaeologies require shallow sub-surface analysis, both seek relatively small anomalies within a wider background, and both require the target area to be manageable – typically 10 grids each of 20 × 20m can be surveyed in the average day. Both too, should ideally use sequences of techniques in order to test for responses of different types, depending on geology, environment and target. Different techniques rely on different phenomena, and often the limitations of an individual technique may preclude its use in the first instance through factors of soil, topography, or background (see Chapter 3). However, there are two significant differences when it comes to searching for modern buried human remains as opposed to archaeological remains: first, there is an additional dynamic – the decay process of the body itself – which may provide a specific or enhanced geophysical signature during the decompositional process (this is discussed further in Chapter 3); and second, in view of the dimensions of a buried body, forensic survey tends to be undertaken at smaller intervals (0.5m minimum depending on target) as opposed to the more usual 1.0m intervals in conventional archaeology.

The advantages of geophysical survey are three-fold. First, the methods are effectively non-invasive and this is particularly useful with GPR in testing areas of driveway, patio, or swimming pool where reinstatement costs would otherwise be prohibitive. Second, fieldwork can be conducted relatively quickly with the data being processed immediately in the field. In fact, GPR data can be seen in real time, although more sophisticated analysis on all methods is best carried out off-site afterwards. Geophysical survey is specialist work and is best carried out by an expert familiar with geophysical data scaling, analysis and interpretation. This is especially important given that the identification of 'anomalies' in the geophysical data will also include geological or other anthropogenic activities which need to be excluded from further attention. Third, geophysics can often be carried out discreetly and without raising suspicion by a minimum of two operators, and the data may be able to identify a small number of 'hot-spots' for detailed targeting and intervention (e.g. Chapter 4, case 19). This offers considerable advantages over large-scale digging which involves not only more manpower resources, but also attracts media attention.

While the forensic use of geophysical survey has increased in the USA and the UK over recent years, there is still a reluctance to deploy geophysical expertise in some other areas of forensic interest in the world. This is partly due to factors of cost, but most usually to lack of awareness and understanding of scientific developments, and is especially the case in the detection of mass graves (Hunter *et al.* 2001). Mass grave locations tend to be identified through witness involvement, although their precise location can be hindered through matters of memory, elapsed time, and fear. Satellite photography also plays a part, but the final pinpointing of a grave tends to be carried out by probing or by machine digging (see Schmitt 2002). There is a clear role for geophysics, especially in the Balkans where the various Commissions are charged with exhumation, identification and repatriation under the terms of the *Banja Luka Agreement* signed in 1996. There, however, as in other parts of the world where mass graves occur, perpetrators have learned to try and deter investigators by machine compaction of the grave infill, by dumping spoil and debris over the surrounding area in order to confuse or distract the effectiveness of search techniques, and by littering the area with metal in order to hinder both the locating and de-mining process. Some graves are even booby-trapped using wires and grenades located within the body mass to deter investigators. In some genocides, bodies are disposed of in existing 'holes' or shafts in the ground. Bodies may be dumped in caves, swallets or wells, and in Rwanda, many were thrown into deep latrines which were then filled in. Clearly, geophysics is of little practical use in such contexts.

2.3.5 Manual evaluation (and other methods)

If the area of investigation can be narrowed down to a relatively small area, the use of invasive techniques becomes justifiable. Augers and ground probes can sometimes be used, but both need to be deployed systematically within a grid system. The latter tests (somewhat subjectively) the firmness of the buried soils or the depth of bedrock, and the former draws a narrow vertical column of soil in order to assess the likelihood of disturbance (see case 12). Both can be effective, but both are of very limited value in untrained hands and in difficult or stoney sub-soils. A more useful primary invasive technique, and the one which presents minimum loss of evidence, is that of the cadaver dog (e.g. Rebmann *et al.* 2000). These dogs are able to detect the gaseous by-products of decomposition of human remains and are either trained on appropriate human materials (e.g. teeth, blood or clothing containing decompositional products), or on materials which have similar properties, notably pig remains. Some trainers use chemical concoctions (pseudo-scent) which simulate actual body decomposition scents, although opinions differ as to the effectiveness of this. In searching for individual graves, there is arguably some dependence on appropriate wind strength, as well as on temperature and humidity, and some research work has taken place (e.g. Komar 1999). However, the application to mass graves seems undervalued, despite the fact that the scent source can be considerably enhanced although in some waterlogged contexts decomposition processes are not 'normal' and can in any case be arrested, and may not produce recognisable gaseous by-products – this needs researching as the potential for success is arguably greater. Dogs also have a value in identifying those locations where bodies have been dumped before being moved elsewhere and buried. Depending on training school, dogs are able to distinguish between animal and human carcass elements in both surface and buried environments, although those in the USA tend to be trained on air-scent only. In the latter, the ground needs to be 'vented' before the dog is brought in to play. This involves probing the ground to as deep a depth as possible, usually to around 1m, using a probing device which leaves an airway at least 1cm in diameter through the ground for the release of decomposition gasses. Venting carried out using an auger or similar device also has the potential to identify disturbed earth.

Some handlers prefer to pepper the ground with a large number of randomly placed vent holes within an area of approximately 2 × 2m at the target area. Other may use a line approach, and place a line of vent holes spaced regularly at 0.5m intervals across a target. Both methods work on the basis that any buried remains will release gasses through the vent holes and enhance the dog's ability to detect buried human remains. The dog is brought to each hole in turn, usually downwind and holes are searched in the same order as they were made. This is to negate the possibility of a dog 'winding' a contaminated hole made by a dirty probe and jumping across the hole containing the scent source, thus giving 'false' indications. The dog's response is judged accordingly. In the same way that geophysical survey requires a skilled interpreter, the responses of cadaver dogs also need a skilled and experienced handler, necessary not only for bringing the dog into detection mode, but also in being able to judge the level of the dog's response as it reaches each vent hole. Sometimes body dogs can be confused by other scents which might either mask the smell of human remains or contain elements of human remains scents (e.g. methane) but which originate from different sources, such as in peatlands. Dogs are not contextually aware; they merely respond to the scents they have been trained to detect. Furthermore, if a dog responds to a particular vent hole, or series of holes, this does not necessarily indicate that the source lies directly below. The gasses to which the dog is reacting may be released through the vent, but the source may lie uphill or in a different part of the hydrological regime which has brought the scent to that particular vent hole. It then becomes the role of the handler to source the remains more precisely using further carefully positioned vents. The movement of scents in such scenarios can be likened to the path taken by smoke from a flare if released inside a dry stone wall, i.e. the path of least resistance.

Dogs are ideally used in combination with other techniques, depending on the importance of the location within an enquiry. In many circumstances, when a specific location has been identified as being potentially suspicious (for example, a back garden), the ground surface can be evaluated and geophysical survey implemented (e.g. cases 4 and 6). Any anomalies identified by the geophysics can then be tested by the dog through the normal venting procedure (Figure 2.5). If the surfaces are dense and GPR has been used, vents can be facilitated using power drills and the dog subsequently

Figure 2.5 Top: using drills to vent solid surfaces for the body dog. Bottom: removal of upper soils can indicate disturbances cut into undisturbed deposits

Source: courtesy of Greater Manchester Police.

brought to each vent in the normal manner. A response by the dog would then necessitate more extreme, but controlled, intervention. If the dog fails to respond to any of the anomalies, then the next stage in the search process will requires the SIO to make a key decision. If the search has been one brought about by generally unfounded allegation or the need to eliminate the garden from an inquiry, then the search may be concluded at that stage. However, if the SIO has strong information in the significance of the garden, he or she may wish to pursue the search effort and input more resources into investigating the garden. This is a management decision and one which must be respected by archaeologists even if they are fully convinced that there are no burials present (but see case 3).

If investigation is to continue, the next stage may involve stripping the topsoil down to undisturbed deposits, usually to bedrock or other undisturbed horizons (e.g., clay, gravel or similar), or even to anthropogenic levels which are known to predate the incident in question. The key factor is to ensure that the horizon is one into which the disturbances caused by burial are readily visible. This is best and most rapidly carried out using a machine, although there are often circumstances of access, or gardens of relatively small size, where this is not always possible, or where there is a clear level of stratigraphy present (e.g. cases 2, 3 and 5). In these cases the topsoil can be removed by hand, most effectively by clearing a 1m wide strip of undisturbed subsurface across one end of the garden by horizontal spading. After this has been exposed and cleaned by trowel it can be covered by the spoil from the next 1m strip, and so on until the whole garden has been systematically stripped, cleaned and covered over again. The method ensures comprehensive coverage and negates the cost of removing spoil on site. On larger sites, the most efficient type of machine is one which can revolve 360° on tracks and offers the facility of a wide, toothless, ditching bucket usually 1m wide (teeth tend to create soil and possible body damage) to scrape away the upper soil horizons. The effectiveness of the process depends entirely on the ability of the machine driver to work carefully and horizontally removing only a few centimetres at a time, and on the archaeologist being able to provide the correct instructions and maintain a thorough watching brief. As with manual clearing, the logistics of the process need to be thought out well in advance. In some instances the spoil will need to be moved off site completely and returned later, in others it will be possible to move the spoil systematically around the site to follow the machine. Either way the machine routing has to be arranged to minimise surface damage. The most efficient way is to clear a corner of the garden to bedrock, trowel it across, and then locate the machine there for systematic movement on to each fresh area as it becomes exposed and eliminated.

When the upper strata have been removed, anomalous features can be quickly cleaned with a trowel and examined, usually by half-section (Figure 2.5; also Chapter 4). In some geological or domestic environments features or intrusions are not always clear-cut and may be blurred by alluvial, root, or even rodent action. Usually there a number of features to be investigated, and there is simply not time to treat each one in painstaking detail. The most practical method implicitly assumes that the feature is there to be tested to determine whether it is a grave or not, rather than to assume a grave in the first instance. The process may lack a degree of archaeological purity, but is a rapid and effective way of eliminating features by using archaeological principles.

Features need not be 'grave-sized' or 'grave-shaped' as victims may be dismembered and body parts buried individually. Neonate and infant victims, however, pose their own problems in that any disturbance is likely to be small and difficult to pick up. However, the smallest burial is unlikely to have sides less than about 20cm (i.e. the width of a typical spade).

If the disturbances are too large to half-section, clarification can normally be made by positioning narrow evaluation trenches across the suspect areas. These trenches can be as narrow as 30–40cm, positioned across the main part of the feature, and can be excavated rapidly until undisturbed soils are reached and the character of the disturbance identified. However, once invasive testing techniques are deployed, there is always a compromise between finding the remains and preserving the full integrity of the evidence. Nevertheless, even relatively deep features can be tested quickly, either by following layers and separating the spoil, or by following 'spits' of convenient depth. In most instances the features will be innocent and can be rapidly eliminated, but they are still potential crime scenes and need to be recorded by note and measured drawing by the archaeologist as part of a brief report. The location may need to be returned to and the notes, no matter how trivial, will be one of the few records of the event maintained in the incident file. They may also be disclosable.

If, through either half-section or trial trench, the features are identified as a grave, then a full archaeological methodology will need to be employed (see Chapter 4) and the location will move into the status of a crime scene. This is the time at which some SIOs may (annoyingly) see no further need for the archaeologist given that the object of the search has been achieved. However, there are now key points of evidential integrity at stake and these illustrate the difficulty of making a hard and fast distinction between the processes of search and recovery respectively. The search process has now identified part of the edges of the grave and, in all probability, has outlined the full extent of the area of evidence potential. Furthermore, the exposed section will show how the grave was filled in, it will also guide the excavators in how to remove the remainder of the fill, and the retained excavated layers or spits will show the material used for infilling. The condition of the human remains will be apparent and further action can be informed accordingly (see Chapter 4, case 19). In short, the search process so far will not only have provided key data about the burial and given guidance as to recovery, but will also have done so with minimal loss of evidence.

A similar approach can be adopted on occasions when it becomes necessary to test targets identified from the air. Police forces have access to skilled military aerial investigators through the Joint Air Reconnaissance Intelligence Centre (JARIC) which is able, at short notice, to take aerial photographs of suspect areas and recommend appropriate points of likely vegetation change or soil disturbance. Once located on the ground, these can then be investigated by either a dog, by using narrow test trenches, or both. A difficulty here is that an experienced aerial observer is likely to be able to identify a number of possible targets even in places which are probably implausible, for example, in an open front garden, or in the middle of a field. As with geophysical anomalies, these will still need to be tested if total elimination is to be ensured. The SIO is effectively committed to this when the decision to use these techniques is made.

2.4 Search advice

Giving search advice requires information under a range of headings and can usually be ascertained by telephone before detailed search has commenced. The FSAG has a *pro forma* for preliminary enquiries of this type which necessitates knowledge of essential data such as the nature and size of the target, the interval since last sighting, the possible interval since death, and the scale of the area under investigation. If the search area is within a building, there is a need to ascertain the nature of the supporting structure, floors and, if possible, sub-floor surfaces. If the area is external, factors of soil, geology, hydrology, vegetation, outbuildings and access will need to be known. It may be desirable to have further information regarding the presumed manner of death as this may affect decomposition rate, as well as possible burial speed (from witness accounts) which may have implications regarding depth and concealment.

Existing acquisition by the enquiry team of OS maps, geological maps, plans and aerial photographs will enable preparation to move quickly, and any information regarding data already acquired can serve as a guide to the required level of thoroughness of search. If any search has already been undertaken, then a log or map, including methodology, is an essential requirement before any further search is conducted. With much of this information to hand, it becomes possible to design a strategy and begin to suggest methods, processes, sequences and prospects, even at the end of a telephone.

At the scene itself, further detail can be gathered to consolidate this information and hone the search design further. There is no substitute for a scene visit, despite any obvious constraints on an inquiry (see Chapter 1), and an on-site briefing will allow all relevant personnel to hear the incident narrative, view maps and photographs, discuss practical issues, and formulate a comprehensive, integrated search strategy (but see case 3). In some instances circumstances may present the need for innovation or lateral thought rather than immediate response (see case 13). Often a first-hand visit will enable a full topographical evaluation to be made (land use, extent, height and variety of any vegetation, the level of undulation, areas of dead ground or concealment, etc.), soil depth and geology can be tested and sampled, and man-made elements can be more realistically visualized (access routes, tracks, buildings, etc.). The SIO will also feel more comfortable discussing sensitive issues of the case which may have implications for disposal face to face (e.g. characteristics of the victim or offender, the integrity of the existing evidence, or the likely manner of death). As the search equation starts to be drawn together, so the search design can be optimised to mutual satisfaction and implemented with appropriate resources, equipment and skilled personnel.

2.5 Case studies

A number of case studies have been listed to illustrate some of the above processes and applications of techniques. There is no such thing as a typical search scenario, but many searches have features in common, and the summaries are intended to depict some of the themes involved, and the breadth of the individual difficulties concerned. They also illustrate the range of experience and understanding needed by the archaeologist. In most instances, the locations and the individuals concerned have been made anonymous. Some of the details have also been changed.

Case 1 *Search for young adult male in a wide rural environment*

A young male adult, part of military platoon, was involved in civil defence work as part of larger military operations within the Falkland Islands in the South Atlantic in 1980. The landscape was almost entirely rural and consisted of scattered coastal settlements typically with populations of around 60 persons and a small number of outlying farms located for the sheep industry. There were no roads as such, transport being by four-wheel drive vehicle across inconsistent trackways. The individual went missing from one of the small communities in 1980 after a local party which took place the night before the platoon's depart by boat. His absence was only noted when the boat had left its berth early the next morning. A subsequent military enquiry came to the conclusion that, having been drinking, he had slipped from the jetty during the night and had been swept out to sea.

Local gossip, subsequent investigation of the sea movements at that point, and further police enquiries suggested that he had met a different fate, that he may have been involved in a fracas at the party in the early hours of the morning which resulted in his death, and that his body had been disposed of locally. Three local men were subsequently arrested, but were later released. All had moved out of the settlement at the time of the search. With no dominant starting point, the search was necessarily restricted to the general environment of the incident (Figure 2.6). This consisted of the immediate settlement locality (some 25 small houses, the estate manager's house and garden, outbuildings, sheds, and substantial sheep shearing facilities), a small number of outlying farms and sheds, and some 250 square miles of low-lying uninhabited landscape containing open plains, rivers, streams, gullies and rock outcrops.

The search design was drawn up by a combination of local police familiar with the scenario, the landscape, and the history of the disappearance, and other specialists including an archaeologist, a body dog handler and a GPR operator. The police made all their files available to the search team and underwrote the costs of a 3-week pro-gramme of search based out in the settlement and arranged appropriate logistics of vehicles, transport, accommodation and provisions. A general plan was drawn up and reviewed on a daily basis at an evening debriefing for all concerned. The search group numbered approximately 10 personnel.

The disappearance occurred in mid-winter when the ground was frozen and vehicle movement difficult. The time-frame of the relevant events was known and it was possible to map two circles of radii c.15km and 20km respectively around the settlement repre-senting the minimum and maximum likely distances that a vehicle could travel in that time and in those conditions. Part of the area could be eliminated immediately as being inaccessible even by four-wheel drive vehicle, and another part could be given priority on the basis of a witness account. The search began in the settlement itself: certain buildings and their gardens associated with potential offenders were targeted, and the estate manager's house with its outbuildings, stables and extensive gardens was given particular attention. Accounts and photographs of the settlement at the time of the disappearance enabled an assessment of suitable areas of concealment to be more accurately focused. Open areas such as gardens were then evaluated using fieldcraft techniques and subsequently vented for the dog. Enclosed areas (e.g. sheds, garages, etc.) which showed evidence for replaced or repaired floors were scanned by GPR and any significant anomaly drilled to allow venting. Much of the locality consisted of a hard near-surface geology. Areas of softer ground were limited, notably ditches, cultivated areas, and the local graveyard, and it was essential to have local (police) involvement in the search who were familiar with the vicinity, its land use and its history. The search team also consulted building records to see if structural changes or alterations

Figure 2.6 Case 1. Top: aerial view of the settlement and the wider environment of search. Bottom: detailed search taking place in one of the secluded gardens

had been undertaken since the event, and as a result a small number of domestic dwellings were also searched for flooring or sub-flooring anomalies. Some 'public' structures were also involved including the Community Hall where the party took place, the various sheep shearing and storage sheds, and external sheep dip facilities. Search was also made of other structures that might have deterred investigation at the time, for example, the extensive kennels for sheep dogs in the estate manager's grounds.

It is almost impossible to eliminate fully a settlement of even relatively small size from a search. The only sure method of elimination is to raze the village to the ground, sieve the debris and take a machine across the whole area to look for disturbances – clearly, an impractical solution. Offenders familiar with a local environment will know exactly where the best disposal locations may lie, and the only realistic way to counteract this is to identify key areas of concealment, flooring and suitable patches of soft land available at the time, preferably with access to local knowledge. This is the best that can be done unless other information is forthcoming.

However, even a small population centre such as this is not a safe disposal environment: buildings change hands; developments occur; too many individuals may witness disposal, and a less central location may be more appropriate for a permanent disposal. The rumour surrounding the event supports this view, namely, that the body was hidden briefly in the settlement until it could be moved to a permanent location elsewhere, probably early the next day. However, an aerial search conducted by the military during the days that followed observed no disturbance of the ground in the vicinity. Nor was any carrion bird activity seen that might indicate a surface disposal.

Outside the settlement, the search concentrated on fixed landscape points adjacent to trackways, the assumption being that disposals are not random, but occur in places which are specific to perpetrators in that the locations are known to them. Knowledge can be through familiarity of workplace, leisure or simply through travel, but allows the place to be returned to for checking and peace of mind. Even uninhabited open landscapes have reference points and, as far as possible, these were investigated using both field craft, the dog and GRP. It was a fairly thankless task and, at the time of writing, the marine still remains undiscovered. The dog responded in areas of peat cuttings at the edge of the settlement, but no remains were forthcoming and the response was eventually attributed to methane released from the peat bogs. It is difficult to see where any search might move next. The primary starting point was that of the settlement, subsequently moving outwards and taking into account known events at the time. The 'obvious' locations have now been eliminated, but any renewed search would need (1) new information or (2) a specific detail of landscape on which to concentrate. The strongly held belief of the search team was that the marine's remains had not been missed, but that the correct area had yet to be targeted.

Case 2 Search for two juveniles in the gardens of urban terraced houses

In the early 1970s two young boys went missing on their way to school, the last sighting being at a bus stop in a terraced part of the city where they lived. Despite intensive enquiries they were never seen again and the investigation was aggravated by a number of other local difficulties. A cold case review in 2001 identified that a convicted paedophile had lived in the immediate vicinity of the last sighting. His house, together with that of a nearby relative, subsequently became the focus of search attention. Both houses had solid floors and generally neglected rear gardens or yards typically containing flagging, hard ground and accumulations of material.

The investigation had been well planned, search officers specially trained, and a sequence of search techniques lined up appropriate to the environment in question. The history of the gardens had been researched as much as possible and the archaeologists were given full details of the case background at the briefing stage. A design was subsequently drawn up which included two archaeologists (one for each house), an anthropologist, GPR operators (both civilian and military), cadaver dog and handler, search officers, scene of crime personnel, forensic scientists, and Operational Support Unit (OSU) officers. It was agreed from the outset that all personnel would be to hand for the full duration of the exercise, even if they were not immediately occupied.

Inside the house the ground floors were cleared and radar transects undertaken. In the few instances where anomalies were recorded, the floor was drilled for venting purposes and the dog brought in. The gardens were also covered using radar, again with the locations of any anomalies vented for the dog. Each garden was then treated as an archaeological site with the various layers, structures, flagging, etc. removed sequentially down to the underlying clay. Any disturbances cut into this clay were sectioned as potential graves (Figure 2.7), but emerged typically as rubbish pits or, on one occasion, the deep burial of a dog. Much of the removal of the deposits was undertaken by the OSU officers under archaeological supervision with the anthropologist to hand. Experience had shown that sites can be investigated fairly rapidly by relatively untrained personnel providing that archaeological supervision is available for trouble-shooting, examination of features and recording. Briefing of the team by

Figure 2.7 Case 2. Half-sectioning a feature in the rear garden

the archaeologist is essential so that all parties know exactly what they are doing, why they are doing it, and the method adopted. In this particular case, the operation was facilitated by several of the local personnel having had experience in Kosovo. Experience has also shown that, in investigations of this nature, the full-time presence of an anthropologist is essential rather than desirable. Animal bone, usually food debris, frequently occurs even in modern gardens and needs to be assessed rapidly. There are often instances, particularly with fragmentary bone, where it is difficult to distinguish between animal and human material and where expert support at the scene negates the delay encountered in taking the material off-scene for examination.

Throughout the search, decisions at the scene were made through discussions between the SIO, the scene manager, and the archaeologist in order to achieve mutually acceptable procedures. This particular investigation took a full working week at the scene. During that time no human remains were encountered and the two properties were subsequently eliminated from the enquiry.

Case 3 Search for a victim in a house, outbuildings and garden

In one particular case a police search was being carried out for cremated human remains in a house and garden, the search being effectively driven by information, rather than a search strategy based upon the characteristics of the search area itself. It occurred in the early stages of forensic archaeological awareness in which the scene officers were not fully familiar with the nature of archaeological input, and the archaeologists were hesitant of their role and status within a major police enquiry.

At this scene, the main focus of attention was a large building at one end of a long narrow garden followed by another construction at the other end. The demolition of the main structure and excavation of late twentieth-century stratigraphy beneath its footprint was ultimately undertaken using archaeological principles and archaeologists but only after the senior archaeologist had advised the Crime Scene manager that the method employed by the police would not allow any cremated bone to be observed. Geophysics was considered but advice was that there were few if any areas that did not have post-disappearance disturbance by services. While the final work on this area was being completed, the archaeologists began to investigate the area immediately adjacent to this structure and located a large ovoid feature of some 1.5m in length. When pointing this out to the Crime Scene Manager, the response was that the feature was a soak-away (which proved to be correct) and, as such was not worth examining. This matter was discussed but the feature left intact. No remains of significance were located beneath the main structure and so focus shifted to the second area of interest. This was excavated archaeologically and produced evidence that was of direct relevance to the case, but included no human remains. Following from this, the rest of the site was excavated systematically by archaeologists working back from the second feature almost to the site of the demolished structure, but no human remains were found. All of this took five weeks. When the excavation was complete back to the area of the soak-away, the SIO decided to halt the work. At this point the archaeologists reminded the police that it would not be possible for them to eliminate the site from suspicion unless the final area was investigated. This was eventually agreed and, some considerable time later than was necessary, the remains of the victim (unburnt) were found in the soak-away inside an oil drum (Figure 2.8; see also Chapter 3, Section 3.9.3).

Figure 2.8 Case 3. A detailed excavation of modern stratigraphy took place in a rear garden over a period of several weeks. The victim was eventually found in an oil drum in an apparent soak-away.

There are three good lessons to be learned from this. The first is that although information can be very highly rated by many police officers, sometimes with very good reason and good outcomes, it can also be very misleading and unreliable, and in some cases it dictates strategy which can ignore the physical characteristic of the site itself. The weight placed on such information may seem odd to archaeologists (who rely more on material than oral evidence) but that is often police practice and has to be accepted as such. This scenario sat in the uncomfortable early years of archaeological input, but now detailed discussion between interested parties before work starts is more likely to iron out differences of opinion and strategy. The second lesson is that the archaeologist is part of a team and one whose advice may well be ignored. That too is the way things are and has to be accepted. The key point to remember from this cautionary tale is that this search strategy, despite being unnecessarily prolonged, was successful and, despite the length of time involved, was not considered expensive for a murder enquiry. The suspect was subsequently convicted of murder and is currently serving a life sentence. Finally, numerous fragments of unstratified cremated bone were found on this site in the upper layers of garden soil, some of this was definitely human. Prior to beginning this investigation the archaeologist had undertaken a check of the local SMR and this indicated that an Iron Age cremation cemetery was known to have existed close to the site. As such, it was concluded that this material was probably derived from that context. Had an SMR check not been undertaken, another murder enquiry might have ensued.

Case 4 Search for a child in a garden in a semi-rural environment

A search for a missing person had entailed the investigation of a domestic garden. The ground consisted mostly of grassy areas, a few flower beds, and some areas of flagging and concrete which were located to the rear of the property in a secluded part of the garden. After earlier discussions with the SIO, a search team was created consisting of an archaeologist, an anthropologist (essential for the interpretation of 'stray' bone), a GRP operator, a dog handler, and the usual scene of crime team. It was agreed to conduct a GPR survey initially, and this was carried out in detail across the concrete and then in more widely spaced traverses across the more open aspects of the garden. This identified a small number of anomalies, although none of them were considered to be of the appropriate size or depth. Nevertheless, the anomalies within the grassy areas were vented for the cadaver dog, and those in the concrete areas drilled to provide the same facility. The dog failed to respond to any of the features. At this point both the GPR operator and the dog handler were content that the garden was clear, but the SIO wished for complete elimination and a machine was brought in to strip away the upper surfaces, including the concrete. Before this occurred the archaeologist dug a series of small test pits to ascertain the depth and character of the natural substrates, and also to identify any layers associated with the construction of either the house or garden. The house had been built in the 1950s on a redeposited clay bed and this was later discovered to lie across the main part of the garden at a relatively shallow depth below the current ground surface. It was also established that the garden had been substantially levelled since the person disappeared and this knowledge was essential when guiding the machining during stripping.

From a search perspective, the stripping transpired to be an interesting exercise in that the only disturbances it revealed were those already defined by the GPR. No others were encountered. On investigation, several of these were pet burials to which the dog, being trained for human decay scent, had properly not responded. The garden was thus eliminated. Like case 2, the search design started in a non-invasive way in order to ensure maximum survival of any buried evidence. The case also demonstrated the value of ascertaining as much history of the site as possible and in being able to understand the basic local stratigraphy before invasive work commences.

Case 5 Search for young female adult in urban environment

A young woman working as a prostitute in the Midlands went missing in 1999. Her disappearance was especially disconcerting as she was bringing up a young child to whom she was devoted. The general area of her last movements could be ascertained from mobile telephone positions and, although a number of males within that area fell under suspicion either for previous offences or through known use of prostitutes, no single one could be targeted. However, the picture changed rapidly when the bedroom of one of the suspect's houses was found to contain blood which had a DNA match with the missing woman. This was approximately six months after the disappearance.

A search was then implemented, the starting point being the house and garden of the suspect, haunts where he was known to take prostitutes, and his work environment. The search assumed that the victim had been disposed of either as a whole body, or as dismembered parts.

The rear garden of the suspect's property measured some 25 × 5m. It was undulating and overgrown and contained deposits of rubbish and rubble, making it unsuitable for any form of geophysics. Parts of it were well concealed from view, but it was unfortunately inaccessible to machine stripping. Initial examination by the archaeologists indicated no obvious disturbance. OSU officers were then brought in to remove overgrown vegetation, and were trained to spade away topsoil horizontally on to undisturbed deposits under archaeological supervision. The exposed horizons were subsequently trowelled by archaeologists and a number of minor disturbances identified. These were then vented for dog work, although no responses were made by the dog, and then tested manually. The garden was then eliminated from the enquiry with a high degree of confidence.

Attention then turned to an area of woodland which the suspect was known to frequent with prostitutes. This posed a number of problems in that it contained several secluded areas, although not all of these were screened by evergreens which would have provided the only appropriate leaf cover at the time she went missing. It was also difficult to define a realistic boundary, given that the suspect was also known to enjoy his activities in the open air as well as in his vehicle. Consideration had to be given to the fact that the woman may have been walked from the vehicle to the place of murder and disposal as opposed to the arguably shorter distance of being carried as a dead weight. The suspect was also a fairly large, strong man and this too had to be fed into the overall equation. On the positive side, the relatively dense woodland also inhibited digging as a result of tree roots, thus narrowing down possible burial places to a relatively small number of clearings and areas of accumulated leaf mould. As a result, a general area of interest could be defined within which certain specific locations could be targeted. While a search strategy was being developed using predominantly field craft, probing and a body dog (the extent of tree roots, rubbish and fly-tipping effectively precluded the use of geophysics), attention turned to the suspect's workplace – an outdoor yard secluded from the road by a high fence – located some distance away in the town.

This covered an area of about 20 × 30m with a compacted earth surface and some patches of concrete. It contained items of plant, building/garden materials, and areas of storage, as well as containing a central bonfire area for burning rubbish. The suspect was known to have lit a substantial fire in the yard the day after the woman disappeared, but the ashes had already been checked as part of the original enquiry, and subsequent bonfires had been lit on top in the weeks that followed. A cursory inspection of the resulting ash tip which was now approximately 2m in diameter and some 20cm deep showed layers of ash representing different burning events. Small fragments of calcinated bone were also evident and these were later identified as animal bone by an archaeozoologist. In view of the potential importance of the ash heap it was agreed to investigate it further, and careful excavation and sieving took place, treating each ash layer separately (Figure 2.9). The work was carried out by a SOCO with a background in archaeology who was able to recognise small items of bone and understand the importance of retaining stratigraphic integrity. A large number of small bone fragments

Figure 2.9 Case 5. Searching of the layered ash tip in the work yard

were recovered, some 15 of which, including a tooth, were recorded from the base ash deposit and were identified by anthropologists as being human. An archaeologist who specialised in cremations was also brought into the enquiry. Further examination of these fragments was able to suggest that the individual was female and of the appropriate age. Analysis of the tooth, and the presence of personal items found within the base ash layer, confirmed the identity of the missing woman. The suspect was subsequently convicted of murder and is currently serving a life sentence. The case shows the value of using archaeological support in certain types of investigation, and the importance of physical anthropologists in the identification process.

Case 6 Elimination of an urban garden during the search for a young female adult

A young female adult had gone missing while walking home to relieve her babysitter. Her body had never been found, there were no particular suspects, and a general air of mystery had developed in the vicinity over the years since she disappeared. Information was eventually received that on the day she vanished a neighbour had heard a disagreement between a female and a male followed by sounds of digging in a nearby garden. The garden in question belonged to a house used by a family well known to the police and it was unclear as to whether the information was genuine or merely an exercise in local hostility. The garden was about 70m long and 8m wide and fenced on all sides. In order not to raise suspicion, a single helicopter pass was used to take a photograph to inform a search strategy. This showed that the garden contained both grassy and concrete areas, a pathway, an area of unkempt ground, sheds and a paved terrace adjoining the back of the house. There were also two areas secluded by trees and a small brick extension adjoining the rear of the property. Reference to planning applications and local building records (this was a local authority house) showed that the extension had been constructed before the woman went missing.

A search design was drawn up using two archaeologists, GRP and resistivity facilities, a body dog handler, an OSU team, and the customary scene of crime presence. Given the narrow shape of the garden and the various impediments and different ground features, proper organisation and integration of the different search elements were critical (see also Chapter 3, Section 3.8.3). The resistivity was undertaken first on the grassy areas while the OSU officers emptied the sheds allowing the GPR survey of the shed floors together with the concrete paths and patio and, subsequently, the rest of the garden to follow on from the resistivity (for details, see Chapter 3, Section 3.8.3). Targets were identified by both techniques and each vented for the dog which only responded to one. On test excavation this response appeared to be brought about by pieces of human excrement caught in a drain area. As the two different geophysics techniques were based on different principles, each had a tendency to identify differ-ent types of feature (hence the importance of using complementary techniques), but they had two in common. Small test excavation showed one of these to be a sump/soak-away pit, the other was the burial of a cat. It was interesting that the dog responded to neither, having being trained specifically not to respond to animal carcasses.

The search lasted for most of the day but was undertaken with minimum disruption, minimum intervention, and entailed minimum reinstatement costs. The garden was confidently eliminated from the enquiry.

Case 7 Investigation of a house containing a possible burial

A police force sought the advice of forensic archaeologists when searching beneath the floor of a particular room in a terraced house with concrete floors. The site had already been subject to survey using GPR which had revealed several anomalies. Each of these had been investigated, and each had revealed a void beneath the concrete. Upon examination of these areas by the archaeologists it was realised that the concrete floor had been laid between and over wooden joists after removing wooden floor-boards and seemed to indicate that in many areas the concrete did not extend right down to the earth floor beneath the joists. The police were, understandably, not keen to remove the entire concrete floor. The application of any other forensic geophysics was not appropriate in this case and the strategy suggested by the archaeologists involved the use of an endoscope to 'see' beneath the layer of concrete. An appropriate endo-scope with a light source was located and used to examine different areas of the floor. No obvious anomalies were apparent. However, when the endoscope was removed from the last area, examination of the head showed that it had accumulated numerous puparia cases. The archaeologists had seen similar evidence before in association with corpses and advised the police to remove the concrete in that area. The remains of the missing person were found beneath the concrete floor; they were almost entirely encased in concrete but fortunately, the perpetrator(s) had failed to entirely enclose the victim and at some stage *Calliphorae* sp. had located the body and ovaposited, resulting in the inevitable barrel-shaped puparium.

The lessons from this case are that an understanding of forensic entomology can be crucial in locating remains and that examining subterranean contexts can involve many different approaches apart from the obvious ones discussed elsewhere.

Case 8 Search for a victim of the so-called Moors Murderers

The so-called Moors Murders hold a place in folklore as much as in real life. Of five children abducted and murdered by Ian Brady and Myra Hindley in the early 1960s, four were concealed in the peat moors in the uplands between West Yorkshire and Lancashire (now Greater Manchester). The landscape is hostile, disorientating, and diffi-cult to search. Apart from streams, it lacks reference points, easily definable boundaries, and is particularly susceptible to rapid changes of weather. The surface vegetation consists of large uneven tussocks which are difficult to walk through, often with hazardous cracking into hidden streams and peat deposits. Despite the expanse of land available, burial is only easily feasible in the areas of exposed peat found in low-lying gullies as well as on higher exposed ground. One characteristic of these peat exposures is the manner in which the exposed turf at the higher end erodes, fractures, and slides down over the old peat, opening up a new peat surface in the process. Comparison of aerial photographs taken since the Second World War demonstrates this phenomenon, and also emphasises the inconsistency and unpredictability of this movement over time. Its effect, however, is to indicate that visible areas suited to burial in the 1960s are not necessarily those apparent today.

Police searching in the 1960s recovered two of the victims, and a third body was found during renewed investigation in 1988. During that period (and since) sporadic, uncoordinated and unrecorded activity has served to make the search task more difficult. The final victim, a 12-year-old called Keith Bennett, was walked across the moors to his fate and the search area becomes much wider than in those instances where a body has to be physically carried from a vehicle. In 1988 police defined much of their search area on information supplied by the two perpetrators. This provided the appropriate (and only) starting point but the search results were negative. One obvious conclusion puts the absence of the child's body down to those natural and animal agencies which might affect a shallow burial. As an added search complication, the sheer physical difficulties posed by the landscape also have the effect of pushing any geophysical techniques to their limits. Most dauntingly, the erosion phenomena and collapse of peat edges have brought about localised disturbance to the bedrock, and in some instances can bring about invertion of the natural deposits. This then appears as background 'noise' and aggrevates geophysical survey.

Renewed search in 2000/1 identified three gullies in order to either discover the body, or eliminate them from any future work. The gullies offered appropriate cover, fitted in with the information available and, most importantly, exhibited a considerable extent of peat movement since the 1960s (Figure 2.10). They also held a particular fascination for Brady, and there is no doubt that the place to which he chose to walk Keith was special to him, not just a place that would suffice in terms of cover and dis-tance from the road. The search was based within a grid framework maintained using GPS and adopted an integrated approach using resistivity, logging of existing peat

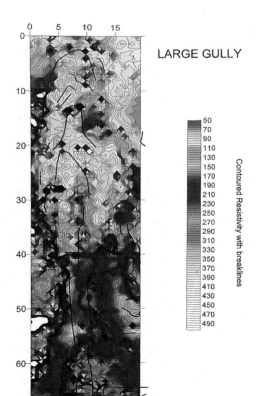

LARGE GULLY

Contoured Resistivity with breaklines

50
70
90
110
130
150
170
190
210
230
250
270
290
310
330
350
370
390
410
430
450
470
490

Figure 2.10 Case 8. Top: general view of the overall environment of Saddleworth Moor. Bottom: geophysics plot of one of the gullies showing both higher and lower resistance values taken at 0.5m intervals illustrating the variability of the subsurface. The gully slopes down to the bottom and the black lines denote current fractures in the turf cover.

edges, and depth probing which had the additional benefit of indicating core composition down to approximately 1m. It was, therefore, possible to correlate the data sets and to identify anomalous points of higher or lower resistance respectively in relation to depth and thus to interpret possible points for targeting. One fundamental difficulty was in not knowing how (or indeed if) the target might respond to resistivity, or whether burial disturbance might itself be detectable. Under typical circumstances, it might be expected that the remains would be relatively well preserved in keeping with other peat recoveries (including the victim recovered in 1988) on the basis of the anaerobic and tanning properties of peat. Clearly there would be difficulty in detecting remains of any type given the variability of the subsurface. Over 11,000 resistivity readings were taken (0.5m intervals at 0.5m traverses). These were interpreted in conjunction with the depth and other data and some 30 points of specific interest were identified. Each of these was then vented for body dog search, the dog ultimately responding to just two. Both were excavated (typically 2 × 1m) down to undisturbed horizons but no human remains were found. The direction of the dog's interest was followed but evaporated as the soil was removed. As in the Falklands, the dog appears to have been respecting gasses emitted from peat or from vegetation within the peat.

The exercise demonstrated the stark difference between classroom theory and the practical application of techniques brought about simply by environment, difficulty of terrain either for conventional or geophysical surveying, access and climate.

Case 9 Search for an alleged neonate burial

It had been alleged that a neonate had been buried many years ago in a very specific location, in fact, in part of a graveyard which had never been used. The target was small, but the part of the graveyard was very specific and measured barely 4 × 4m. The strategy adopted was to use magetometry initially in that there was some evidence of a possible small ferrous object associated with the burial, followed by resistivity. Given the sensitivity of the operation the police were anxious to avoid public interest and erected a large perimeter screen supported by metal (iron) posts which had the effect of completely negating the value of any magnetometry. This was an issue of lack of communication, particularly on the part of the archaeologists who discovered this on arrival and who should certainly have ascertained the provision of a viable working environment during earlier briefings. Given the size of the target, resistivity survey was carried out at 25cm intervals and three 'hot spots' identified. In each instance the turf was carefully removed and the anomaly investigated. In two cases the anomalies were found to be the result of tree root effects, the third being a gravel-filled hole. As the area was small, it was then agreed to remove the turf across the whole area by hand, and carefully trowel away the topsoil to undisturbed levels. This was achieved fairly rapidly and no disturbances were encountered. The question was asked of the archaeologists as to why this was not carried out initially, rather than go through the whole process of geophysical survey and data analysis first. Put simply, moving from non-invasive to invasive techniques had enabled the integrity of any data to be maintained. To have excavated from the very outset would have entailed putting any evidence at risk, particularly as the target was so small and fragile. The area was subsequently eliminated from the enquiry.

Case 10 Dismembered remains uncovered by animals

One winter in the 1990s a search was required as the result of partial human remains being discovered at the top of a wooded motorway embankment. A head and part of a limb had been dragged from a shallow burial site by foxes and had been reported by a member of the public walking his dog. The individual had been dismembered and it was not clear how much of the body had been buried in that particular place. Full identification was never made despite the use of intensive publicity, DNA, and facial reconstruction. Moreover, the need to locate any other body parts (either dragged into the woods by animals or buried in the vicinity) caused additional problems in that the search boundary necessarily contained the whole wooded area which was several hectares in size. This was exacerbated by the presence of overgrown scrub and heavy vegetation. The search for further surface remains was undertaken using Operational Support Unit Officers working systematically in a line using the original burial location as the starting point. However, the officers were generally unfamiliar with subtly disturbed ground, and their movement was necessarily destructive, given the thickness of the woodland that required searching. A useful working arrangement was devised whereby the area was divided into taped sectors, each sector being checked first by an archaeologist who marked any possible disturbed ground with a flagged cane. The sector was then thoroughly line-searched and the marked areas subsequently investigated individually.

No further buried remains were recovered, but a small number of scavenged human bones were identified on the surface. One of these was discovered on the second day of the search but in an area which had already been searched and cleared the previous day. This was attributed to animal activity and highlights the problems of surface search in contexts which require more than a single day's investigation. Ultimately, it was concluded that only the one burial site had been involved and that it had only contained some of the body parts – namely those which had been recovered. The field investigation lasted for several days to ensure complete elimination. Any subsequent finding of human material by the public would have required a major search exercise to be repeated.

Case 11 Some issues of scavenging and decomposition in a search enquiry

In a very complex case involving a missing person, a body was eventually discovered many weeks after the person had gone missing. The discovery was made in a woody area which had been intensively searched on several occasions and, although the body lay quite close to a footpath, it had lain unnoticed. In the meantime a person had been arrested and charged with the offence. The case naturally brought to light the question as to why the body had not been found earlier, one possible solution being that it may have been moved there from a primary location during the period of search. Another solution maintained that it may have been partly concealed and dragged into a more open place by animals, or failing that, that the search techniques had been inadequate.

The issue involved examination of the entomology, the extent of the decay, the metrology, the scavenging and animal behaviour patterning, the botanical environment, and the soil on and around the body, but all appeared to give inconsistent answers. The case demonstrates the complexity of such scenarios and the number of specialists required. In fact, the wide range of specialists may be a problem *per se*: although each expert can report on their own particular field, it is perhaps the overview and the interaction of the various disciplines that need to be considered in order to provide a more accurate understanding of such phenomena.

Case 12 Investigation of a cemetery for an illegal burial

Some experts advocate the use of probes in searching for buried remains, although this is not a technique that a UK-trained forensic archaeologist would normally employ. However, the use of an auger can be applicable in certain contexts. For clarification, an auger is not a probe as its purpose is to remove a stratified sample (a core) of the substrate, while a probe is a solid rod which is customarily 'sniffed' or used to detect differences in resistance to force from above.

In this case it was suspected that a missing person may have been interred within one of a series of graves in civil cemeteries, probably being interred above a recent burial (recent at the time of the victim's disappearance). Two factors were pertinent: the depth of the legitimate burials was known with confidence (in most cases it was between 3–4m deep – too deep for a sondage), and, for reasons of sensitivity and public relations, there was no question of any excavation being undertaken unless there was a high degree of certainty that an additional burial might be present. As a result an auger was used to core down systematically (0.5m at a time) to a level just above the anticipated depth of the legitimate burial. While undertaking this it was considered that coffins collapse with time and that the top of the remains would be several centimetres lower than at the time of deposition. In one grave, differential resistance to the auger was noted at a depth above that of the legitimate burial and augering stopped immediately. When the auger was removed, it contained fragments of wood and plastic, and smelt strongly of decomposition. The officer in charge of the investigation, being a cautious man, double-checked the information regarding depth given by the cemetery authority. This proved very sensible as it transpired that the wrong grave number had been given to the police and that in the grave in question there had been a legitimate burial at the depth at which augering had produced a 'result'. None of the other graves investigated indicated a secondary illegal burial and, in view of the success in locating this shallower burial, both archaeologists and police were confident that the cemetery could be successfully eliminated.

This case exemplifies the need for forensic archaeologists to have a wide-ranging experience of archaeological methods, and demonstrates that an archaeologist with experience of augering can use an auger as a sensitive and effective search tool. The auger has a particular role to play in establishing the presence of absence of human remains in burials lying below a depth which would normally be assessed by sondage. Although successful augering to some extent depends upon the substrate, in this case, most of the graves were dug into gravels. Despite the instability of the medium, the method still worked.

Case 13 Investigation of a house containing a possible burial

A request was made for archaeologists to assist an investigation beneath the floors of a 1930s house. It was considered possible that a person missing for a decade or more years might have been buried beneath the floorboards. The police proposed to remove the floorboards allowing the archaeologist access to the ground beneath, but the archaeologist advised that an alternative approach should be considered. This involved an assessment of the floor by an experienced joiner with experience of local properties including those extending in construction date back to the decade in which the house was built. Such an expert would be able to approximately 'date' repairs to the floor by the use of certain techniques and nails. This approach was adopted and any disruptions and repairs that dated to the period in which the person disappeared were removed and the ground beneath assessed by the archaeologist. Those repairs that could be confidently assigned to have pre-dated the presumed event were not examined. This investigation took five hours, no grave was found and the cost to the police was minimal in comparison to the likely costs that would have resulted from the original strategy. The lesson from this example is that it is imperative to think laterally and involve appropriate expertise (not necessarily that of a forensic scientist) that will ensure a confident result.

References

Brown, A.G., Smith, A. and Elmhirst, O. 2002. 'The combined use of pollen and soil analyses in a search and subsequent murder investigation', *Journal of Forensic Sciences* 47:3, 614–618.

Buck, S.C. 2003. 'Searching for graves using geophysical technology: field tests with ground penetrating radar, magnetometry, and electrical resistivity', *Journal of Forensic Sciences* 48:1, 5–11.

Cox, M. 2001. 'Forensic archaeology: a United Kingdom perspective', in Godwin, M.G. (ed.) *Criminal Psychology and Forensic Technology*, New York: CRC Press, pp. 1–14.

Davenport, G.C. 2001. 'Remote sensing applications in forensic investigations', *Journal of Historical Archaeology*, 35:1, 87–100.

Davis, J.L., Heginbottom, J.A., Annan, A.P., Daniels, R.S., Berdal, B.P., Bergan, T., Duncan, K.E., Lewin, P.K., Oxford, J.S., Roberts, N., Skehel, J.J. and Smith C.R. 2000. 'Ground penetrating radar surveys to locate 1918 Spanish flu victims in permafrost', *Journal of Forensic Sciences* 45:1, 68–76.

France, D.L., Griffin, T.J., Swanburg, J.G., Lindemann, J.W., Davenport, G.C., Trammell, V., Travis, C.T., Kondratieff, B., Nelson, A., Castellano, K., Hopkins, D. and Adair, T. 1997. 'Necrosearch revisited: further multidisciplinary approaches to the detection of clandestine graves', in Haglund, W.D. and Sorg, M.H. (eds) *Forensic Taphonomy*, Boca Raton, FL: CRC Press, pp. 497–509.

Gaffney, C. and Gater, J. 2003. *Revealing the Buried Past*, Oxford: Tempus.

Gill-King, H. 1997. 'Chemical and ultrastructural aspects of decomposition', in Haglund, W.D. and Sorg, M.H. (eds) *Forensic Taphonomy*, Boca Raton, FL: CRC Press, pp. 93–108.

Godwin, M. and Canter, D. 1997. 'Encounter and death: the spatial behaviour of US serial killers', *Policing: An International Journal of Police Strategies and Management* 20, 28–38.

Haglund, W.D. 1997. 'Dogs and coyotes: post-mortem involvement with human remains', in Haglund, W.D. and Sorg, M.H. (eds) *Forensic Taphonomy*, Boca Raton, FL: CRC Press, pp. 367–381.

Haglund, W.D. 2002. 'Recent mass graves, an introduction', in Haglund, W.D. and Sorg, M.H. (eds) *Advances in Forensic Taphonomy*, Boca Raton, FL: CRC Press, pp. 242–261.

Haglund, W.D., Connor, M. and Scott, D.D. 2001. 'The archaeology of contemporary mass graves', *Journal of Historical Archaeology* 35:1, 57–69.

Haglund, W.D., Connor, M. and Scott, D.D. 2002. 'The effect of cultivation on buried human remains', in Haglund, W.D. and Sorg, M.H (eds) *Advances in Forensic Taphonomy*, Boca Raton, FL: CRC Press, pp. 133–150.

Haglund, W.D. and Sorg, M.H. (eds) 1997. *Forensic Taphonomy: The Postmortem Fate of Human Remains*, Boca Raton, FL: CRC Press.

Haglund, W.D. and Sorg, M.H. (eds) 2002. *Advances in Forensic Taphonomy. Method, Theory and Archaeological Perspectives*, Boca Raton, FL: CRC Press.

Horrocks, M. and Walsh, K.A.J. 2001. 'Pollen on grass clippings: putting the suspect at the scene of crime', *Journal of Forensic Sciences* 46:4, 947–949.

Hunter, J.R., Brickley, M.B., Bourgeois, J., Bouts, W., Bourguignon, L., Hubrecht, F., De Winne, J., Van Haster, H., Hakbijl, T., De Jong, H., Smits, L., Van Winjngaarden, L. and Luschen, M. 2001. 'Forensic archaeology, forensic anthropology and human rights in Europe', *Science and Justice*, 41:3, 173–178.

Hunter, J.R., Roberts, C.A and Martin, A. 1996. *Studies in Crime: An Introduction to Forensic Archaeology*, London: Routledge.

Janaway, R.C. 1996. 'The decay of buried human remains and their associated materials', in Hunter, J.R., Roberts, C.A. and Martin, A. 1996. *Studies in Crime*, London: Routledge, pp. 58–85.

Janaway, R.C. 2002. 'Degradation of clothing and other dress materials associated with buried bodies of both archaeological and forensic interest', in Haglund, W.D. and Sorg, M.H. (eds) *Advances in Forensic Taphonomy*, Boca Raton, FL: CRC Press, pp. 379–402.

Killam, E.W. 1990. *The Detection of Human Remains*, Springfield, IL: Charles C. Thomas.

Komar, D. 1999. 'The use of cadaver dogs in locating scattered, scavenged human remains: preliminary field test results', *Journal of Forensic Sciences* 44:2, 405–408.

Morse, D., Duncan, J. and Stoutamire, J. 1983. *Handbook of Forensic Archaeology and Anthropology*, Tallahassee: Rose Printing.

Murad, T.A. 1997. 'The utilization of faunal evidence in the recovery of human remains', in Haglund, W.D. and Sorg, M.H. (eds) *Forensic Taphonomy*, Boca Raton, FL: CRC Press, pp. 395–404.

Nobes, D.C. 2000. 'The search for "Yvonne": a case example of the delineation of a grave using near-surface geophysical methods', *Journal of Forensic Sciences* 45:3, 712–715.

Rebmann, A, David, E. and Sorg, M.H. 2000. *Cadaver Dog Handbook*, Boca Raton, FL: CRC Press.

Schmitt, S. 2002. 'Mass graves and the collection of forensic evidence: genocide, war crimes, and crimes against humanity', in Haglund, W.D. and Sorg, M.H. (eds) *Advances in Forensic Taphonomy*, Boca Raton, FL: CRC Press, pp. 277–292.

Scollar, I., Tabbagh, A., Hesse, A. and Herzog, I. 1990. *Archaeological Geophysics and Remote Sensing*, Cambridge: Cambridge University Press.

Skinner, M., York, H.P. and Connor, M.A. (2002) 'Postburial disturbance in graves of Bosnia-Herzegovina, in Haglund, W.D. and Sorg, M.H. (eds) *Advances in Forensic Taphonomy*, Boca Raton, FL: CRC Press, pp. 293–308.

Stoffel, R. (ed.) 2001. *The Handbook for Managing Land Search Operations*, Cashmere: Emergency Response International, ERI Publications and Training.

Turton, S. 2004. 'The scavenging of human remains in forensic contexts'. Unpublished MPhil thesis, Institute of Archaeology and Antiquity, University of Birmingham, UK.

3

FORENSIC GEOPHYSICAL SURVEY

Paul Cheetham

3.1 Background

Chapter 2 has presented a general overview of search methodology and outlined a number of case studies demonstrating the breadth of techniques available. Geophysical survey features prominently among these techniques but is an emerging area of science in its forensic application and is still in its infancy. The topic is highly specialised, appropriate information is not always easy to come by, that which is available is sometimes apparently contradictory, and there continues to be a number of popular misconceptions regarding its role and relative value within well-resourced multi-disciplinary search strategies. This situation is exacerbated by some well-intentioned commentators straying into geophysical discussion without the appropriate background. Equally, some excellent work within this specialism is not filtering through into operational practice.

With this in mind, this chapter is intended to present an overview of the current status and role of forensic geophysics. It draws on the contributor's personal experience of working as a forensic geophysicist and as a forensic archaeologist – an experience gained in tandem with a wider background of archaeological geophysics and archaeological field techniques ranging from aerial photography transcription and analysis through to directing excavation projects. One of the key features in the development of forensic geophysics in the UK has been its association with archaeological geophysics – a strand that runs throughout this chapter. Moreover, for a number of years this contributor has lectured on forensic geophysical survey to both professional and student audiences. This has provided a good appreciation of which aspects of the topic need only be covered in general, and which aspects demand more detailed explanation. This chapter aims to discuss specific issues of geophysics as applied in a forensics context and pursues in more detail the use of certain methods outlined in Chapter 2. A more detailed scientific understanding of individual techniques can be gained through the sources referenced.

3.2 Forensic geophysics

A review of forensic literature illustrates remarkably little overall coherence in geophysical research but points towards a slowly emerging discipline. As early as 1973, Alongi demonstrated that a very early 'portable' horn antenna ground penetration radar (GPR) system with a single trace oscilloscope output could detect the presence of the buried carcass of a dog and suggested its potential for the detection of buried human cadavers. Fourteen years later, Strongman (1992) in trials for the Royal Canadian Mounted Police on the potential of GPR, using a more sophisticated GPR system, clearly demonstrated its effectiveness in a series of successful trials to locate animal carcasses. Positive results have also been obtained and commented on by France *et al.* (1992, 1997) and these have laid the ground for continued experimentation (e.g. Freeland *et al.* 2003) leading to a much better understanding of both the nature of the problem and the effectiveness of GPR as the solution (e.g. Mellett 1996; Hammon *et al.* 2000; Millar *et al.* 2002). As this listing suggests, GPR has seemingly become the *de facto* geophysical technique for forensic grave detection. However, it may be argued that this is simply the consequence of less thorough effort being put into examining the other potential techniques even although, for example, good earth resistivity results for the detection of pig test graves were reported by Lynam as early as 1970 (see below). In the UK earth resistivity continues to be shown to be successful and reliable in favourable survey situations. There have been two recent papers that have attempted to compare multiple techniques (Buck 2003 and Nobes 2000), both of which are discussed here. It might also be noted that while geophysics is normally associated with detecting buried human remains, it is equally useful for other types of buried forensic evidence (firearms, drugs, stolen goods, etc.). However, for these purposes it has not received the same attention in the forensic literature.

3.3 Geological geophysics

Geophysics is widely used by geologists. However, there is need to exercise caution about some aspects of the relevance of geological geophysical expertise in the search for, and recovery of, human remains. This is due to the differences of scale, geophysical methods employed, instrument configurations and field survey and ground-truthing methodologies. The growth area in geophysics has been the smaller scale near-surface survey in what is loosely termed applied engineering, environmental or industrial geophysics with a coincident decline in mineral exploration work (Milsom 2003: xi; Reynolds 1997: 2). This has required new texts to cover the appropriate techniques and methodologies (e.g. Milsom 2003; Reynolds 1997) and clearly some of this material has relevance to forensic applications of geophysics. More generally, Donnelly (2002) rightly championing the discipline of geoforensics and stressing the wide range of expertise that the geologist can bring to forensic investigations, also acknowledges the need to work closely with specialists from related disciplines as there is inevitably some overlap. Forensic archaeologists (including in the UK archaeological geophysicists) have already acknowledged this by virtue of their participation within organisations such as the multidisciplinary Forensic Search Advisory Group in the UK (see Chapter 1, Section 1.7) and NecroSearch International in North America (France *et al.* 1992). While geological principles and methods have much to contribute to forensic investigations, logic dictates that with respect to the detection of graves by geophysics it should be a case of applying archaeological principles and methods. This is because burials are essentially anthropogenic, shallow, sub-surface features, and not larger natural geological phenomena.

3.4 Archaeological geophysics

Ground-based geophysics has a long and distinguished history of use and development within the discipline of archaeology, and has become recognised as *archaeological geophysics* or even *archeogeophysical prospection* (Herz and Garrison 1998: 147). Within European archaeology, geophysics has been for some time considered a mature and fully integrated area of specialism closely allied with other major archaeological prospection techniques. These include aerial photography, field survey in all its forms, geochemical prospecting and other remote sensing techniques. The journal *Archaeological Prospection* and the biannual Archaeological Prospection international conference are the main expressions of this central position and of the integration of geophysics with other prospection techniques within mainstream archaeology. Curiously, this situation relates primarily to Europe (see below), and this partly explains the different manner by which geophysics has been developed and become incorporated into forensics, compared to North America. For a more thorough treatment of the history of archaeological geophysics the reader is directed to Gaffney and Gater (2003).

The first properly documented example of archaeological geophysics took place in the USA in the late 1930s, and was a form of earth resistivity survey that aimed to locate a stone vault beneath a church in Williamsburg, Virginia (Bevan 2000). In the mid-1940s in the UK, crop mark ditches at Dorchester-on-Thames were shown to be detectable by earth resistivity survey (Clark 1996: 11). By the 1950s magnetometry had been added to the list of principal techniques followed by electromagnetics (though with very limited uptake), topsoil magnetic susceptibility and latterly GPR introduced in the 1970s, but with minimal impact initially. Although much of the early geophysical instrumentation was developed for geological and engineering applications, archaeologists have always been quick to borrow and exploit developments in other fields and geophysics has been no exception. Close alliances between archaeologists, archaeological scientists and geophysicists in the UK, France and Germany have led to a breed of archaeological scientists specialising part- or full-time in archaeological geophysics. In the UK the work and seminal publications of Arnold Aspinall and his research students (e.g. Aspinall and Lynam 1970), Martin Aitken (1974), Anthony Clark (1990) and that of many others helped develop and bind archaeology and geophysics together in a way that resulted in the development of new instruments and the honing of techniques to meet the specific requirements and challenges that archaeology presented. Although similarly important routes of development occurred in France, Germany, and Austria (e.g. Doneus *et al.* 2001a), there continues to be a somewhat curious disparity in the development of the relationship of geophysics and archaeology between Europe and North America. This seems to have arisen mainly because of the different ways archaeology (in particular its relationship with anthropology) sits in the study of the past in these two continents. As a consequence, the value of archaeological geophysics requires better appreciation by other geophysicists, including forensic operators (NRC 2000: 27), while the contribution of forensic geophysics also needs to be taken on board by archaeologists (*contra* Hildebrand *et al.* 2002).

In North America archaeology tends to be housed within anthropology faculties that are essentially humanities-based rather than science-based, and this contrasts somewhat with the situation in the UK where in the 1950s the Department of the Environment set up an Ancient Monuments Laboratory to be a focus for scientists pioneering the transfer of new scientific developments into the service of archaeology. A geophysics section followed in 1967 (Clark 1996: 20) and a small number of university programmes (notably at Bradford) in the 1970s began teaching undergraduate and postgraduate programmes in archaeological sciences. Thirty years later, all areas of archaeological science, including geophysics, are now taught in mainstream archaeology programmes in the UK. This close association between archaeology and geophysics has not only resulted in new instruments and configurations but also in a philosophy of multi-method high intensity survey with rigorous spatial control, quite unlike most geophysical work in other disciplines. In archaeological applications the various methods of geophysical survey often aim at maximising the general information about the character and extent of a site rather than details of any specific features, and hence the instrument configurations and survey methodologies are selected with this in mind. However, as a consequence of this, not all features (including graves) may be detectable by such surveys. Schmidt and Marshall (1997) provide an unsettling example that demonstrates how problematic the generalist approach can be.

3.5 Geophysical phenomena and geophysical contrast

It is important to define the relevant terminology and to obtain a clear understanding of what is meant by geophysical survey in the context of detecting clandestine graves and other buried targets. *Geophysical* simply refers to *the physics of the earth* and so in this context geophysical survey is the investigation of the earth by the measurement of its physical properties. Such physical properties are many and varied. Acoustic, electrical, magnetic and electromagnetic are some of the most relevant properties and these are related to a greater or lesser degree to chemical properties (geochemical survey is a topic in its own right and will not be covered in this chapter). The use of geophysical survey techniques in a forensic context most frequently demonstrates two important aspects of the technique, one effectively following on from the other. The first is that survey is conducted on or just above the ground surface and that as such it is non-, or at least only minimally, intrusive. Second, each technique will, when combined with positional information, allow the geophysicist to create a 'map' of the sub-surface. Different techniques will create 'maps' which can vary in both visual form and content. What the geophysicist is looking for are measurements that by virtue of their magnitude or form can be considered different and stand out from the 'natural' variations that will be found to exist in any survey area. If such measurements are identified, then these will constitute 'hot-spots' or, in the language of geophysics, *anomalies*. It must be stressed that if the natural variations are extreme, then the often subtle contrasts that result from minor sub-surface disturbances (including graves) may well be drowned out by this background geophysical 'noise' and may consequently remain undetected.

A most important point to appreciate is that anomalies relate to the physical properties being measured and the way they are measured; they should not be considered to represent in any way 'visual' images of the feature. Put another way, a geophysical image is not like the faithful optical image that the comic book X-ray vision of the Superman variety creates, but is an image created via an intermediary in a geophysical visual language. An analogy would be that it may be possible to get some impression of what a person is doing in the next room even though they cannot be seen, if they can be heard creating familiar sounds that can be interpreted as being associated with various activities such as pacing around, or sitting down at a table and eating. However, two activities (e.g. slow dancing and pacing) may produce very similar sounds, or there may be other perhaps new or unusual sounds, and this illustrates one of the many problems in inferring the presence and interpreting the nature of buried features by geophysical means. Geophysics can be used to infer a presence, but this needs to be interpreted by a process of conjecture, and the interpretation must subsequently be confirmed.

If there is not a contrast in the physical property being measured between a grave (including its contents) and the surrounding medium, then it will not be possible to detect the burial using the geophysical techniques. In this respect simple graves of archaeological date (shallow graves which only contain the body with minimal wrapping such as a fine textile shroud) are inherently problematic, as the fill of the grave will normally consist largely of the same material that was removed, plus a small proportion of bone. Even if this fill is now a different mix, because the material it was dug into was stratified to some extent, its bulk properties may remain very similar and so be undetectable by some geophysical techniques. Lack of contrast makes graves one of the most difficult archaeological features to detect geophysically and most attempts to locate or map individual simple graves within ancient cemeteries have been largely failures, although there are some notable exceptions (see below).

3.6 Geophysical detection of archaeological and historic graves

Readers familiar with Channel 4's *Time Team* television series may recollect that early programmes in the series included a number of attempts to detect graves of Anglo-Saxon, medieval and later periods, including colonists' graves in Maryland, USA, none of which were particularly successful. More recently the Team's use of ground-penetrating radar has been successful in favourable situations but latterly there has been tacit recognition of the limitations of the techniques for the detection of individual archaeological graves (Gaffney and Gater 2003: 136). In respect of work undertaken in the United Kingdom, David (1995) provides a very useful table listing a range of archaeological features together with the likely success of detection of each when using five geophysical techniques frequently used in archaeological work. This is based on the compilation of results from a large number of survey reports. The entries for graves and cremations, reproduced here in Table 3.1, illustrate that graves are not easy to detect. Only resistivity and ground-penetrating radar are reported to be successful, and then only under favourable conditions. Unfortunately 'favourable conditions' are not, and probably cannot, be defined in a satisfactory way that will lead ultimately to some sort of predictive use of the results. The situation for the detection of cremations is even more daunting. In respect of historic burials, the situation is rather more promising with some notable successes documented in a paper covering a number of case studies of grave surveys undertaken by Bevan (1991), the oldest discussed dating from the seventeenth century. Although Bevan concluded that GPR had the greatest success rate, no technique provided a guarantee of not missing graves that were there, or of interpreting the presence of graves where there were none.

66

Table 3.1 The effectiveness of detecting graves and cremations with the most frequently used archaeological geophysical survey methods

Feature/Method	1	2	3	4	5	6
Graves	?	–	–	y	–	y
Cremations	n	–	–	–	–	–

Source: Extracted and adapted from David (1995, Table 2).

Key to Techniques: 1. Magnetometer area survey. 2. Magnetometer scanning. 3. Magnetic susceptibility survey. 4. Resistivity area survey. 5. Electromagnetic survey. 6. Ground-penetrating radar.

Key to effectiveness: Y. Responds well in a majority of conditions and is usually recommended (note that none of the techniques listed in this table are this effective for either graves or cremations); y. Can respond effectively in many conditions but is best used with other techniques; ?. May work well in some conditions, but its use is questionable in most circumstances; n. May work in some conditions but is not usually recommended. Blank boxes indicate where the techniques are probably not effective, or their effectiveness is unknown at present.

All in all, it may well appear that the detection of graves with geophysical techniques has a very low chance of success, because of the accepted lack of geophysical contrast of the grave and its contents. However, if there is a significant geophysical contrast then the situation is reversed. Certain types of deposit will be disrupted to such an extent by the digging of a grave that the fill, although essentially the same material, will provide a physical contrast. A contrast in porosity will allow individual graves to be detected by aerial photography (see Chapter 2, Figure 2.3). Such visible graves should also be detectable by geophysical techniques that measure the electrical properties of the ground, given that it is the moisture differences that these techniques largely measure and such moisture differences are also responsible for the creation of crop marks. However, the relationship between geophysical and vegetational effects may not be directly equitable. For example, a crop mark effect may still be evident for a period after moisture level differences between a grave and the surrounding material are reduced to a point where the difference would be undetectable by geophysical survey. Additionally, the moisture difference may never have been enough for geophysical detection despite causing the development of a crop mark.

In archaeological and historic contexts graves may be more readily detectable because of their associated contents rather than the difference of the fill or presence of any skeletal remains. Thus, the presence, for example, of stone coffins, stone cappings or ferrous grave goods (e.g. Clark 1996: 98) can allow graves to be detected with relative ease. More recently, Neubauer *et al.* (2003) have reported detecting patterns of anomalies that were seen to define cemetery areas, with some graves 'commonly' producing anomalies detectable by high resolution, high sensitivity gradiometry, although not all the graves produced such responses. Although less well studied, cremation cemeteries are, if anything, even less productive with examples of the detection of individual cremations not confirmed in the literature, although the larger pyres are detectable both in archaeological and modern experimental contexts (Marshall 1998). Despite this lack of success in archaeological contexts, in forensic contexts the situation turns out to be more rewarding. The reason for this is that graves of forensic interest are often fundamentally different in nature when compared to those that the archaeological geophysicist traditionally encounters.

3.7 Geophysical detection of recent graves

The major difference between an archaeological grave and a recent grave is the presence of a body which can present additional effects during the decomposition process. In a shallow grave the bulk of the grave fill may well be the body itself and in the early stages of decomposition, long before skeletonisation has been reached, the body will predominate in determining a grave's geophysical characteristics.

That said, it is still the case that the disruption of strata caused by digging the grave, and the less consolidated fill that results, will contribute to a grave's geophysical properties. They will become the predominant geophysical factors when skeletonisation has occurred. However, in the UK, ground and climatic conditions can result in reduced rates of decomposition (Turner and Wiltshire 1999) and the body may take many years to decompose fully (see also Chapter 2, Section 2.1). Therefore, for recent graves the effect of the presence of the body must be taken into account in determining the methodology and likely responses. Because the condition of the body changes over time, a recent grave constitutes a feature with dynamic geophysical properties. This is something infrequently encountered in archaeological situations because although an archaeological feature's geophysical response may vary due to changing ground conditions (e.g. moisture levels), if the same ground conditions occur again, then the response should be the same. The importance of these characteristics (the presence of the body and decomposition dynamics) are not always appreciated or fully understood.

Understanding decomposition dynamics has significant implications in modelling for 'real' scenarios. France *et al.* (1997: 506) recommend the construction of empty calibration graves adjacent to likely clandestine graves. However, there are reasons why this concept may be flawed. It is likely that such empty graves will produce geophysical responses that do not correspond to a grave containing decomposing remains. Conversely, if the remains are old enough to be skeletonised, then it is likely that the grave fill will have settled and consolidated and so again be very different in geophysical response when compared to a newly dug grave. The importance of the presence and effects of decomposition may not have been fully considered in the results reported by Hildebrand *et al.* (2002) when surveying 'archaeological' test graves in which pigs had been buried for only one year because their decomposition states may not have stabilised. In other studies (e.g. Buck 2003 and Davis *et al.* 2000) it would appear that most of the graves surveyed had little in common with recent shallow forensic graves.

In general, it can be argued that while work on historic and archaeological cemeteries and graves is of interest to forensic geophysicists, in most respects these targets will be poor analogues of forensic graves. For forensic research, experimental graves using human or animal remains would seem the way forward (e.g. Freeland *et al.* 2003), with field and computer grave simulations gaining in importance, but only if the fullest range of decompositional effects is appreciated (*contra* Hammon *et al.* 2000). The importance of decompositional effects was noted by Rodriguez and Bass (1985) who predicted changes in electrical conductivity and also suggested the application of archaeologically successful geophysical methodologies to locate graves. To date, research in this area has been dominated by GPR work, but the dramatic effects on electrical conductivity caused by decomposition in a microbially active soil (Kirby forthcoming), has highlighted the potential of other techniques that exploit this physical property.

A further, if less fundamental, aspect of difference between forensic and archaeological graves may be that the 'cut' of a forensic grave may still be present in the topsoil. This is because bioturbation, repeated cultivation and biochemical topsoil forming processes all take time to return a disturbed topsoil/subsoil mix to a homogeneous state. Hence, a forensic grave can potentially produce an anomalous response from the immediate surface rather than having to be detected through a layer of masking topsoil as is normally the case with archaeological features. It is sometimes forgotten that if the top of a grave can be found, then finding the body in the bottom becomes relatively straightforward.

While much of the preceding discussion, and the chapter as a whole, inevitably focus on a target that is a single adult inhumation, many searches involve much more varied scenarios. These include locating single inhumations ranging in size from neonates through to overweight adults; remains that have been burnt and/or dismembered; remains wrapped or buried in containers; multiple and mass burials; empty graves (used and unused); and sites of burning of bodies or evidence such as clothing. Searches can include finding associated evidence such as weapons, spades and shovels, keys, in one case a dog lead was sought, structures such as shafts, or even vehicles buried or dumped in rivers and lakes. Unfortunately if the manner of disposal is not known, as is often the case, then the forensic geophysicist must avoid making assumptions about the nature of the target. However, if there is good intelligence concerning the nature of the grave and contents, then the most appropriate geophysical methods can be employed using the most suitable survey methodology.

3.8 Earth resistivity

3.8.1 Principles of earth resistivity

Earth resistivity survey uses an electrical current passing through the ground to measure the electrical properties of the subsurface. Moist soil will conduct electricity more easily than dry soil or solid rock and, by taking a number of readings across the surface of an area, it is possible map subsurface structures that are more conducting or less conducting than the material in which they lie. In practical systems two electrodes inserted into the ground provide a known electric current while two others are inserted to measure any voltage changes. The arrangement of these electrodes is termed the array configuration. It is both the spatial ordering and relative separations of the electrodes that define a particular array, and there are many variants. Milsom provides a useful overview of the range of arrays (2003: 98) while Gaffney and Gater (2003) and Clark (1996) focus more on those of archaeological interest. The conventional earth resistivity array, in which all four electrodes are placed equally spaced in a line with the current electrodes positioned at each end, is called the Wenner array (Figure 3.1). The depth of penetration of any array depends on the separation of the electrodes as well as the array configuration itself. For the Wenner array an electrode separation of 1m is employed for much near-surface archaeological work and forensic research has employed the same separation (e.g. Buck 2003).

The array traverses the survey area taking readings at set intervals, normally 1m in archaeological evaluation surveys, to produce a grid of readings that can be displayed as a plan. If a deeper or shallower survey is required, then the array spacing can be

Figure 3.1 Illustrations of the Wenner configuration (top) and twin-electrode array (bottom) in use

expanded or narrowed and the survey repeated. In fact, it is possible to take many readings at increasing electrode separations at individual points along a single line to create a vertical section down into the earth. This is termed an electrical pseudosection (Aspinall and Crummett 1997). Many such sections can be put together to allow a three-dimensional interpretation of the substrate.

3.8.2 Selection of array for forensic grave detection

Although the earth resistivity technique has had a number of successes, both in experimental trials and real investigations, it appears to be the Cinderella of grave detection geophysical techniques, a fact perhaps best illustrated by its limited mention in a recently published manual (Davenport 2001a: 29–30). No mention of it is made in either of the France *et al*. papers on grave detection methods (1992, 1997). Killam covers the technique well although he notes it as slow (1990: 228) and it fails to feature in his final list of recommended techniques. His view may be based on the use of the Wenner configuration which, in North America, has been considered the most common array and used along with the double-dipole for archaeological work (Herz and Garrison 1998: 159). In the UK and Europe, however, the twin probe array has been the preferred resistivity array for archaeological survey for more than 20 years.

One reason for the difference between North American and European applications is that the majority of geophysical work undertaken in North America, both archaeological and forensic, has been by geophysicists primarily drawn from the geological, engineering and environmental disciplines who are most familiar with the Wenner array. While it may be that some of these practitioners are unaware of advances in archaeological geophysical survey methods in Europe, it may also be that resistivity has been of limited value in hot arid summers which characterise the North American fieldwork season, and in which other methods are more appropriate. In Europe the twin electrode array has now gained wider acceptance in other disciplines exploiting high-resolution near-surface geophysical techniques and is now covered by Milsom (2003: 98 and Figure 5.1) while not being covered in the first edition of his book published in 1989. Practitioners such as Kvamme (2003) have introduced the regular use of the twin electrode array for archaeological surveys in North America but, given that Buck (2003) does not seem aware of the array, its use may not be yet that widespread.

While the Wenner is a very effective array configuration for some applications it does have its limitations when used for forensic grave detection. It is not an efficient nor effective survey array for intensive high-resolution surveys required to detect individual graves, especially in areas with space restriction and physical obstacles frequently encountered in forensic work. Buck (2003) reports that it took two people two hours to survey a 7 × 6m area at a 1m reading interval (a total of 42 readings) using a 1m separation Wenner array. Not only is this unacceptably slow, but the sampling interval of 1m is unlikely to be enough to be capable of defining a grave effectively. Even the 1m spacing of the Wenner electrodes employed is probably too wide to ever resolve a grave effectively and its resolution also varies depending on the traverse direction across a feature. After setting up the instrument and laying out the grid, a conservative estimate for the time taken to survey the same area using a standard 0.5m separation twin array configuration (e.g. the Geoscan Research RM15) by one operator would be less than 2 minutes. Increasing the sample to a more appropriate 0.5m reading interval it would still take less than 10 minutes to survey the same area. The twin electrode array only requires the movement of two (mobile) electrodes during survey (the other two remaining fixed outside the survey area) and the effects of the array orientation are much reduced when compared to the Wenner. To obtain a similar depth of penetration to the Wenner, it only needs half the electrode separation and consequently has better lateral resolution. The mobile electrodes are normally set 0.5m apart and fixed in a frame that also holds the resistivity meter with its built-in data logger. Readings are taken automatically a short time after the electrodes are pushed into the surface and when the survey is complete, downloading and display of data should take no more than a few minutes. For detecting single shallow forensic graves the 0.5m twin-electrode is the most appropriate array configuration. However, the twin electrode array is less sensitive and subject to a greater extent in both the unwanted effects of both topsoil and deeper geological variations than the equivalent penetration Wenner array. There are other arrays, e.g. the square array, that may be suitable for forensic work; interest in alternatives to the twin electrode is a recurring theme in archaeological geophysics (e.g. Gaffney and Gater 2003: 180; Cheetham 2001).

3.8.3 Grave detection by earth resistivity

Earth resistivity detects graves due to changes in the resistance to an electric current that the grave causes. That said, exactly what this change will be is not always going to be possible to predict (see Chapter 3, Section 3.6 above). Normally it would be expected that a grave being more porous, due to the loose backfill, holds excess water and, together with the presence of a decomposing body, will ease the passage of electric current and so produce a low resistance anomaly. However, the process can be more complex. Initially a grave may appear as a high resistance anomaly because the fill is very loose and contains air pockets and the body is intact so the electrical flow is inhibited. As the fill initially settles and the body begins to decompose and rupture, decomposition fluids will flow into the grave, increasing its conductivity and so produce a low resistance anomaly. As the soft tissue decomposition is completed and skeletonisation takes place it is only the effect of water trapped in the more porous grave fill that will allow the grave to continue to be detected as a low resistance anomaly. However, in dry conditions the more porous grave fill may dry out, leaving air cavities and thus producing a high resistance anomaly. A heavy downpour of rain may within a few hours reverse this again to a low resistance anomaly. If the grave has been filled with stones above the body then these will tend to create a high resistance element within the grave, causing a shift to a higher resistance in each of the cases discussed above. As the grave response moves from low to high or back again there will be times when the grave has a similar resistivity to the material into which it is cut and at these times no measurable anomaly may be present.

A series of resistivity surveys of a buried pig at an FSAG test site in Lancashire was undertaken over a 5-month period to illustrate this phenomenon (Bray 1996). As predicted (Figure 3.2), the surveys indicate a slight high resistance anomaly shortly after burial, but after the first month the grave could not be detected. At two months a low resistance anomaly started to appear and this increased in intensity in months three and four, and was still visible after the fifth month. Another pig that had been buried six months previously was also surveyed at the same time. This showed as a low

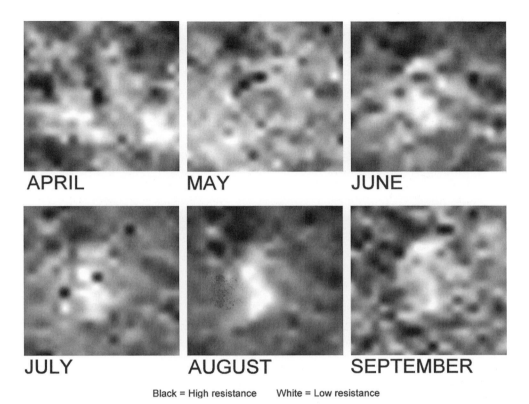

APRIL   MAY   JUNE

JULY   AUGUST   SEPTEMBER

Black = High resistance   White = Low resistance

Figure 3.2 Earth resistivity plots over a single pig grave at the Lancashire test site. The first plot is a 10 × 10m area surveyed at 0.5m reading intervals, whereas the remaining plots are 5 × 5m areas surveyed at 0.25 × 0.25m intervals. The plots vividly capture the changing response due to the remains decomposing.

resistance anomaly from the start of the surveys but in the last month its contrast reduced, suggesting that the main phase decomposition may be coming to an end.

Similar work was carried out by Lynam and was one of the first surveys ever undertaken with the twin-electrode array (1970: 119–201). Here some of the shallow graves, dug on a test site at Havant in Hampshire, contained pigs that had only recently been buried and others were backfilled empty. Although magnetometers and a number of electromagnetic instruments traversed the graves at the time of the survey, resistivity was the only successful technique and in this remarkable survey all three graves that were in the survey area are clearly delineated by low resistance anomalies (Figure 3.3). Lynam predicted that as decomposition progressed 'the release of body fluids might be expected to provide a considerable contrast in polarisation' (1970: 201). However, he did sound a cautionary note pointing out that other areas of low resistance were present that did not result from graves. If Lynam's survey had been part of an authentic investigation, then all the anomalies would have been vented, checked by cadaver dog, then ground-truthed by rapid evaluation trenches, and hence in this case all the graves present would have been located.

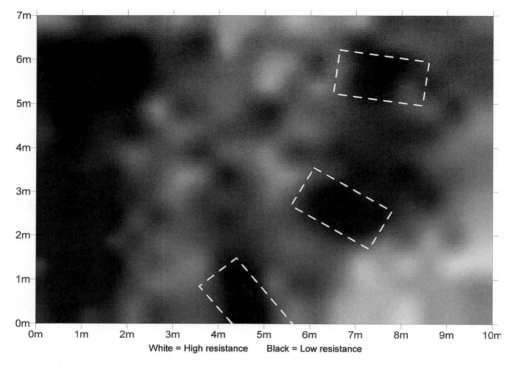

White = High resistance   Black = Low resistance

Figure 3.3 Earth resistivity survey of test graves at Havant, Hampshire. Black corresponds to low resistance compared to the background levels. The test grave locations are indicated by dashed white lines. All three are clearly delineated by low resistance anomalies, while similar anomalies on the left of the plot do not represent test graves.

Source: Replotted from data given in Lynam (1970, Figure 7.18).

In an actual forensic case earth resistivity provided a number of geophysical anomalies resulting from the search of a garden for the body of an adult female (see Chapter 4, case 19). A vegetable plot had been cleared in an area where the missing woman's husband had been seen digging a hole around the time of her disappearance and was surveyed at 0.5m reading intervals using an autologging 0.5m twin electrode array resistivity system. The survey results shown in Figure 3.4 indicated a number of low resistance anomalies that were systematically examined by evaluation excavations. Although a former pond and two wooden posts found *in situ* towards the west each produced a grave-like anomaly, it was the less obvious anomaly detected at the eastern edge of the survey area that was ultimately the more relevant. The survey could not be extended in this direction because of a concrete area that abutted the west and south of the area surveyed. Of note is the high resistance anomaly at the northern edge of the survey that was caused by banked-up topsoil placed there during the search. This provides a good example of how some search activities can adversely affect others if the techniques are not sequenced correctly.

In another scenario, earth resistivity was deployed alongside GPR (see Chapter, 2 case 6). While GPR covered the hard surfaced areas, the lawn and garden area were

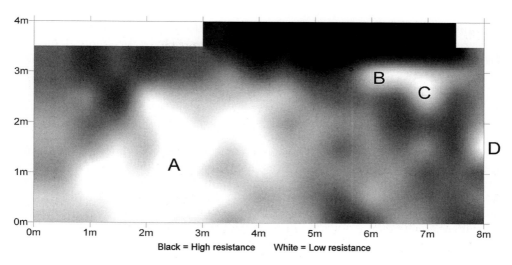

Black = High resistance   White = Low resistance

Figure 3.4 Resistivity survey of a garden vegetable plot. Low resistance anomaly A resulted from an infilled shallow garden pond, B and C postholes still contained rotting timbers, and D the edge of what evaluation excavation showed to be a cut feature and, after further excavation, the grave itself (see Chapter 4, case 19).

first surveyed by resistivity at a reading interval of 0.5m and this was then followed by real-time interpretation GPR traverses while the resistivity data was being processed. Both techniques detected a grave-like anomaly near the end of the garden. This turned out to be an undisturbed gravel-filled slot dug as a soak-away. This was partially excavated, then augered, checked by a cadaver dog and deemed to not contain human remains. Further investigations showed that the construction pre-dated the disappearance of the female being sought.

As well as searching for individual graves, earth resistivity has also been used to map near-surface deposits and so help define where it may be possible to bury remains, for example within an area of peat moorland (see Chapter 2, case 8, Figure 2.10). If resistivity is simply used to define the extent of deposits, then a coarser reading interval of 1m or more may be appropriate.

In respect to forensic search, earth resistivity comes with a raft of advantages and disadvantages. On the positive side, despite its lack of use on many actual cases it has been demonstrated in tests to perform well, and with resistivity being less affected by site interference, it can be used in tight urban garden situations where electromagnetic and magnetic methods cannot. The instrument can be up and be running in minutes and can cover reasonably large areas in a day, the exact coverage being dependent on the array used and the reading interval chosen. For example, 400m² per hour taking readings at 0.5 metre intervals will allow an area of 40 × 60m or more to be fully surveyed in a day, using the twin electrode array. The results of such a survey can be downloaded, plotted and interpreted within minutes. Resistivity cannot be used inside buildings, on areas that will not allow for the insertion of the electrodes (e.g. concrete), or in very dry soil conditions when electrical contact cannot be made. Extreme waterlogging and frozen conditions cause problems and responses are sensitive to general moisture changes in the subsurface that may hamper or enhance the detection in an unpredictable fashion. However, where conditions are appropriate for its use, earth resistivity does produce reliable results and deserves to be used more frequently for locating forensic graves.

3.8.4 Recomendations

In the application of earth resistivity survey in forensic applications, a reading interval of 0.5m as opposed to the more usual 1m interval used in archaeological work is advocated here as being essential. Only under very favourable conditions will a greater reading interval be even theoretically capable of detecting a grave-size target. Areas should be accurately surveyed in grids using guide lines with markers at 0.5m intervals. Reducing the reading interval to 0.25m would further improve the results, but quadrupling the number of data point and reduced rate of coverage may often make this unfeasible in practice. Only when very small targets such as child graves are been sought would a 0.25m reading interval be essential. Because of the asymmetrical nature of some graves (i.e. long and thin), an array that has an isotropic response (i.e. orientation independence) and good lateral resolution characteristics is preferable. In most cases this would make the twin electrode array not only the most practical and rapid, but technically one of the most appropriate.

3.9 Magnetometry

3.9.1 Underlying magnetic principles

The basic principle of this technique relies on the presence of the earth's magnetic field and on its consequent effects. It is the earth's internally generated field that provides a uniform background response upon which is superimposed the often much smaller changes that are to be detected – in the UK this background level is around 48,000nT (nanotesla). To put this into perspective, the changes caused by digging a grave may be as little as 1nT (a 0.002 per cent change) or even less. The earth's magnetic field is then responsible for the two effects that can be exploited for detection. The first is the effect of the presence of the earth's magnetic field on magnetically susceptible materials: these are materials that become magnetised to various degrees in the presence of an external magnetic field and thus create their own magnetic fields resulting from the induction caused by the earth's field. The resulting interaction of the primary earth's field and this new superimposed secondary magnetic field creates small variations (anomalies) within the otherwise uniform background level. This magnetic effect is essentially temporary and only exists while the external field (the earth's) is present, so if the earth's field was removed, this magnetic effect would disappear. The second is that magnetic particles in rocks and soils can become preferentially aligned with the earth's magnetic field when they are formed and this results in a relatively weak, but permanent, magnetism. This magnetism is 'locked' in the material and will still be present even if the earth's field were to be removed. In this latter form, the effect is most commonly brought about by heating to high temperatures and cooling, and is termed thermoremanent magnetism (TRM). There is, however, a much weaker effect in sediments in which small particles have been allowed, by either fluidity in formation (fine wind-blown or water-lain sediments) or subsequent settling, agitation or diagenic processes of some form, to create a naturally formed remanent magnetism (NRM).

Both of these principal effects are of interest here but how they are exploited depends on the local conditions. NRM, for example, is not present in some superficial sediments and is not generally considered important in most archaeological survey. A further mechanism is more important in the detection of 'cut' archaeological features, and this relies on the phenomenon of topsoil magnetic susceptibility enhancement. While there is more than one mechanism that causes the magnetic susceptibility enhancement of topsoils (see Gaffney and Gater 2003: 37–39), here it is only necessary to know that this enhancement occurs. This means that in many environments the naturally formed topsoil is often more (often orders of magnitude more) magnetically susceptible than the subsoil or rock from which it is derived and which it overlies. Archaeologically, if pits or ditches are cut and then become filled with enhanced topsoil material, then they will be detectable if the magnetic contrast is great enough to be detected by a particular sensor type and provided natural variations in the deposits are small. Unfortunately, although this mechanism is responsible for the highly effective nature of many archaeological magnetic surveys, it does not necessarily occur in the case of most graves. Archaeological effectiveness does not always equate with success in forensic application.

Magnetic variations in the near-surface can be exploited by using magnetometry. A full discussion of this technique is beyond the scope of this chapter and the reader is directed initially to sources such as Clark (1996) or Scollar (1990) for an archaeological perspective, to Davenport (2001a) with forensics in mind, or to Reynolds (1997) and Milsom (2003) for a more general treatment. Magnetometry is a specific technique that uses sensors (magnetometers) singly or in combination to survey changes in magnetic field strength in the proximity of the sensor. This technique can be exploited in forensic contexts in a number of ways but is barely covered in the relevant literature. One reason for this omission is that magnetometry presents certain problems not encountered, or not as extreme as those encountered, with other geophysical methods.

From an archaeological standpoint, magnetometry is rightly regarded as both the workhorse and racehorse of archaeological geophysics in the UK (Clark 1996: 69) and Europe. All the other techniques arguably pall into insignificance in terms of the number of sites surveyed, the size of areas surveyed, and the resolution of the data recorded. Published forensic texts pay little regard to this wealth of experience that has led to highly effective and efficient instrumentation and well developed field methodologies. As already emphasised, exactly how an instrument is used is paramount in terms of its actual effectiveness, as is the specific configuration of the instrument in question. In the case of magnetometry, even the type of sensor (there are four primary types commonly in use) is a matter that requires knowledge and consideration. With differences in sensor come differences in cost as well as performance characteristics, and this has led to a specific sensor being dominant in archaeological applications.

3.9.2 Grave detection with magnetometry

The human body has a low magnetic susceptibility and so the direct detection of the remains by magnetometry is not possible. However, associated items may exhibit an effect and this is considered below. If the sediment into which the grave is cut has NRM, then the removal of the material and the refilling of the grave will disrupt the magnetically aligned particles, replacing them randomly, resulting in the loss of the coherent permanent magnetic effect. When the magnetometer passes over a grave, then this will result in a *negative* magnetic anomaly. The inclusion of a body at the expense of some of the spoil removed (the excess presumably being deposed of through removal or spreading near or around the area of the grave) will also enhance this negative anomaly effect. However, sediments in the UK with little or no NRM (e.g. glacial tills and coarse water-lain sand and gravel deposits, together with chalks, limestones and gritstones, etc.) may show virtually no change and so the grave is likely to remain undetected. Nevertheless, in Colorado, France *et al.* (1997: 505) noted the NRM effect created by graves dug at their test site, and hence its potential effect should always be considered.

Alternatively, if the ground simply possesses a high magnetic susceptibility down to the depth of the grave then, as in the previous scenario where the fill of the grave is less dense or the grave contains a body or a void formed as the body decays, it would also be detected as a negative anomaly (Breiner 1973: Figure 48).

On sites where there is a strongly developed topsoil enhancement, then the process of digging a grave may cause a redistribution of the more magnetically susceptible topsoil deeper into the ground while bringing the less magnetically susceptible subsoil to near the surface, thus diluting the topsoil enhancement above the grave. This will also produce a negative magnetic anomaly over the grave. This effect is unlikely to occur in archaeological situations due to bioturbation, argricultural activities and other soil formation processes acting over a long period of time leading to a return to a homogeneous topsoil above the grave. However, over forensic timescales this will not occur and Figure 3.5 shows an example on chalk (which exhibits a strong topsoil/subsoil magnetic susceptibilty contrast) where despite the turf being replaced the grave feature is identifed clearly as a negative anomaly. If a perpetrator carefully removes turf and topsoil and replaces these exactly as found then such a grave is likely to go undetected, at least due to this mechanism.

There is one other possible way that a grave may be detectable and that is if the decay of the remains causes iron oxides in the soil to be converted to more magnetic forms by reduction and reoxidisation. While such a process is theoretically a possibility, such an effect has not been demonstrated. Archaeological graves occasionally exhibit magnetic properties (e.g. Neubauer *et al.* 2003a) that may possibly result from such a mechanism, but most do not. If such enhancement does occur, it may take a long period of time to develop or it may be that the nature of the decay process of human remains alone does not lead to any magnetic enhancement. Over forensic timescales such a mechanism may be irrelevant for single graves. However, in mass graves the large number of bodies decaying rapidly may cause anaerobic conditions within the grave. This in turn may cause the reduction of the iron oxides in clay soils around and above the grave, a process which could result in magnetic enhancement and may offer potential for detection by magnetic methods.

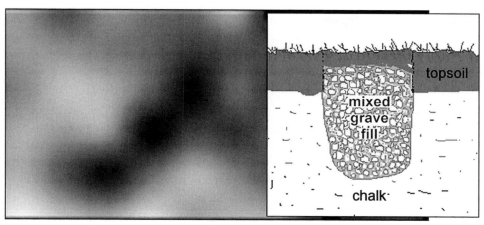

1m   White = Positive   Black = Negative

Figure 3.5 Top: this extract from a larger survey clearly delineates the position of a training grave cut into chalk which is showing as a negative magnetic anomaly. The negative response results from a reduction in the volume magnetic susceptibility in the topsoil over the grave caused by the lack of compaction together with the dilution due to the mixing with the chalk fragments. Bottom: Forensic archaeology students excavating the grave.

3.9.3 Magnetometers as ferrous metal detectors

As iron, and, to a lesser extent, steel and cast iron, are relatively highly magnetically susceptible, they will cause strong magnetic anomalies. If a grave contained a knife, hammer or similar ferrous items, then a magnetometer will, acting as a very effective ferrous metal detector, detect them and thus the grave. However, the size, depth and orientation will affect detection, while non-ferrous metals such as copper, aluminium and non-ferrous alloys will not produce a magnetic effect and thus cannot be detected at all with a magnetometer. It is noted by Sutherland and Schmidt (2003) that there are limitations in using magnetometers to locate and study mediaeval battlefield sites because so few ferrous military items are to be found. Most material located on such sites by metal detectorists tends to be non-ferrous copper alloy clothing items such as buttons, buckles and strap-ends. Similarly, lead bullets and brass shell cases will not be detected by magnetometers. However, despite these limitations, there have been a few instances when magnetometers used as metal detectors have or could have been used in forensic search.

In one case in the UK, a victim was entombed within a concrete-filled 56-gallon oil drum buried at a depth of 1.5m in a soak-away at the end of a garden (see Chapter 2, case 3). Although eventually found by archaeological excavation, had the nature of the burial been known or even the involvement of an oil drum suspected, then magnetometry may well have been a most effective and efficient technique to locate the drum and thus the body.

Another case required the location of a large buried steel tank which was specified by a witness to be near the edge of a field. Such a tank should be detectable 10m or more away with a magnetometer. Initial scanning followed by a 20 × 40m area 1m reading interval survey of the area in question detected no anomalies or any disturbance that would suggest a large buried tank was (or had ever been) in the area specified. The survey did detect a linear anomaly that rapid evaluation excavation showed to be a narrow trench, suggesting that any greater disturbances should have been detected by the survey. It later transpired that the tank was situated in a completely different area.

Davenport (2001b) reports the use of a gradiometer (see below) mounted in an aluminium boat that was also towing a marine magnetometer. Their purpose was to locate a vehicle that was reported to have been pushed into the Missouri River with a murder victim in the boot. The marine magnetometer detected five anomalous areas and upon prioritising, the first anomaly investigated turned out to be the vehicle in question and the body was recovered. GPS and a laser range finder were used to provide positional information.

3.9.4 Instrument configurations

Magnetometry can be conducted with single sensor instruments, two sensor differential systems or two (and three) sensor gradiometers. However, for archaeological applications, the two sensor vertical gradiometer has been the preferred configuration. The configuration used for archaeological survey is significantly different from that used in geological survey and ensuring that the correct configuration is used largely determines the effectiveness of the instrument for near-surface applications, both archaeological and forensic. In a vertical gradiometer configuration two sensors are fixed in a single tube one above the other, normally with a 0.5m–1m separation between the two, although this separation can be greater in some cases. Most important is that the lower of the two sensors should be close to the ground at a height of around 0.3–0.4m (Davenport 2001a: Figure 4.3).

By contrast, in geological work the vertical separation will often be 1m or more and the lower sensor will be set on a pole some 2m from the ground surface (ibid., Figure 4.5). Such a geological configuration has little chance of detecting shallow low contrast anomalies found in archaeological and forensic contexts. The downside to having the lower sensor too near the ground is that while sensitivity is increased, inhomogeneity in the near-surface, including small but shallow ferrous items, will have a disproportionate effect in the data. However, in forensic contexts, this can be exactly the type of effect required. Generally, as the instrument is used nearer to the surface, increased sampling resolution is required to take advantage of the higher lateral resolution of vertical gradiometers.

One of the most problematical aspects of the use of magnetometry in forensic contexts is the interference often classified under the term 'cultural noise'. This is caused by human activities that result in magnetic effects that can appear in the survey. The most obvious are visible ferrous items such as wire fencing, vehicles and surface rubbish, possibly compounded by invisible buried ferrous rubbish and objects ranging in size from a nail, that may affect only a single reading, through to buried tanks and pipelines that will cause effects tens of metres from the source. Electrical equipment such as transformers can also affect the magnetometer if approached too closely. Even when such cultural noise is absent, there are natural variations in the strength of the ambient (the earth's) magnetic field that exceeds by up to two orders of magnitude the more subtle variations caused by a forensic grave. These natural variations are often noted in the literature under labels such as 'magnetic storms' and are quoted as a major problem with using magnetometry (e.g. Killam 1990: 86; see also Breiner 1973 and Clark 1996, for a more complete examination of natural variation).

Both cultural and natural variations can be eliminated or significantly reduced by use of the gradiometer configuration which, added to its greater lateral resolution and increased sensitivity to near-surface anomalies at the expense of larger but more distant (deeper) sources, makes it the most logical choice for forensic investigation. This is a view with which Davenport also concurs (2001a: 60) and is further supported by the problematic surveys undertaken using magnetometry reported by Buck (2003) who attempted unsuccessfully to use a single sensor instrument in three investigations of known grave sites. Buck's experience illustrates the importance of having access to appropriate equipment and processing facilities, and of familiarity with current practice in archaeological geophysics where high-resolution magnetic data have been regularly collected, downloaded and interpreted within minutes in the field for many years. Scanning, the sweeping of the magnetometer over an area and observing the response without taking regular gridded readings, is sometimes used in archaeological work to locate features such as kilns, furnaces or areas of activity. However, there appears to be general agreement that this type of 'real time' magnetic scanning is simply not an option given the improbability of detecting weak and subtle anomalies either for forensic (Buck 2003) or for archaeological purposes (David 1995: 18).

A totally different approach to surveying magnetic variation in the topsoil is by measuring the magnetic susceptibility of the soils directly using a magnetic susceptibility meter that has a coil placed in contact with the soil surface. One frequently employed instrument is the Bartington MS2 meter which, when attached to the MS2D search coil, can provide volume susceptibilities of the soil down to a depth of around 10cm. There can be problems if the vegetation is other than well-cropped and uniform, as inconsistency of instrument height above the ground surface can create large variation between one reading and the next. In archaeological work topsoil magnetic susceptibility survey is used to detect enhancement caused by anthropogenic activity, frequently through the heating of the soil by fire, and so the technique has potential for locating the sites of fires of forensic interest. For a full discussion of topsoil magnetic susceptibility see Clark (1996: Chapter 4).

3.9.5 Recommendations

A 0.5m vertical gradiometer held with the bottom sensor some 30–40cm from the ground surface would provide the appropriate resolution and sensitivity to detect smaller ferrous items within a shallow grave. It will also be capable of detecting magnetic changes if these are present and if a contrast between the grave and the surrounding soil is sufficiently strong. Readings should be taken at 0.5m intervals or more frequently when logging data automatically. Caesium sensors are ideal but the more compact fluxgate instruments are more convenient to use in many survey situations. A 1m gradiometer has a better signal to noise ratio but can be affected more by magnet gradients caused by ferrous clutter in the survey area. If areas of burning are sought, then a topsoil magnetic susceptibility survey at a reading interval of 0.5 or 0.25m could be used to try to locate the seat of a fire long after any vegetation has re-grown.

3.10 Electromagnetic systems

3.10.1 Principles of electromagnetic systems

The family of electromagnetic (EM) instruments, including metal detectors, currently has relatively little impact on archaeological geophysics in the UK. Metal detectors and EM systems work by using electromagnetic fields generated by passing an alternating current through a transmitter coil. This electromagnetic field induces small electrical currents (termed eddy currents) into conducting targets thus creating secondary electromagnetic fields that are detected in a second receiving coil. Soil will also conduct electricity allowing EM systems to map subsurface changes that are largely due to moisture differences and so produce results that can be similar to earth resistivity survey. In metal detectors the frequency of the transmitting source is around 40kHz whereas, in more general EM survey instruments, this is reduced to around 14kHz. This lower frequency allows better transmission of electromagnetic fields in soils and also has the added effect of allowing such systems to detect changes in magnetic susceptibility as well as conductivity. This means that that an EM instrument can, in theory at least, substitute both for a magnetometer, and also for a deeper penetrating resistivity instrument when its coils have their axes vertical. Equally, it can substitute for a magnetic susceptibility meter, and also a shallower penetrating resistivity instrument when the axes of its coils are horizontal. The instrument electronics can extract the appropriate magnetic susceptibility and electrical conductivity (the reciprocal of resistivity) component of the signal received in the detection coil. For a more complete discussion of EM systems including comparisons to other techniques in an archaeological context see Clark (1996) and Cole *et al.* (1995).

Metal detectors have their place in locating small metal items around and within graves and other forensic scenes but can only detect to a relatively shallow depth (approximately 20cm for a shell case). In archaeology their main use has been to provide portable find distributions more effectively under the portable antiquities recording schemes. Metal detectors have also demonstrated their worth in work on battlefield archaeological surveys from such disparate sites in time and space as the medieval battle of Towton (Sutherland and Schmidt 2003) to the Battle of the Little Big Horn (Scott and Connor 1997). Because targets only have to be able to conduct an electric current, EM instruments will detect all types of metals, unlike magnetometers which will only detect ferrous items. Good electrical conductors such as gold, silver and copper are obvious targets for the treasure hunting enthusiast often to the detriment of some archaeological sites.

Unfortunately for these users, EM instruments of all kinds will also respond to far more ubiquitous conductors such as iron and steel. However, because iron and steel have high magnetic susceptibilities (unlike the non-magnetic metals gold, silver and copper), they also create a magnetic effect in the presence of the metal detector's electromagnetic field. As mentioned above, it is possible to differentiate electronically between the magnetic and conducting effects and this ability is employed in most metal detector systems to provide a discrimination facility to help decide on whether a conducting target is ferrous or non-ferrous. While such a facility can be useful, it should be noted that such discrimination systems are not wholly reliable due to the complexities of the responses from combinations of material, to materials in close association, or to the shape and orientation of objects. One metal detection manual candidly reminds users that 'the only 100% reliable discriminator is called a shovel.' (Rowan 1991: 20). The shape, orientation and state of preservation can also affect detection: objects that are in good condition lying flat in the ground and disk- or ring-shaped will be detected more easily than a corroded, thin object (e.g. a knife) orientated vertically in the ground. This is because of the greater difficulty in inducing eddy currents into such a shape from a coil placed flat on the ground directly above the target.

As with many active geophysical techniques, increasing the depth of detection rapidly leads to a loss of resolution and therefore diminished sensitivity to smaller targets. With metal detectors, the size of the search coil influences depth of detection, with larger coils giving greater depth while progressively reducing the ability of the detector to pick up smaller targets. Many higher quality systems have a range of interchangeable, and in some cases multiple-sized but integrated search coils; some deeper 'hoard hunting' systems use configurations similar to those used in the more sophisticated ground conductivity EM systems described below, but use the higher frequencies more appropriate for metal detecting.

Like all geophysical instruments, the ability to use this equipment effectively relies on the familiarity of the user with both the instrumentation and the response of that particular system to specific targets. In forensic and archaeological situations it is obviously important that the coverage is objectively systematic and thorough, and this can only be ensured by setting down an appropriate gridding system for survey, using a full coverage sweep pattern as advocated by Davenport (2001a: 111). Choice of instrument, coil size, whether to employ discrimination in the selection of targets, and search methodology are all decisions that must be made by someone who is informed enough about the technique. A metal detector is a specialised variety of EM instrument, each make and model having individual strengths and weaknesses. Although metal detectors have been advocated for use in locating and recovering bullets from the base of graves (e.g. Morse *et al.* 1983) recent work by Vingerhoets (2004) shows that in some soils the depth of penetration of hand gun rounds that miss or pass through only soft tissue can be far greater than the detection depth of metal detectors.

3.10.2 *Grave detection with electromagnetic systems*

EM instruments proper were originally designed as ground conductivity meters. For both archaeological and forensic use, the 1m coil separation instrument such as the Geonics EM38 would appear to be the instrument of choice, although the Geonics EM31 has documented forensic success by Nobes (2000) and is illustrated in Davenport (2001a: Figure 5.3). However, Clark (1996: 34) comments that the resolution of the EM31 with its 3.66m coil separation was likely to be too low for archaeological use and it would follow that its usefulness for detecting single graves would therefore be limited. The Nobes publication shows an anomaly near (but apparently not over) a location where human remains were eventually found by extensive digging, and it is unclear whether, had the survey been used, it would have led to the discovery of the remains in question. Even the relatively close 1m coil separation of an EM instrument causes problems in resolving many archaeological features of comparable dimensions to a grave, this being exacerbated by its anisotropic response which ideally requires the averaging of two orthogonal readings at each survey point to reduce this problem. This issue is noted by Davenport (2001a: 81), who suggests that the most efficient field methodology is to survey a grid in one orientation and then repeat it in the other.

EM instruments will detect electrical conductivity contrasts that will arise from either the differing porosity of a grave fill compared to the surrounding medium (drier or wetter) or the presence of the decaying cadaver (wetter and conductivity-enhancing due to the decay products) in a similar way to earth resistivity (Figure 3.6). They are continuous reading non-contact systems that can be used over hard surfaces or in very dry conditions and so are more flexible in use than resistivity systems that require the insertion of electrodes into the ground to make a good electrical contact. Their ability to detect metals of all kinds allows EM instruments to also act as metal detectors for medium to large targets. Although large metal objects in the survey area can cause survey problems, the effect is less than that encountered when using magnetometers. There are a number of makes and designs of EM instruments that need to be considered for both archaeological and forensic applications, depending on circumstance (below).

3.10.3 *Recommendations*

Because of the lack of published results of using EM instruments in forensic contexts, any recommendations can only be preliminary. Ideally, for single adult grave detection, a 0.5m coil separation instrument would seem ideal but until one is made available a 1m instrument would seem to be the most appropriate. An instrument that allows

Figure 3.6 Electromagnetic images of a test grave

both conductivity and magnetic susceptibility changes to be exploited should be employed in this mode. For shallow burials the horizontal dipole mode may turn out to be better than the deeper-seeking vertical mode. Readings should be taken at 0.5m intervals (or less if used in continuous reading mode) and for the highest quality results two surveys should be performed orthogonally to one another and the results merged. In searching for mass graves, an instrument with a greater coil separation would be more suitable because of the greater depth penetration. However, if areas of burning are sought, then in a similar way to employing a topsoil magnetic susceptibility survey (above), an EM system surveying in horizontal dipole mode with a reading interval of 0.5 or less could be used to try to locate the seat of a fire.

3.11 Ground-penetrating radar (GPR)

3.11.1 Principles of GPR

Without doubt, ground-penetrating radar (GPR), also variously known as sub-surface interface radar (SIR) or, in the recent archaeological literature, georadar, is the most flexible and potentially most effective geophysical survey technique available for both archaeological and forensic applications. The reason for this is that the way GPR works is fundamentally different from the methods so far discussed. Earth resistivity, magnetic, and electromagnetic techniques all measure the bulk properties of the subsurface such that the value of the property being measured will often be at least in part a combination of the physical property of the feature of interest, and the properties of the surrounding medium(s) in which it lies. As far as the relevant instruments are concerned, this final combination is indistinguishable from such a value derived from a homogeneous medium. The reading of the instrument can only detect the final 'sum' value and not disentangle the differing contributing values of the individual parts. We therefore talk of *apparent* resistivities and conductivities. GPR, on the other hand, directs electromagnetic (microwave) pulses into the ground. These pulses travel and directly interact with subsurface changes in properties that correspond to features of interest and so have the potential of much greater lateral and vertical resolution. While GPR is both in principle and practice the most complex of the geophysical techniques to be covered here, a basic understanding is all that is required to appreciate both the strengths and weaknesses of the technique for forensic archaeological investigations.

The principles of GPR are deceptively simple: a pulse of microwaves is projected (transmitted) into the ground and this pulse continues to be transmitted through the ground materials but undergoes reflection and refraction at interfaces between materials that alter the velocity of the microwaves until all its energy is dissipated. Reflected parts of the microwave will return to the surface and are detected by the GPR receiver. By looking at the strength of the reflection and the time taken for the reflection to arrive back at the instrument after being transmitted, it is possible to detect both the presence and depth of interfaces between materials beneath the GPR. By taking many such readings along a single survey line (a survey traverse) at intervals of as little as 5cm or less, an effectively continuous profile down into the ground can be created.

However, depth and level of detail (resolution) are more difficult to determine. The method by which microwaves travel through materials is complex and beyond the scope of this text, but it will suffice to say that some materials are poor transmitters of microwaves, hence the depth achieved will depend primarily on the general make-up of subsurface layers. In general, dry, uniform materials with low electrical conductivities will allow deeper penetration of microwaves. Air and dry sand are excellent materials for both the transmission (passage through) and lack of attenuation (signal loss). To compare the difference between the ability of a material to transmit microwaves but to have different attenuations ice, fresh water and salt water are good examples. Table 3.2 shows that the relative dielectric permittivity (RDP – the measure of a material's electromagnetic transmission properties compared to air – hence the value for air in Table 3.2 is 1) for ice is 3–4, indicating good transmission and also that the electrical conductivity is also very small and hence a good depth of penetration is possible. On the other hand, the different structure of liquid water (RDP factor of 80) allows less penetration than ice, and while salt water has a similar RDP, due to its high electrical conductivity the signal is highly attenuated and penetration is consequently extremely limited.

Another factor that affects the depth of penetration is the frequency of the transmitted microwave. The lower the frequency, the greater the depth of penetration. Wavelength is related to frequency and it is the wavelength of the microwave that determines the detail that can be resolved in the radar image. As the name microwave suggests, the wavelengths used in GPR are relatively short (compared to radio waves) and are of the order of 10cm at 500 megahertz (MHz = millions of cycles per second – the units of frequency used in GPR work). However, the wavelength also depends on the velocity of the microwave through a medium – if the microwave passes through a material with half the velocity of the previous material, then the wavelength will halve, thus doubling the resolution. Consequently, as with many real systems, the selection of the frequency for a GPR survey is a compromise between depth of investigation and resolution and this is conditioned by the depth and size of the target sought and the

Table 3.2 Radar parameters for common materials

Material	Relative Dielectric Permittivity – RDP	Conductivity (mS m^{-1})	Velocity (m ns^{-1})	Attenuation (dB m^{-1})
Air	1	0	0.30	0
Ice	3–4	0.01	0.16	0.01
Fresh water	80	0.5	0.033	0.1
Salt water	80	3000	0.01	1000
Dry sand	3–5	0.01	0.15	0.01
Wet sand	20–30	0.01–1	0.06	0.03–0.3
Shales and clays	5–20	1–1000	0.08	1–100
Silts	5–30	1–100	0.07	1–100
Limestone	4–8	0.5–2.0	0.12	0.4–1
Granite	4–6	0.01–1	0.13	0.01–1
(Dry) salt	5–6	0.01–1	0.13	0.01–1

Source: Based on Milsom (2003: Table 10.1).

material in which it resides. The aim, therefore, is to use the highest possible frequency as this will produce the maximum detail while ensuring the depth required to detect the target is achieved.

3.11.2 GPR in archaeological and forensic contexts

For most archaeological applications a 400–500 MHz frequency would appear to be the starting point with such a frequency having been utilised successfully in many surveys (e.g. Hildebrand *et al.* 2002; Neubauer *et al.* 2002; Piro *et al.* 2003). However, three recent forensic studies are somewhat at odds in this respect. Nobes (2000) used a 200 MHz antenna in the search for a murder victim, suggesting that such a 'moderate' frequency was often preferable for forensic applications. However, Buck (2003) on her test sites, utilised a 400 MHz antenna for the surveys although she had a 900 MHz antenna available which was only reported to have been used on a site which turned out not to contain graves. These need to be reconciled with each other and with Hammon *et al.* (2000) who recommend a frequency of 900 MHz whenever possible. As noted above, in most archaeological GPR work a frequency of around 500 MHz is used, but lower frequencies are regularly used where soil conditions cause restricted penetration of the higher frequency. Where conditions are more favourable, then an 800–1000 MHz antenna would be more appropriate. While in most soils penetration at these frequencies will normally be restricted, a shallow grave may well be within the depth achievable at around 900 MHz, and it may be that the detection of disturbances within or just below the topsoil are all that are required to locate a grave.

A major advantage of GPR is its ability to perform well in confined spaces and even within buildings (e.g. examining basement floors or looking into walls for cavities), its ability to see through dense materials such as concrete or tarmac, and its real-time display. It is the latter that is of some concern, not because such a real-time output should not be used but because it does not do justice to the information that is available if more detailed survey is undertaken and appropriate processing is applied. The ability to run a GPR over a patio and immediately check whether anything akin to a grave exists beneath it is obviously a very attractive operational benefit when compared to the time involved in traversing the patio with 10 or 20 carefully located and aligned traverses that may then take a little time to put together. However, the latter will undoubtedly provide a much better basis for deciding whether a clandestine grave exists below the patio. In practice, if an SIO decides that a body may reside under a patio, then the patio will be lifted no matter what the GPR produces, but in those circumstances the importance of the GPR survey lies in being able to more accurately define the position and extent of any burial in order to support the most appropriate recovery operations (see Chapter 2, Section 2.3). The physical nature of graves (i.e. size and shape) is such that although single profiles can contain much detail along a single GPR traverse, if the traverse misses or cuts the grave only partially then the grave may be missed entirely. Only by accurate closely spaced and (ideally) orthogonal survey methodologies can GPR produce the best results. It may be prudent and excusable to use a less precise methodology in some situations but the inadequacies of such approaches need to be addressed and justified.

The development of the use of GPR in archaeological work is worth summarising as it has, and will continue to have, an effect on the use of GPR in forensic work. GPR has been available since the 1970s but its impact on archaeological geophysical survey has until recently been very limited. In both Clark's first edition (1990) and Scollar (1990), GPR barely featured because it had not proved itself to be useful in many archaeological survey situations, particularly those requiring lateral spatial mapping.

The only application area in which it was thought GPR could really make an impact was in urban archaeology. Small awkwardly shaped sites, often crammed between, and sometimes under, buildings in areas of intense cultural noise, together with the realities of often deep urban stratigraphy meant that conventional archaeological geophysical survey techniques offered little help. It was hoped GPR profiles would be able to see at depth and help untangle the deep stratigraphy giving excavators some idea of what lay at what depth beneath their sites. However, it soon became clear that despite the optimistic claims being banded about, the complexities of urban stratigraphy made useful interpretation effectively untenable. The York experience reported by Stove and Addyman (1989) in retrospect seems to have been rather over-optimistic with Atkin and Milligan (Atkin and Milligan 1992, and Milligan and Atkin 1993) giving a more measured assessment of its effectiveness in urban archaeological situations. Hence, while GPR found success in regard to some specialist applications, for example, locating voids and larger stone features that represent structures such as crypts and tombs, as a general area survey technique, it seemingly had little to offer.

Things began to change in the mid-1990s in a way that would put GPR firmly alongside the other leading techniques. This was pioneered largely by archaeologists who managed to get some access or input into how GPR surveys were to be undertaken and processed. Up to this point, most GPR operators were unfamiliar with the concept of high intensity archaeological survey where full area coverage, high resolution and high spatial accuracy were the norm, because without this intensity the relatively fine and, in terms of geophysical contrast, subtle features sought by archaeologists were simply not being detected. When archaeologists managed to get hold of GPR systems and collect data with the frequency and precision that archaeological survey demands, the situation changed rapidly. In 1992 at the Computer Applications and Quantitative

Methods in Archaeology Conference in Aarhus, Denmark, Milligan and Atkin (1993) presented a paper on using digital GPR data and introducing a technique of combining many parallel depth profiles and slicing them horizontally to provide plans at various 'depths'. These 'depths' were in fact electromagnetic pulse travel times that could be equated broadly with an actual depth, provided that the velocity of electromagnetic waves were known or could be established for that medium. These slices that combined the GPR reflections over a specific time span (and hence at an approximate depth range) resulted in two major advantages over the inspection and interpretation of individual GPR profiles. First, they allowed the spatial extent of anomalies to be seen and therefore be identified for what they were much more effectively and, second, they made possible the identification of subtle anomalies and patterns of otherwise uninterpretable anomalous responses that made no sense when identified only in individual profiles. This mirrors the modern archaeological excavator's wariness of placing any reliance on interpretations based the inadequate and misleading information contained with individual archaeological sections, and which has led to the widespread adoption of the methodology of open area excavation.

Further work, notably by Conyers and Goodman (1997), Nishimura and Goodman (2000), and Neubauer *et al.* (2002), but also by many other practitioners, has used high resolution and appropriate time-slice processing and visualisation techniques to transform the importance of GPR as an archaeological geophysical survey technique (Figure 3.7). By this method, sites can be almost surgically dissected as slices are peeled off, with animation down through the slices sometimes providing breathtaking detail. Once GPR data is collected in such a detailed way, then it can be processed not only to produce the time-slices discussed above but also to enable the data to be analysed in a way that will allow features to be extracted. Leckebusch (2003) has been using such approaches for some time, but in the forensic domain the application of such techniques appears to be relatively undeveloped. Such methods will allow all features

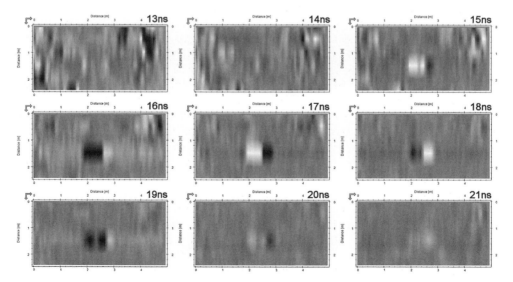

Figure 3.7 GPR time-slice images of a test grave

to be extracted or narrowed down to those that meet certain parameters determined in advance. Thus, in terms of graves, size, depth and shape parameters can be used to help extract relevant anomalies from the otherwise confusing mass of data. While all data processing techniques should be used cautiously, such approaches can give the search team starting points by highlighting anomalies of potentially high priority. This is an excellent example of archaeology being at the forefront of development (NRC 2000), largely as a result of the demanding nature of highly intensive archaeological surveys.

Time-slice approaches have slowly been leaking out to other users of GPR but there has been surprisingly little application regarding the detection of clandestine graves and similar small forensic targets (but see Figure 3.8). This may perhaps have arisen because many practitioners undertaking forensic GPR work have done so without knowledge of developing archaeological methodologies. Equally, and probably linked, is the fact that archaeologists have not had access to the high costing GPR equipment long enough to develop wide expertise in the routine use of the technique even within the archaeological geophysics community. To some extent GPR's undoubted forensic potential awaits the further benefits of archaeological experience, although there have already been notable GPR successes (e.g. Davenport 2001b; Mellett 1996). The University of Texas team's simulation work (Hammon *et al.* 2000) has in some ways laid down the gauntlet for forensic GPR practioners by requesting 10cm reading interval data in order to determine the diagnosic features of an imaged human.

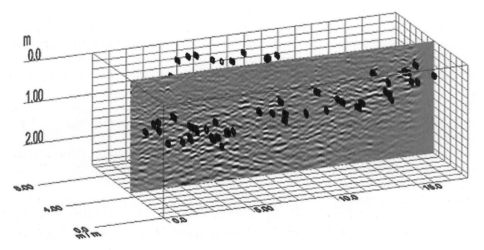

Figure 3.8 Feature extraction from 3-D GPR time-slice survey of burials.
Source: From Watters and Hunter (2004).

3.11.3 Recommendations

Taken together, the extensive literature on the use of GPR for the location of recent burials of forensic interest can be used to provide some practical guidance to ensure that practitioners can aim for a choice of equipment and survey methodology that will provide the best chance of success. These might be summarised as follows, but readers should consult the original papers and any new sources in order to be aware of all relevant aspects that affect the final choice. It would appear that under ideal conditions (shallow burial in a uniform dry sand matrix), then an antenna around 900MHz should give excellent results. Provided survey traverses are taken close enough together (c.10cm) and reading intervals along traverses are 10cm or less (with stacking and recorded in step mode rather than continuous movement), then it may be possible not only to locate the remains but obtain information on the orientation in the grave by imaging individual elements of the body. Migration of GPR data followed by three-dimensional analysis in the form of amplitude time-slicing would be most likely to provide the best imaging of the remains. However, as GPR is often employed as a tool to prioritise areas for more detailed search when factors such as the depth or even the presence of a burial are perhaps not known, then such a detailed survey methodology is clearly impractical. A more general search specification would utilise a 500MHz antenna surveying at a 5cm reading interval along traverses set 0.5m apart. Again, migration of GPR data followed by three-dimensional analysis in the form of amplitude time-slicing would be most likely to provide the best imaging of the grave and remains. However, in search areas that exhibit distinct horizontal stratigraphy then a 250MHz antenna may show the disruption of digging a grave through such layers more effectively when compared with the more cluttered responses produced by higher frequency antennas.

3.12 Integration of geophysical survey into forensic search

Geophysical survey is best utilised as part of a sequence of search techniques according to scenario. Apart from being used to locate buried remains, and with the full recognition that using geophysical survey for eliminating areas to be searched with 100 per cent confidence is not possible, negative results can have a role in prioritising areas for more intensive scrutiny so ensuring the most effective use of resources. In all circumstances, however, using appropriate equipment and methodology under optimum site conditions (above) is paramount. Compromise in any of these may lead to a burial being missed completely when it should have been detected. The use of geophysics also commits the enquiry to testing any anomalies which are produced. This need not be either a lengthy or expensive process (*contra* Hammon *et al.* 2000: 171–172) and can be conducted in a number of ways (see Chapter 2, Section 2.3.5). Moreover, 'best practice' follows a route which leads from the non-invasive to the invasive in order to minimise loss of evidence, and this also accords with Code B of the Police and Criminal Evidence Act (PACE; Home Office 1997a) which requires searches to be conducted with the minimum of disturbance to property. However, in situations where a large number of anomalies is produced, there is a danger that the geophysicist may be asked to prioritise them on grounds of time (e.g. the PACE 'clock' – see Figure 7.3) or cost. This may even be a decision that will need to be defended in court. Furthermore, in order to conform to the terms of the *Code of Practice of the Criminal Procedure and Investigation Act* (CPIA) 1996 *Code of Practice* (Home Office 1997b), all data (including raw digital data) will have to be stored safely as it may need to be disclosed for scrutiny by other geophysicists. Adequate documentation is essential (Davenport 2001b: 124–126) and forensic geophysicists may need to adopt a documentation and archiving approach similar to that recommended for archaeological geophysicists (Schmidt 2002).

3.13 Concluding notes

To put all of this material into context, it has to be re-emphasised that the use of geophysical survey in forensic situations should not be considered simply as a bolt-on, stand-alone, technique (see Chapter 2). Within archaeology, geophysical survey has always been integrated into wider search and excavation strategies, working in parallel with complementary techniques, as this is when it offers most benefit. Archaeology provides a good model of how geophysical survey should be incorporated into forensic search. The aim of this chapter has been to stimulate further research and also to provide some guidelines for operational use, but these are no more than reasonable starting points. In respect of the latter there are no hard and fast procedures to adopt. As with the recovery of forensic remains (see Chapter 4), such a mechanistic approach has no place in a situation where every case is different and where adaptation and flexibility are the rule rather than the exception. The ability to integrate geophysical survey into search and recover requires the user to be conversant with many other techniques and methodologies to ensure the geophysicist's specialist expertise can contribute most effectively within an investigation as a whole. Table 3.3 gives a brief summary of key aspects of the topic in the form of a checklist. Some items on the list have been barely touched upon in this chapter, but the forensic geophysicist should be aware of and familiar with them all.

Table 3.3 A forensic geophysics checklist

To be competent in the application of geophysical survey in a forensic context the forensic geophysicist should:

- be appropriately competent in, and knowledgeable of, the technical aspects and forensic application of the techniques employed so as to be able to be considered an expert in the eyes of the court.
- be able to communicate this expertise effectively in operational, media and courtroom contexts.
- fully understand both the legal and law enforcement operational frameworks within which they are required to operate.
- appreciate the role of geophysical approaches within the wider universe of search and recovery strategies, techniques and methodologies.
- make themself aware of all local conditions that might influence the effectiveness of the proposed geophysical survey strategy, e.g. former land use.
- be aware of likely geophysical response(s) and the possible changes of this response over time.
- understand both the strengths and weaknesses of employing control or calibration graves to investigate potential geophysical responses.
- aim to undertake surveys when conditions are optimal for that particular technique.
- employ reading intervals and instrument configurations appropriate for the detection of the target sought.
- avoid employing techniques or methodologies that do not have a proven record of success.
- recommend and use multiple complementary techniques whenever possible.
- understand both the strengths and weaknesses of geophysical survey in providing negative evidence.
- be aware of the need of, and be able to undertake, discreet or clandestine searches effectively.
- appreciate the likely media responses to the use of geophysical techniques.
- appreciate that instrument data, field notes, plots, and reports are disclosable evidence.
- have considered the courtroom presentation of geophysical evidence

References

Aitken, M.J. 1974. *Physics and Archaeology* 2nd edn, Oxford: Clarendon Press.

Alongi, A.V. 1973. 'A short-pulse high-resolution radar for cadaver detection', *Proceedings of the 1st International Electronic Crime Counter-measures Conference, Edinburgh, Scotland, July 18–20, 1973*, University of Kentucky Press, pp. 79–87.

Aspinall, A. and Crummett, J.G. 1997. 'The electrical pseudosection', *Archaeological Prospection* 4:1, 37–48.

Aspinall, A. and Lynam, J.T. 1970. 'An induced polarisation instrument for the detection of near surface features', *Prospezioni Archeologiche* 5, 67–75.

Atkin, M. and Milligan, R. 1992. 'Ground-probing radar in archaeology – practicalities and problems', *The Field Archaeologist* 16, 288–291.

Beavis, J. and Barker, K. (eds) 1991. *Science and Site: Evaluation and Conservation*, Proceedings of the Archaeological Sciences Conference 1993, Bournemouth University, Bournemouth.

Bevan, B.W. 1991. 'The Search for Graves', *Geophysics* 56, 1310–1319.

Bevan, B.W. 2000. 'An early geophysical survey at Williamsburg, USA', *Archaeological Prospection* 7, 51–58.

Bray, E. 1996. 'The use of geophysics for the detection of clandestine burials: some research and experimentation', unpublished MSc dissertation, Department of Archaeological Sciences, University of Bradford, UK.

Breiner, S. 1973. *Applications Manual for Portable Magnetometers*, Sunnyvale, CA: GeoMetrics.

Buck, S.C. 2003. 'Searching for graves using geophysical technology: field tests with ground penetrating radar, magnetometry, and electrical resistivity', *Journal of Forensic Science* 48:1, 5–11.

Cheetham, P.N. 2001. 'A symmetrical response, high resolution and reduced near-surface noise multiple potential electrode earth resistivity array for archaeological area survey', in Doneus, M., Edler-Hinterleitner, A. and Neubauer, W. (eds) *Archaeological Prospection*, Vienna: Austrian Academy of Sciences, pp. 79–80.

Clark, A.J. 1990. *Seeing Beneath the Soil: Prospecting Methods in Archaeology*, London: Batsford.

Clark, A.J. 1996. *Seeing Beneath the Soil: Prospecting Methods in Archaeology*, 2nd edn, London: Batsford.

Cole, M.A., Linford, N.T., Payne, A.W. and Linford, P.K. 1995. 'Soil magnetic susceptibility measurements and their application to archaeological site investigation', in Beavis, J. and Barker, K. (eds) *Science and Site*, Proceedings of the Archaeological Sciences Conference 1993, Bournemouth University, pp. 144–162.

Conyers, L.B. and Goodman, D. 1997. *Ground-Penetrating Radar: An Introduction for Archaeologists*, Walnut Creek, CA: AltaMira Press.

Davenport, G.C. 2001a. *Where Is It? Searching for Buried Bodies and Hidden Evidence*, Maryland: SportsWork.

Davenport, G.C. 2001b. 'Remote sensing applications in forensic applications', *Historical Archaeology* 35, 87–100.

David, A. 1995. *Geophysical Survey in Archaeological Field Evaluation*, English Heritage Research and Professional Guidelines, No. 1, London: English Heritage.

Davis, J.L., Heginbottom, J.A., Annan, A.P., Daniels, R.S., Berdal, B.P., Bergan, T., Duncan, K.E., Lewin, P.K., Oxford, J.S., Roberts, N., Skehek, J.J. and Smith, C.R. 2000. 'Ground penetrating radar surveys to locate 1918 Spanish flu victims in permafrost', *Journal of Forensic Sciences* 45:1, 68–76.

Doneus, M., Edler-Hinterleitner, A. and Neubauer, W. 2001a. *Archaeological Prospection in Austria*, in Doneus, M., Edler-Hinterleitner, A. and Neubauer, W. (eds), *Archaeological Prospection*, Vienna: Austrian Academy of Sciences, pp. 11–33.

Doneus, M., Edler-Hinterleitner, A. and Neubauer, W. (eds) 2001b. *Archaeological Prospection: Fourth International Conference on Archaeological Prospection*, Austrian Academy of Sciences, Vienna.

Donnelly, L. 2002. 'Finding the silent witness', *Geoscientist* 12:5, 16–17.

France, D.L., Griffin, T.J., Swanburg, J.G., Lindermann, J.W., Davenport, G.C., Trammell, V., Armbrust, C.T., Kondratieff, B., Nelson, A., Castellano, K. and Hopkins, D., 1992. 'A multidisciplinary approach to the detection of clandestine graves', *Journal of Forensic Science*, 37:6, 1445–1458.

France, D.L., Griffin, T.J., Swanburg, J.G., Lindermann, J.W., Davenport, G.C., Trammell, V., Trammell, C.T., Kondratieff, B., Nelson, A., Castellano, K., Hopkins, D. and Adair, T. 1997. 'NecroSearch revisited: further multidisciplinary approaches to the detection of clandestine graves', in Haglund, W.D. and Sorg, M.H. (eds) *Forensic Taphonomy*, Boca Raton, FL: CRC Press, pp. 479–509.

Freeland, R.S., Miller, M.L., Yoder, R.E. and Koppenjan, S.K. 2003. 'Forensic application of FM-CW and pulse radar', *Journal of Environmental and Engineering Geophysics* 8:2, 97–103.

Gaffney, C. and Gater, J. 2003. *Revealing the Buried Past: Geophysics for Archaeologists*, Stroud: Tempus.

Haglund, W.D. and Sorg, M.H. (eds) 1997. *Forensic Taphonomy: The Postmortem Fate of Human Remains*, Boca Raton, FL: CRC Press.

Hammon, W.S., McMechan, G.A. and Zeng, X. 2000. 'Forensic GPR: finite-difference simulations of responses from buried remains', *Journal of Applied Geophysics* 45, 171–186.

Herz, N. and Garrison, E.G. 1998 *Geological Methods for Archaeology*, New York: Oxford University Press.

Hildebrand, J.A., Wiggins, S.M., Henkart, P.C. and Conyers, L.B. 2002. 'Comparison of seismic reflection and ground-penetrating radar imaging at the controlled archaeological test site, Champaign, Illinois', *Archaeological Prospection*, 9, 9–21.

Home Office, 1997a. *Police and Criminal Evidence Act 1984 Codes of Practice*, London: The Stationery Office.

Home Office, 1997b. *Criminal Procedure and Investigations Act 1996 Code of Practice*, London: The Stationery Office.

Killam, E. 1990. *The Detection of Human Remains*, Springfield, IL: Charles Thomas.

Kirby, A. forthcoming. 'Conductivity changes in decomposing remains', unpublished MSc dissertation, School of Conservation Sciences, Bournemouth University, UK.

Kvamme, K. 2003. 'Multidimensional prospecting in North American Great Plains village sites', *Archaeological Prospection* 10:2, 131–142.

Leckebusch, J. 2003. 'Ground-penetrating radar: a modern three-dimensional prospection method', *Archaeological Prospection* 10:4, 213–240.

Lynam, J.T. 1970. 'Techniques of geophysical prospection as applied to near surface structure determination', unpublished PhD thesis, University of Bradford, UK.

Marshall, A. 1998. 'Visualising burnt areas: patterns of magnetic susceptibility at Guiting Power 1 round barrow (Glos., UK)', *Archaeological Prospection* 5, 159–177.

Mellett, J.S. 1996. 'GPR in forensic and archaeological work: hits and misses', *Symposium on the Applications of Geophysics to Environmental and Engineering Problems*, SAGEEP '96 Environmental and Engineering Geophysical Society, Keystone, CO, 487–491.

Millar, M.L., Freeland, R.S. and Koppenjan, S.K. 2002. 'Searching for concealed human remains using GPR imaging of decomposition', *Ninth International Conference on Ground-penetrating Radar*, Proceedings of SPIE, 4758, 539–544.

Milligan, R. and Atkin, M. 1993. 'The use of ground-probing radar within a digital environment on archaeological sites', *Computing the Past: Computer Applications and Quantitative Methods in Archaeology* CAA92, 21–32.

Milsom, J. 1989. *Field Geophysics*, Milton Keynes: Open University Press.

Milsom, J. 2003. *Field Geophysics* 3rd edn, Chichester: John Wiley.

Morse, D., Duncan, J. and Stoutamire, J. 1983. *Handbook of Forensic Archaeology and Anthropology*, Tallahassee, FL: Rose Press.

Neubauer, W., Edler-Hinterleitner, A., Seren, S. and Melichar, P. 2002. 'Georadar in the Roman civil town Carnuntum, Austria: an approach for archaeological interpretation of GPR data', *Archaeological Prospection* 9:3, 135–156.

Neubauer, W., Edler-Hinterleitner, A., Seren, S., Becker, H. and Fassbinder, J. 2003. 'Magnetic survey of the Viking Age settlement of Haithabu, Germany', *Archaeologia Polona* 41, 239–241.

Nishimura, Y. and Goodman, D. 2000. 'Ground-penetrating radar survey at Wroxeter', *Archaeological Prospection* 7, 101–105.

Nobes, D.C. 2000. 'The search for "Yvonne": a case example of the delineation of a grave using near-surface geophysical methods', *Journal of Forensic Sciences* 45:3, 715–721.

NRC, (National Research Council) 2000. *Seeing into the Earth*, Washington, DC: National Academy Press.

Piro, S., Goodman, D. and Nishimura, Y. 2003. 'The study and characterisation of emperor Traiano's villa (Altopiani di Arcinazzo, Roma) using high-resolution integrated geophysical surveys', *Archaeological Prospection* 10:1, 1–25.

Reynolds, J.M. 1997. *An Introduction to Applied and Environmental Geophysics*, Chichester: John Wiley.

Rodriguez, W.C. and Bass, W.M. 1985. 'Decomposition of buried bodies and methods that may aid in their location', *Journal of Forensic Sciences*, 30:3, 836–852.

Rowan, M. 1991. *Guide to the Eagle Spectrum and Engineers Report*, Inverness: Whites UK.

Schmidt, A. 2002. *Geophysical Data in Archaeology: A Guide to Good Practice*, Oxford: Archaeology Data Service Oxbow [also available online at: http://ads.ahds.ac.uk/project/goodguides/geophys/].

Schmidt, A. and Marshall, A. 1997. 'Impact of resolution on the interpretation of archaeological data', *Archaeological Sciences 1995: Proceedings of a Conference on the Application of Scientific Techniques to the Study of Archaeology, Liverpool, July 1995*, Oxford: Oxbow, pp. 343–348.

Scollar, I. 1990. *Archaeological Prospecting and Remote Sensing*, Cambridge: Cambridge University Press.

Scott, D. D. and Connor, M. 1997. 'Context delicti: archaeological context in forensic work', in Haglund, W.D. and Sorg M.H. (eds), *Forensic Taphonomy*, Boca Raton, FL: CRC Press, pp. 27–38.

Stove, G.C. and Addyman P.V. 1989. 'Ground probing impulse radar: an experiment in remote sensing at York', *Antiquity* 63, 337–342.

Strongman, K.B. 1992. 'Forensic applications of ground penetrating radar', *Proceedings of the 2nd International Conference on Ground Penetrating Radar, Geological Survey of Canada*, Paper 90–4, 203–211.

Sutherland, T. and Schmidt, A. 2003. 'An integrated approach to battlefield archaeology', *Landscapes* 4:2, 15–25.

Turner, B. and Wiltshire, P. 1999. 'Experimental validation of forensic evidence: a study of the decomposition of buried pigs in a heavy clay soil', *Forensic Science International* 101, 113–122.

Vingerhoets, R. 2004. 'A study of bullet penetration into soil in the context of forensic archaeology', unpublished MSc dissertation, School of Conservation Sciences, Bournemouth University, UK.

Watters, M. and Hunter, J.R. 2004. 'Geophysics and burials: field experience and software development', in Pye, K. and Croft, D. (eds) *Forensic Geosciences*, London: Geological Society of London, pp. 21–31.

4

THE RECOVERY OF FORENSIC EVIDENCE FROM INDIVIDUAL GRAVES

Case studies 14–29

4.1 Background

Details of the various archaeological approaches to recovering evidence from individual graves are discussed in various texts too numerous to mention (e.g. Sigler-Eisenberg 1985; Hunter *et al.* 1996; Haglund 2001). A key factor in the development of the subject is that there has, until recently, been a difference in approach reflecting whether those undertaking such work have a UK or North American training. Within the UK intellectual and professional context, the grave itself, plus other forensic evidence contained within and around the grave, whether environmental or anthropogenic, is considered as important as the human remains themselves. In North America, the approach has, until recently, tended to view the excavation process as a means of recovering a body and did not accord the grave itself, and its fill, the same level of importance compared to the UK. In forensic terms there is a major distinction in that

> the *exhumation* of human remains is simply the retrieval of remains, whether archaeological techniques are used or not. The *excavation* of human remains results in the retrieval of the remains, but also in the reconstruction of human activity at the site and beyond.
>
> (Connor and Scott 2001: 4; our italics)

This is the contextual paradigm. It is the latter aspiration with which this chapter is concerned.

The key point in the investigation of a grave, as with any forensic scene, is to adopt a multidisciplinary approach in which experts integrate with crime scene personnel in a well-managed team framework. Archaeology as a discipline brings with it a wide understanding of buried environments, and experience has shown that a forensic archaeologist may emerge as a facilitator within this framework, identifying the potential range of other evidence within buried deposits (e.g. soil, plant and insect remains) that might exist in a recoverable and recordable form, presenting a case for specialist personnel to be introduced or a sampling strategy to be implemented by crime scene personnel. This is not a case of the archaeologist playing the detective, merely ensuring, as on any archaeological site, that the most complete range of evidence is collected in order to provide the fullest possible archaeological picture. This entails the archaeologist having an awareness of other forms of evidence, in this case insect, soil and plant remains, and an understanding of their analytical methodology (e.g. Hall 1997; Hutter 2001; Greenberg and Kunich 2002).

This collection of evidence may also extend to an area considerably wider than the grave itself and will also be the subject of examination by scene of crime personnel whose interests may be in conflict with the stratigraphic interests of the archaeologist (see case 14). In the case of much older graves, this may be less problematic but nevertheless, some evidence may still survive. In mass grave scenarios, there may be evidence of an execution scene evidenced by the distribution of cartridge cases at a short distance from the grave itself (see Chapter 5, Section 5.5.2), or an area denoted by significant soil biochemistry changes where bodies were 'processed' prior to interment (e.g. chopped into pieces with a machine bucket). Alternatively, the relevance may be one of *context*, for example, in assessing localised vegetation and woodland with a view to identifying any differential plant colonisation or growth which may offer dating evidence, or which might require specialist attention. Even if nothing anomalous is observed, species can be sampled and preserved, and the record can act as a control against any botanical remains found within the fill of the grave itself. The location of these contextual samples will constitute part of the wider record of the site as a whole (see below).

The surrounding area can also act as a guide to the soil characteristics and hydro-logical regime to be expected and this can be established by the excavation of a small test pit. These are key elements in understanding the burial environment, and hence the likely condition of the remains (see Haglund and Sorg 1997, 2002). A waterlogged clay environment, for example, will lead to the longer-term survival of soft tissues and other organic materials, and can induce saponification of soft tissues, while by contrast, a free draining chalk or gravel can lead to more rapid skeletonisation and decay processes. This site background is important for deciding on ultimate recovery strategies, logistics, and for informing which type of equipment, materials, or even personnel (e.g. an anthropologist) might be needed to support the forensic pathologist during recovery. Equally important, but from a forensic science perspective, is the need to understand the characteristics and properties of the local soil or sediment. This can also be established from the test pit and will enable distinction to be made between natural local soils and those accidentally introduced via a vehicle or on clothes during the perpetration of the crime. Comparative criteria can include mineral, chemical and organic contents of soil as well as pollen and leaf mould. A test pit will also have the benefit of allowing the archaeologist to recognise the nature and depth of natural substrates, and to be guided, according to soil condition, as to the likely survival of such environmental evidence as pollens.

4.2 Excavation: information and logistics

The procedure adopted in the excavation of a gravesite will be dictated to some extent by what is known of the case in question. In some instances, a possible gravesite may have been located as part of a thorough search for a specific missing person where the probable post-mortem interval (and by implication post-depositional period) is known. Alternatively, and more frequently, a suspect site may be located serendipitously by a member of the public with nothing known of the period of deposition or even the name of the likely victim. Archaeological expertise thus needs to be applied as appropriate but with a breadth of adaptiveness not often encountered on traditional archaeological sites. The ability to think laterally and apply techniques with confidence, adjust approaches, or adopt a different strategy if circumstances dictate are paramount (e.g. Hoshower 1998) and are well recognised in the registration criteria established for forensic archaeologists by the Council for the Registration of Forensic Practitioners (see Chapter 1, Section 1.5). All forensic cases are unique and the greater the background field experience that the archaeologist can bring to a scene, the more likely it is that he or she will be able to recognise the wider implications of the evidential requirements that the scene presents, the role of other specialists, the range of archaeological methods that can be applied, and the relevance of the legal parameters in the recovery and recording process. The approach taken will invariably be dictated by the information needed and the objectives of the investigation, rather than by a steadfast adherence to archaeological purity. These objectives need to be transparent to all concerned from the outset, although unfortunately, biases can creep into the process. The SIO, for example, may retain certain information about a case for various strategic reasons, and these reasons may also impact on archaeological strategy. Recognising this situation, it is imperative that archaeologists ask the right questions, particularly those relating to circumstances of the case, local factors, or the time intervals involved.

4.2.1 Equipment, contamination, and health and safety

Most archaeologists have their own excavation equipment (e.g. spade, hand shovel, hand mattock, trowels, plasterers' leaves, sieves, brushes, etc. as well as more technical equipment such as GPS and EDM). Increasingly, the police have sophisticated surveying equipment and appropriately skilled personnel, although, ironically, not all forces seem able to distinguish between a spade and a shovel. Wheelbarrows are a constant difficulty and may need to be purchased specially. Two barrows are minimum. Most scene managers will be happy to purchase a list of equipment in advance, but the archaeologist needs to be in a position to insist on certain specifications and the appropriate number of items (see also Chapter 5, Section 5.2). Failure to do this has, in the past, resulted in trowels the size of dinner plates, a single bucket for a major excavation, a large number of spades but no shovels (alternatively a large number of shovels but no spades), and, on one occasion, an unrequested Operational Support Unit (OSU) armed with flame-throwers and chain saws. Experience suggests that the archaeologist is best advised to appear on site prepared with enough equipment to be self-sufficient, including basic items such as buckets. Much of this equipment may never be seen again, either because it will be retained in order to hold evidential material, will become contaminated, lost, wrecked, or simply put in someone else's vehicle at the end of the exercise. Some items may become sufficiently unpleasant for the archaeologist not to want them back. They are best treated as disposable and charged accordingly. From the point of view of contingency, it is also preferable to maintain a stock of variously sized sealable finds-type bags and sample bottles. Most scene of crime vans are well stocked, but there may be several incidents running simultaneously and facilities may be stretched. Containers may be needed for the collection of microscopic evidence and of environmental indicators such as pollens and spores. Equipment and containers need to be either new or spotlessly clean as even the remote possibility of contamination may be seized upon avidly in cross-examination. Best practice is to maintain an equipment log that records the cleaning of equipment after each usage (using distilled or de-ionised water), and the storage of items in a clean and secure location.

Rubber gloves are essential for all scene of crime work and are best worn doubled up when dealing with human remains. This provides a reasonable compromise between finger movement and safety, and allows the outer glove to be replaced without risk of contamination or risk to the individual. Latex gloves are not overly durable, and thicker Marigold-type gloves are preferable for heavier work. Alternatively kevlar-type gloves (gash-proof) may be preferable in certain environments. Unlike more traditional archaeological scenarios, there are *no* occasions at a scene of crime where it is permissable to use bare hands. Masks may also be an essential item to filter vapours and other particles, rather than simply being a desirable extra for those particularly sensitive to the stench of decomposition. Any mask needs to be a high efficiency particulate air filter respirator to at least PPE (personal protection equipment) level 3 if it is to be effective in screening out infectious pathogens, fungi and moulds, and dangerous particulates that may be found at recent gravesites. Health and safety measures continually strive to maintain a position one step ahead of litigation, and the scene of crime manager may insist that all personnel wear appropriate safety equipment in order to minimise risks.

Investigation of gravesites has become increasingly sophisticated, particularly with regard to issues of contamination, partly through fibres, but now also through the sensitivity of DNA developments. Appropriate clothing is imperative and typically consists of disposable forensic over-suits which minimise fibre transfer from clothes, and overshoes which avoid shoe-print recognition issues. Experience suggests that police stocks of these tend to consist of sizes L and XL only, and that specialists would do well to provide their own sizes which are readily available from most DIY and industrial clothing retailers. Over-suits which are either too small or too large can impede progress.

Health and safety has serious implications for archaeologists and anthropologists at a scene of crime (see Crist 2001; Galloway and Snodgrass 1998) and extend well beyond issues of hard hats, appropriate footware, and up-to-date tetanus immunisation. While the UK police are generally improving their protocols for the health and safety of their staff, the archaeologist is in effect a sub-contractor to whom they have no mandatory obligations, and the onus is therefore placed on the individual. The same is true of many organisations who contract archaeologists in international investigations (see also Chapter 5, Section 5.3). Perhaps the most obvious risks are from contact with the remains of recently deceased individuals who suffered from an infectious disease at the time of their death. While some viruses and bacterium cannot outlive their host, others can, for example, the now-extinct smallpox virus (see Young 1998). Galloway and Snodgrass (1998) cite data from a study conducted in a post-mortem examination context which indicated that 33 per cent of all autopsies tested positive for potentially dangerous viral infections, including hepatitis A and B and HIV. There is also the potential for post-traumatic stress disorder for which appropriate support and treatment are now becoming increasingly available.

Furthermore, graves attract insects or rodents which may be vectors of disease: in the UK rats, for example, carry Weil's disease and some rodents in the USA carry the virus that causes the Hantavirus Pulmonary Syndrome (Crist 2001). Gravesites also present a variety of potential traumas: accidental injury through piercing of gloves or protection; deliberate booby-trapping of graves and bodies; disease or poisoning from contact with contaminated substrates (e.g. from rubbish tips, land-fill and weapons testing areas); or poison gasses such as methane which can build up in shafts or wells in which human remains have been dumped. Methane can persist for long period, is heavier than air, odourless, and potentially fatal.

4.2.2 Verifying the grave

Once the wider area has been assessed and treated appropriately, steps can be taken to verify the grave. To some extent the method used may depend on the reliability of the information known. Strategies may differ between, for example, a specific location which has been pointed out by an offender who has been taken to the scene, a potential grave discovered by a member of the public, and a 'grave' which may be one of several anomalies that need to be tested as the result of a search programme (see Chapter 2, Section 2.3.5). However, before any invasive work is undertaken, the area will be treated as a provisional scene with appropriate photography/video and recording undertaken by scene of crime personnel. It is in the legal interests of the archaeologist that this occurs. Under most circumstances, the surface area will then be carefully cleaned and recorded, the edges outlined, and a sondage, or narrow trench, excavated across the suspect area (Figure 4.1). This need be no more than 50cm wide to serve its purpose but needs to extend across and beyond the suspect area in order to find, or confirm, the edges of any possible grave cut. Not all graves are rectangular or of a size approximating to an extended adult. Unpremeditated murders frequently result in very rushed grave construction where the grave is no more than a shallow 'scoop', little deeper than the body itself and of varied dimensions and shape (see case 15). In some cases, whether premeditated or not, bodies may be buried in all variety of position and in some cases the body may be incomplete, or may be complete but disarticulated (see case 16). Digging a grave can take a considerable time, depending on substrates, for example, digging a deep rectangle of any size through chalk or clay can be extremely time-consuming even for fit, strong people. An offender will need to balance the need to conceal a body well with the time taken to carry out the disposal. The deeper and more securely the body is buried, the longer it takes, and the greater the likelihood of being observed. In gravels it may be virtually impossible to dig to any depth at all, and the sides may become fluid and cause difficulty in maintaining either depth or contour. Similar problems may be evident in alluvial silts in riverine flood plains, or valley mires, where highly mobile sediments are in constant flux due to recharge hydrology as well as the impact of precipitation. Archaeological excavation of these will be confronted by the same difficulties: the grave cuts may be indistinct, even if very recent, and this further demonstrates the importance of the test pit in order to evaluate likely characteristics and indicators of disturbance.

Excavating a sondage assumes that the feature in question may be a grave. Deturfing, and the removal of soils either in obvious layers or, more often, in arbitary 'spits' of some 10 cm depth, need to be undertaken carefully with the individual deposits removed from the scene and preserved as separate contexts. This usually entails polythene sheeting, where individual contexts/spits can be kept discrete, or plastic dustbins. The latter tend to be preferred by scene of crime personnel as they are relatively cheap, can be lidded and made secure, stored easily, and can be lifted and carried by two persons

Figure 4.1 A sondage or narrow trench being excavated across a suspect area

even when full. Using the sondage method, part of a grave cut and any subsequent burial will be readily apparent with minimal loss of evidence. However, if undisturbed natural layers are reached and no grave is located, excavation can cease and a negative result recorded. In warning, however, there have been occasions where a grave has been dug and never used (for example, because of tree roots, lack of appropriate depth, etc. – see cases 17 and 28), or even where the body had been 'robbed' from the grave and the empty grave infilled (case 18) – an event rare in the UK but often a more common feature of mass graves (e.g. Skinner *et al.* 2002). However, in the event of human remains being discovered, the investigation develops from one of simple search into a 'major incident' which may bring with it the potential for increased funding and prioritisation of resources. The scene will be secured, an approach route established, cordons put in place, personnel access logged, and the scene almost certainly tented to preserve evidence and inhibit public and media view.

4.3 Excavation strategy

Once human remains have been encountered, the SIO will be reluctant to allow further work within the grave unless the pathologist is either present or agreeable. Given the length of time that it may take the pathologist to reach the scene, it may be possible, by telephone agreement, to uncover the remainder of the body. This will only be permissable if the pathologist can be assured that the integrity of the body is retained for his or her own examination – an agreement best achieved if the archaeologist and pathologist have worked together previously. Such an arrangement is of mutual advantage: it allows the archaeologist to excavate and record the remainder of the grave down to the body at a professionally acceptable speed; and it minimises the time the pathologist has to wait at the scene in order for the body to be uncovered in full. The interval also allows the archaeologist to plan a recovery strategy on the basis of known stratigraphy, soil profile, and taphonomic state. It is also the opportunity to set up a recording system: to identify either an EDM or manual system; and establish a base line and prepare contexts sheets, planning boards, and other appropriate logging systems.

Specific techniques for excavating a grave after evaluating a suspicious feature that proves to be positive are discussed in depth in such work as Hunter *et al.* (1996), and as such are only repeated here as key issues arise. Clearance of the surface of vegetation and any detritus, suitably recorded, across an area of approximately 3 × 3m allows a disturbed feature to be clarified. The intention here is to provide a background against which any disturbance will stand out, and also create a visual workspace within which non-participant personnel can be excluded. If the disturbance transpires to be 'grave-shaped', then the proportions of the cleared area can be altered accordingly.

There may well be sediment or soil layers that overlie the grave and its adjacent land surface. Under ideal circumstances these can be excavated individually and sieved for any material evidence, as well as sampled for botanical or entomological reasons. These layers may have no bearing on the crime, but could contain material that helps define a date before which the burial occurred. Alternatively, they may have been deliberately deposited by the perpetrator with the intention of concealing the grave, hence any evidence regarding their nature, date of deposition, or place of origin is important. On removal of these layers, the top of the grave will become apparent and, according to the drift geology, may be clearly or less obviously defined. The fill of the grave is likely to be different in terms of colour, compactness, moist/dryness, and texture to the undisturbed soil around it. Degrees of difference will reflect local conditions and features of the burial (e.g. if wrapped).

Graves should only be excavated by experienced archaeologists using appropriate equipment such as metal trowels, plasterers' leaves and brushes, although often the upper fills or a half-section can be removed more rigorously during initial testing. In most situations half-sectioning is the optimum way forward: it allows the archae-ologist to determine whether the feature is a grave or not without removing the whole fill, and it provides a section which not only illustrates how the feature was infilled, but also provides some guidance as to how the other half might be best excavated (Figure 4.2). In either event, excavation continues to be conducted according to any layering or arbitary spits which are stored as separate contexts. Each context needs to be uniquely numbered in order that all materials, exhibits and samples seized can be recorded in terms of precise contextual location. Archaeology is a destructive process and this ensures that all items and samples taken can be sourced to their particular context enabling the record to be modelled in three dimensions. This is useful for the court as well as the investigating authority. All of the fill must be retained for appro-priate sampling and, if required, for legal purposes. If a grave is deep, it may be necessary to deconstruct one of the sides in order to recover the body (see case 19). This can potentially destroy evidence of the type of implement used to dig the grave or the direction of digging, and has to be balanced against damaging the remains by excavation in a confined space (see case 20).

Figure 4.2 Half-sectioning a potential grave

Once the fill above and to the sides of the body has been removed and the remains exposed as much as possible, then the body can be lifted. This is a critical point in the excavation process in that the key item of evidence (i.e. the human remains) has now been revealed for the first time and needs to be recorded carefully through photographs, video, documentation, etc. Like any other scene of crime, nothing can be disturbed until this process has been completed. The removal, for example, of individual bones, checking of pockets, or lifting of body parts to clean and expose them better is un-acceptable until the recording (and subsequent briefing) are complete. The skill of the archaeologist can be measured by the extent to which the remains can be exposed and presented without jeopardising the integrity of the scene. It should be noted that unlike in traditional archaeology, where skeletons devoid of a speck of soil seem desirable, in forensic cases over-cleaning can all too easily remove valuable trace evidence from such surfaces as clothing, thus destroying contextual relevance. The point at which lifting occurs, and the method of lifting will normally be defined by the pathologist. Methods of lifting will reflect both the environment and the condition of the remains. In some instances the body can simply be lifted out whole (e.g. case 15) or by using straps if the space is confined (e.g. case 20). Where the remains are likely to disarticulate, a thin metal sheet can be carefully slid underneath in order to provide support (e.g. case 19), or, if the remains are skeletonised they can be lifted individually, checked off and bagged (e.g. case 21). Failure to recover all the skeletal material can result in later difficulties in interpretation (see Cox and Bell 1999).

Before lifting commences, the pathologist may wish to undertake a fairly detailed examination within the grave itself, often to ascertain how the body is positioned and how it can be freed without damage. Soil pressure and decay may have served to contort the remains badly, often to the extent that the position of limbs is difficult to establish and may require the pathologist to feel around and under the body in order to understand the configuration of deposition. Clothing, if predominantly of artificial fibres, can facilitate this by acting as a type of semi-waterproof sack containing the remains, but natural fibres tend to survive less well, and part-decayed clothing has a tendency to confuse rather than assist in interpretation (see also Janaway 2002). In the event of the body being completely or substantially skeletonised, the pathologist may wish to gain the support of a physical anthropologist to aid in interpretation, recovery, and analysis both in the grave and the mortuary.

After the body has been removed, any remaining fill can be excavated in the normal way and the grave recorded in detail. These lowest layers are crucial contexts as they are those most likely to contain personal or identifying items (see above). Once the grave has been completely cleared, it can be photographed, measured and planned in the normal way, and checked against fixed reference points (Figure 4.3). At this point there is perhaps some merit in considering the possible action of bioturbation, particularly in older graves, or in shallow graves dug into relatively soft or loose substrates. The phenomenon of small objects being moved from out of the grave by the activities of insects and small mammals, or even earthworms is not unknown (e.g. Johnson and Watson-Stegner 1990), although this diminishes with depth. The same principle applies with remains deposited on the ground surface, for example, bone can be moved beneath the sward by the same mechanism (Cole 2000). The extent of bioturbation is not well understood and, once the grave is fully recorded, additional excavation of the grave-sides and base for a few centimetres will effectively close a possible avenue of approach in cross-examination, even if nothing is found.

The recording process at a gravesite follows the usual procedure of any traditional archaeological site. It will require at least two fixed reference points and the use (ideally) of a total station electronic distance measurer (EDM). This can also be used to plot the locations of any samples taken for botanical or other purposes. Forensic life is not impossible without an EDM, in fact, the required speed of investigation may necessitate more manual methods (triangulation, offsetting, use of dumpy level, etc.) and the archaeologist should be familiar with the underlying principles of geometry on which electronic systems are based. Although GPS instruments can be used to position the grave itself, accuracy is not great (usually to 5–8m at best unless extremely expensive systems are purchased) and it is probably no less accurate to locate the position of the grave by measurement to fixed points marked on an OS map. It can be stressed yet again, that forensic archaeology often requires archaeologists to be creative and to improvise. In some respects a gravesite requires a very simple level of recording for which using expensive electronic instrumentation can be argued as 'overkill'. It is perhaps worth pointing out that scenes tend to occur in enclosed or confined areas within which the error encountered by holding a prism too close to the instrument is probably greater and less effective than using a tape measure. Plans and section drawing will almost certainly need to be undertaken manually at an appropriate scale (Figure 4.4). A scale of 1:10 is probably optimum and is at a reasonable size in its original state for a jury to understand. Sketches and rough drawings need to be marked

Figure 4.3 The fully excavated grave ready for planning and photography

up as 'not to scale' in order to avoid opening issues up accuracy in cross-examination. Although scale plans of skeletal remains are normally made on archaeological sites and look very impressive, these are generally agreed as unnecessary at a scene of crime. However, a detailed record of skeletonised remains will almost certainly be essential for anthropological purposes in order to determine cause of death differentiating between anti- and peri-mortem trauma to bone, deliberate excision of bone, etc. Mass grave excavations (see Chapter 5, Section 5.5) document each skeleton in sufficient detail in order to ensure that this type of evidence is recorded, usually by a physical anthropologist, or by an archaeologist with a thorough understanding of skeletal anatomy if an anthropologist is unavailable. Comprehensive detailed and high quality photography (including video) is seen as acceptable, but must be taken by someone with an understanding of anthropological objectives to be effective, whereas the planning of individual skeletal items is tainted with subjectivity, not to mention errors of non-parallelax.

A photographic record is a key part of the crime scene record and will be maintained by crime scene personnel throughout the whole process irrespective of archaeological involvement. At the time of writing digital photography is not admissible in court as it offers the potential to be 'doctored'. Nevertheless, it is in the archaeologist's interests

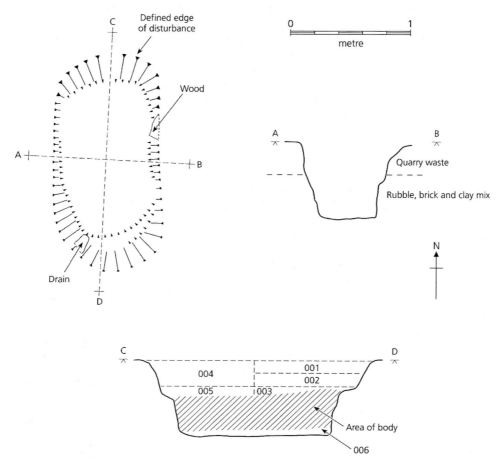

Figure 4.4 A typical plan of an excavated grave with section

to ensure that the official photographic record includes those taken at appropriate points during the recovery. These are not arbitary points, but specific times when the archaeologist feels the record is changing, or has changed, for example, at the removal of individual layers or spits, or at the exposure of specific features or objects. Many crime scene photographers tend not to use scales, and it is useful to have a 0.5m calibrated scale available for general photography and a smaller (e.g. 10cm) scale available for more detailed photographs. In photographing the grave or body itself, it is usually prudent to insist that the photographer takes records shots from a specific fixed point as the excavation progresses. This has to be defined early in the investigation and any half-sectioning needs to be undertaken in awareness of appropriate space and lighting for the camera positioning. Once this position has been established a sequence of photographs can be taken as the excavation continues, as the fill is systematically removed, and as the body is gradually exposed and the grave emptied. If these photographs can be taken to reflect specific archaeological events in the recovery process, they can ultimately be viewed in reverse order and indicate how a grave was dug, a body deposited, and the grave infilled. This record can provide a remarkably effective reconstruction of events when shown in reverse order and has a major part to play in any homicide investigation. The archaeologist may also wish to take his or her own photographs, although this will need the approval of the SIO. Unlike the official photographic archive these are deemed as being for record purposes and can be digital. However, like all other documentation, drawings, plans, notes etc, these photographs will be potentially disclosable under the terms of the Criminal Procedure and Investigations Act (1996).

As the excavation process is itself destructive, it is as always imperative to record the rationale of approach, process and results extremely clearly, including any change of approach. This is important not only for the archaeologist's own personal records and to provide an *aide-mémoire* after the tensions of the site have been left behind, but also to provide an intelligible, transparent and disclosable record for cross-examination purposes, or for any appeal. There are different approaches to recording on forensic scenes but perhaps the safest is to use a purpose-designed, page-numbered and securely-bound excavation log that incorporates especially designed context records, plan and section forms of all relevant types, including checklists of specific types of information that can sometimes be forgotten under pressure, such as details of weather conditions, quality of light, etc. This has the advantage of placing all the documentation in one place, it ensures attention to basic detail including cross-reference to exhibits and exhibit numbers which will be maintained separately by the exhibits officer, and allows for straightforward photocopying in order to retain a personal copy. An alternative is to use carbonised paper in such a log and remove one copy of each page by that method. Any alterations need to be crossed out, explained in the log, and signed. It is absolutely not acceptable to erase text or figures or have pages torn out. In court, changes of mind that are not justified may be viewed as incompetence, while what can be construed as attempts to conceal such changes of strategy or errors may even be seen as an attempt to pervert the course of justice. There will also need to be cross-reference to other scene records, notably the presence of other scene personnel, times of entry and exit, and the times at which specific events (e.g. commencement of the excavation, or exposure of the body) occurred. The exhibits officer is also required to record (to the minute) the recovery of individual exhibits, and it is as well to ensure that records concur as the excavation progresses. An alternative and perhaps safer approach is to rely on the exhibits officer for that level of detail. The record is confidential and *sub-judice* throughout the period of an investigation and during any possible appeal thereafter. It is also likely to be required to be disclosed.

4.4 Identifying evidence

Before excavation proceeds it is important to remember the processes that took place in creating the grave – the digging, the deposition, and the infilling respectively – and applying a reverse of that process in the recovery exercise. Critical in the excavation process is maintaining the integrity of the grave; this necessitates that during excavation, where practically possible, every care must be taken to ensure that the sides of the grave right down to the base are revealed and maintained. Failure to ensure this lays the process open to accusations of contamination from surrounding layers that may be earlier or later than the grave itself, or of inefficient collection of evidence, especially directly above the base of the grave below the body where items such as buttons, coins, or even projectiles can collect when the body decomposes (see case 21). The grave as a feature will hold such clues as the mode of digging, the tools used and the direction of digging (Hochrein 2002). The grave cut itself, the fill, and evidence on and around the body will potentially hold the majority of the evidence available to an enquiry, particularly when the grave is a serendipitous find and there is no criminal context for the burial. Conversely, if the grave is the result of a concerted search effort, the missing person will be known, there may be a suspect, and the timeframe of disappearance will already have been recorded. In the former, there is always a danger of making assumptions and hence of not being entirely objective (e.g. case 22). Either way, the potential of the available evidence within the grave will only be realised if excavation is conducted by appropriately experienced experts. The buried evidence will be interrogated and the following questions, while not exhaustive, are typical of those which will need to be addressed:

- *How was the grave dug and with what implements?*
  Digging a grave can be undertaken using a variety of different implements, ranging in size from a machine with a bucket or front loader, down to a small collapsible military-style trenching spade. Depending on soils and substrates these can leave characteristic tool marks or patterns in the grave-sides. Detecting and excavating machine teeth marks represents a standard feature of mass grave work (see Chapter 5, Section 5.5.3; Figure 4.5) but marks of smaller implements are usually harder to detect even in compacted deposits such as chalk or clay. Nevertheless, it is often possible to distinguish between the use of a spade, a shovel, and a garden fork and this itself may be an important piece of evidence. Most implements exhibit characteristic wear marks and are potentially identifiable (e.g. Humphrey and Hutchinson 2001), although little research has been carried out on the wear patterning of garden tools (but see Hochrein 1997, 2002).

- *Was the grave dug in a hurry or was it carefully prepared?*
  This ostensibly simple question is heavily loaded as it implies that (at one extreme) a shallow irregular grave was dug in haste, whereas (at the other extreme), a deep grave with clean sides was carefully prepared in advance. Taken further, the implication is that the former reflects an unpremeditated act (manslaughter), whereas the latter assumes a premeditated act (murder). Archaeological opinion can only be restricted to commenting on the speed with which the grave in question might be dug, not to the implications of that speed. Those are for the barristers. It is, however, important in advance discussion with barristers, that the archaeologist makes clear the limitations of opinion. There are other reasons why graves may be shallow (tree roots, laziness, water table, etc.), and there are equally reasons why they might be deep (softness of substrates, avoidance of scavengers, etc.). In one instance where the offender was a professional hole-digger (case 23), the burial was probably carried out in haste, but to a depth of over 2 metres with almost sheer sides.

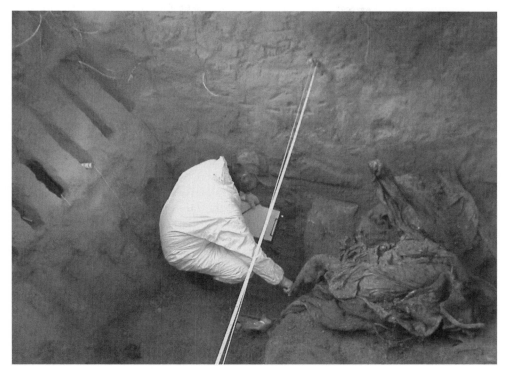

Figure 4.5 The excavated machine tooth marks from a mass grave

- *Is there evidence of the grave being left open before burial of the body?*
  Recognition of a grave which has been left open before burial is probably the only way to indicate a premeditated act, and is difficult to prove. The main pointers can include the presence of silted deposits in the grave base, accumulation of blown material such as leaves, twigs, etc. in the bottom, and weathered grave-sides (see also Hochrein 2002). Silted deposits, however, may be impossible to identify unless carefully excavated and will become completely unrecognisable once body fluids have been released and the soil biochemistry has been altered. Leaves and twigs can be argued to have fallen as part of the action of depositing the body, and weathered edges are extremely difficult to define objectively. Difficulties of this nature were encountered in a case where a victim had been seemingly buried in the ground but had been discovered trussed up on the ground surface adjacent to the grave (case 17).

- *Is there evidence of post-mortem interval?*
  This effectively assumes that the time of death and the time of burial are largely synchronous. A fresh disturbance, a spread of spoil in the vicinity, and surface trample can point towards a very recent deposition, but in most instances there is little or no visual surface evidence. Excavation, however, may be able to provide

a *terminus post quem* or a *terminus ante quem* for the burial from material located within the grave itself and from layers around and above the grave (see case 24), although this may necessitate excavation wider than the grave itself. Many modern items contain dating evidence, either from batch numbers, 'sell by' dates, wrapper styles, etc. Material is often thrown into the grave as a useful dumping site during burial and this has been known to include pages from magazines and newspapers. Many non-archaeologists (e.g. a jury) find these *termini* confusing and it is as well to rehearse a simplified explanation before any court appearance. Alternatively, there may be good stratigraphic evidence to indicate that the grave is cut through, or is sealed by, layers which can be related to specific events, for example, building activity or land use. The use of section plans, or even measured drawings are essential if this line is followed.

Tree or plant roots may also be of some value if they demonstrate having been severed during the digging of the grave, or if they are seen to penetrate the remains (Willey and Heilman 1987). This is a specialist area of expertise, as is interpretation of the vegetation on the grave surface, but is one which the archaeologist should be able to recognise, record and sample for specialist input as routine. On a broader front, it may be possible to determine season of burial through presence of plant macrofossils, pollens, spores or leaves compressed and sealed within the grave fill. In fact, they may indicate an ecological profile of the murder scene which may be different to that of the burial. Less helpful, however, is taphonomic evidence (but see also Hopkins *et al.* 2000). Rates of decay can vary very significantly reflecting a combination of extrinsic variables (e.g. depth, clothing, climate, wetness, soil environment, etc.) and intrinsic variables (e.g. age, sex, health status, diet, genetics presence of gut flora, etc.). All these can act singly or in combination and consequently this subject is far from being an exact science (e.g. Haglund and Sorg 1997, 2002).

- *Is it a burial, and, if so, is it criminal or archaeological?*
  In the case of accidentally discovered remains, these are questions which almost everyone at the scene will ask, but which only the archaeologist is likely to be able to answer, if indirectly. There is a substantial archaeological difference between remains which have been deliberately buried and those which have become buried through natural processes (see Chapter 1, Section 1.4.3; Figure 1.5) and which may not have a criminal origin (e.g. case 25). It will be the role of the archaeologist to establish whether a grave cut exists or not, and whether any 'disposal' was originally on the ground surface. This issue is mostly restricted to articulated remains and can be resolved by careful excavation of any overlying soils and materials. A botanist may often have an important role to play here in analysing both surface remains and those which may underlie the body. In cases of disarticulated or scattered remains (e.g. case 26) it may be harder to identify any original grave site (for possible analysis see Morse 1983: Table 6.1; Haglund *et al.* 1989).

  By maintaining the integrity of any grave edges and base, it may be possible to show that the burial occurred within a timeframe which is not modern and which, for the purposes of police enquiry, occurred more than approximately 70 years ago. Remains discovered before this (arbitary) date are considered not worthy of investigation on the assumption that any perpetrator is unlikely to be still living. However arguable this premise might be, there needs to be a line drawn somewhere. In the absence of such features as modern dental restorations or other protheses, stratigraphic evidence is likely to be the best absolute method of differentiating between forensic and archaeological contexts (e.g. case 27), but in the absence of any useful buried context, other evidence needs to be forthcoming. Archaeologists familiar with period cultures will also be familiar with specific burial configurations (e.g. crouched burials) although these too can be forensic, the nature of associated grave furnishings such as weapons or personal adornment, or burial features which may leave characteristic traces even when ploughed out, such as mounds or cairns (see case 29). On rare occasions when none of these evidence types are forthcoming, for example, in the case of some bog burials (e.g. Brothwell and Gill-Robertson 2002), other criteria need to be employed. The most obvious of these is to employ absolute dating methods although this presents a major challenge within the required modern timeframe. However, radiocarbon dating has the advantage of being able to distinguish between deaths occurring before around 1955 and those occurring after 1955 owing to the amount of weapon radiation present in the atmosphere (Ubelaker 2001). This is a part solution to the problem only and is useful, for example, in eliminating 'ancient' human material unearthed during building operations. A similar need arises where the archaeological context has been lost as in numerous cases where bones are recovered by workmen or other members of the public and handed into the authorities (e.g. case 27 discussion). However, on those occasions where it indicates human remains dating to post-1955, it initiates further enquiry and poses even more questions. Strontium 90 dating of bone offers limited potential because it is vulnerable to its environment context (Pollard 1996: 148) but work on radio isotopes, particularly lead isotope analysis of bone (^{210}Pb) with a half-life of around 22 years, and also polonium (^{210}Po, with a half-life of 138 days), based on human biokinetic ingestion now shows greater potential with the ability to date accurately within the last 50 years (Swift *et al.* 2001).

- *Is there evidence of either cause or manner of death?*
  Preserving the integrity of the grave effectively also preserves the integrity of the body and allows it to be examined by the pathologist (and anthropologist) in the configuration in which it was deposited. Careful excavation will ensure that individual elements or skeletal parts will not have been disturbed, thus allowing clear identification of any peri-mortem trauma, and exclusion of obvious post-depositional effects. This will be particularly relevant in examination of the hyoid (often broken during strangulation) or other fractures, including entry and exit wounds. Maintaining this integrity will enable the pathologist to view the individual as a whole and consider the wider implications of how the victim died using the totality of evidence within the defined boundaries of the grave itself. There are, however, two possible exceptions to this: first, projectiles (bullets) fired at point-blank range into the grave may have permeated the body and become embedded in the grave bottom, and, second, toxins from the body may have seeped into undisturbed deposits below the grave. The former may be identified by scanning the emptied grave using a metal detector (and is one good reason why the

archaeologist should remain available until the autopsy is complete). A ballistics expert will be able to provide a better opinion on the depth to which projectiles from different firearms can penetrate certain substrates. The latter can be tested by sampling which is now carried out routinely in most homicide work. It is, nevertheless, useful to co-ordinate the toxicology sampling with the excavation stratigraphy (or spits) as this can provide a better contextual understanding of the burial as a whole (e.g. case 15).

- *Who is the victim?*
  Retaining the integrity of the grave and the position of the victim also serves to ensure that the remains belong to the same individual and that the integrity of the remains for measurement, general identification and DNA sampling purposes can also be guaranteed. If the integrity of the grave is broken, there is a valid cross-examination argument not only that identification may be flawed, but also that items pertaining to identification do not necessarily belong to the victim in question. Although it is not possible to disprove their stratigraphic association, it is not possible to prove it either. Items in question can include surviving elements of clothing such as buttons, zips, belt buckles, etc., or personal items such as ear rings, watches, finger rings, contents of pockets or metal piercings, which may have fallen from soft tissue and become deposited in the bed of the grave. Recent research (Jackson 2001) has shown that even such personal items as soft-contact lenses can also survive within a burial environment in association with decomposing tissues and still be read for their diopter strength. Clearly, these are only of value if their context is indisputable but they can prove important in ruling various missing persons in or out of the equation. Although not conclusive in their own right, all such information can enable an enquiry to move forward, particularly if the burial has been discovered accidentally without a named missing person or date of disappearance. Conversely, ignoring the integrity of the burial and inadvertently introducing material from layers which are stratigraphically earlier or later can have the effect of sending the enquiry off in completely the wrong direction.

- *Was there a transfer of material from offender to grave or victim?*
  Digging a grave requires manual labour and can be hard work for even the fittest of individuals, given that an estimated 'average' grave measuring $2 \times 0.5 \times 0.5$m will require removal and replacement/disposal of a minimum of some 0.5 tonnes of earth. During this process the individual will undergo intensive exertion using arms, back and legs during which fibres from clothes, and head hair, may be transferred or dropped to the grave infill, footprints may be left on the graveside or in the grave itself before the body is interred. This is in addition to any accidental transfer of objects from pockets, or through deliberate discarding of material (e.g. plastic gloves) into the grave fill for purposes of concealment. These will almost certainly be recovered during excavation or subsequent sieving (below), but fibres and hair will be more difficult to observe. The former may be recovered through taping of layers or arbitary surfaces during the excavation process (Wells 2002). Hair is more difficult to identify and recover, even with sieving, although a single head hair has been recovered from grave fill by one of the authors. Similarly, inexpensive garden spades (or similar) may leave flakes of paint adhered to the

sides of a grave. These are potentially recoverable and can be useful evidence (see case 28).

Footprints tend to be a neglected area of interest but can often underlie human remains in graves of any depth if the substrate is malleable enough to imprint and stable enough to retain that print (e.g. clay). In order to facilitate shovelling soil out of a grave during digging, it invariably becomes necessary to place one foot, or even both feet, in the base of the grave. Footprints, in theory, underlie burials, although the possibility of their survival depends upon the nature of the substrate and other variables. These include difficulties in lifting human remains, wetness brought about by decompositional products, and bioturbation in shallow graves which all make them difficult to identify or preserve (Figure 4.6). Their potential presence, however, adds further emphasis to the need for retaining the integrity of the grave and its boundaries during excavation.

- *Is there foreign material in the grave fill and from where did it originate?*
  Excavation of the grave will be conducted according to well-established principles and by adhering to a defined recording process. All deposits from within the grave will be retained *in toto* according to layer/spit definition and preserved for future sieving and any pertinent analysis. Reference to test pitting (above) will be able to identify any foreign or unusual soils which can then be earmarked for further investigation, and any obvious or visually distinctive material can be separated out for analysis. They may, for example, represent soils or sediments transported with a body from a former location. Experience has shown that on occasions, foreign material (e.g. bricks, hardcore, timbers, etc.) can be introduced into the grave fill either to provide additional volume to fill up the grave (see case 24), or to provide a false horizon with the fill of the grave (see case 19; Figure 4.7). The corollary of this, however, is in being able to track soils or sediments from a vehicle or clothing back to the grave and demonstrate association. In short, not only will a control sample from test pitting identify material which is alien to the grave, but it will also provide a control for material found elsewhere which may have originated from the grave.

4.5 Collating and reporting evidence

Like any other excavation, the archaeologist's work moves into post-excavation mode once the excavation aspect of the work is over but, unlike most excavations, the written report or statement will need to be produced as soon as possible after the event. By virtue of working in the grave the archaeologist is likely to be a significant expert witness, and the SIO will want to ensure that all the evidence from the various scene individuals is collated and tied together rapidly. Crime scene personnel are accustomed to completing necessary paperwork before moving to the next scene, and the archaeologist will need to ensure that he or she can also respond appropriately by making the necessary records throughout the excavation process. Some scene specialists prefer to use dictaphones, other prefer making written notes, but both types of record, together with other material, will be disclosable (see Chapter 7, Section 7.4). There is a delicate balance here, on the one hand in avoiding production of a text from memory and retrospect on the basis of a few notes and records taken at the time, and on the other, creating too much text during the recovery process.

Figure 4.6 The recovery of a footprint underneath a buried body

Source: courtesy of Durham Constabulary.

Figure 4.7 A deliberately placed layer or false horizon in the fill of a grave (case 19)

Most UK police forces use a bound and page-numbered standard crime scene recording log and some forensic archaeologists have adopted this strategy. Alternatively, the archaeologist's notes can be included in the actual Crime Scene Log avoiding unnecessary duplication or contradiction. Reasons for using pro formas are varied but one notable aspect is that it allows the record to be used as an *aide-mémoire* to ensure that all important aspects of recording are considered, even if subsequently rejected for good reasons. Working at a crime scene can be stressful and it is all too easy to forget the obvious when under pressure. Further, having a bound and page-numbered system ensures that the complete record will be submitted and cannot be 'doctored' either by addition or omission at the point of disclosure. Essentially this strategy is 'back-covering' as well as efficient. To keep too scant a record can be criticised as being an inadequate record and therefore unprofessional, while over-recording exposes itself to cross-examination if it contains excessive interpretation and hypothesis. The correct balance provides objective observation and record which can be transferred quickly into simple narrative, irrespective of the recording medium used.

The minimum level of essential site documentation is likely to include completed context recording sheets, appropriate plans and sections which incorporate an overview of the site in relation to fixed points together with any outlying sample locations, any notes and narrative, and photographs. All this information is disclosable and, as on any other archaeological site, all the documentation should have internal consistency of cross-reference. Bound sets of context cards, other records, drawings and plans, or any photographs are all likely to require exhibit numbers and will require adherence to continuity procedures (e.g. Melbye and Jimenez 1997; see also Chapter 7, Section 7.5). They constitute primary evidence and are afforded the same processual status as exhibits recovered from within the grave, or even a murder weapon. They will be numbered and tagged as such, and any transfer from one person to another will need to be logged, recorded and signed for. Copies of records can be retained by the archaeologist, and it is in the interest of the archaeologist to do so, and to produce the records in a form which is amenable to photocopying in the first place.

In reality, most clandestine burials will contain very few individual contexts, real or arbitary, and the number of context sheets is likely to be fairly small. The context record is also likely to be relatively simple and reflect straightforward superimposition of layers, rather than the complex stratigraphy encountered, for example, on many medieval sites. It is, however, important that the records are completed adequately, even if the information required by standard archaeological forms may seem superfluous. Key aspects for recording are the relationships of layers (e.g. 'sealed', 'cut by', etc.), soil descriptions (usually according to soil science handbooks and Munsell charts), listing of seized exhibits per context, and the archaeologist's interpretation of each layer or spit recovered in terms of its overall significance in the excavation. It is preferable to write 'N/A' (not applicable) against many of the usual prompts asked by standard context forms rather than leave them blank, which is an open invitation in cross-examination. No *pro forma*, even one dedicated to forensic work, is necessarily exactly suited to every particular job, and there needs to be a section on each which allows the archaeologist freedom to make specific observations or notes.

The rules of disclosure, however, have a tendency to limit expression of ideas or hypothesis. The UK legal system prefers evidence to be submitted in terms of black and white rather than shades of grey, and this runs counter to archaeological phraseology which relies heavily on relative terms such as 'likely', 'probably', 'often', or 'normally'. The archaeologist is advised to take care when making observations which may indicate subjective or reflective standpoints. Like any other expert witness, the role of the forensic archaeologist is that of an independent scientist who can recognise and record 'facts' but who may differ in the interpretation of the implications of those 'facts' with other scientists. There are numerous purist and theoretical archaeological standpoints on this, but anyone wishing to pursue them in a forensic context will also have to convince a lay jury of their importance, value and applicability. In such circumstances, it is probably best to keep things simple.

The file of archaeological evidence will almost certainly be represented by a written (and signed) statement which documents, in simple narrative, the process that has been undertaken from the beginning to the end of the recovery process (see Chapter 7, Section 7.3). This will outline how the grave was dug, used, and filled in according to the archaeological evidence and will provide the jury with an objective account of events. This is the statement that will be seen in court, although all the exhibits, including records, context sheets and plans can also be produced, if necessary, by either party. The statement needs to be straightforward and simple, and cover the main elements of what happened, the timing, the processes undertaken, the reasons why the processes were undertaken, and the outcomes. It will provide the platform on which both prosecution and defence base their questioning. It is up to the two sets of barristers to try and ascertain what may, or may not, be interpreted from the evidence within that statement. The archaeologist provides the 'facts' and is there to answer questions as to how those 'facts' might be interpreted. It is not the role of the forensic archaeologist to take sides and to provide proactive theories.

Unlike 'traditional' archaeology, however, the archaeological reporting needs to be set within, and tied to, the wider scene of crime investigation. Scene of crime personnel and other specialists will also be producing their own reports which, for legal consistency, need to be dovetailed. Key elements here are, for example, the time at which work started, paused or stopped, the names of the individuals concerned (for example, the name of the pathologist and his or her time of arrival), the time at which individual items were seized, and the presence of use of machinery, tents or other activity. These points need to be recorded throughout and routinely cross-referenced. Any specific activity (for example, the lifting of the body) will be recorded separately by several individuals at the scene who will each record the time and the other personnel involved. Like the input of any other person at the scene, the archaeological work and those carrying it out will be tightly documented within the wider scene of crime framework. Furthermore, this may also continue well after the event, for example, if sieving of the burial soils is undertaken and further exhibits seized.

Production of the signed statement and submission of the appropriate file of exhibits (records) effectively signals the end of the archaeologist's involvement. Only when the case comes to court, months or even years later, may he or she be involved again (see Chapter 7, Section 7.5). At that point, familiarity with the incident and the ability to answer questions about it will depend wholly on the value of the statements and reports submitted. For an archaeologist, this is an excellent test of having recorded accurately, written lucidly, and reconstructed objectively. There is no second chance.

4.6 Case studies

As in Chapter 2, a number of case studies have been listed to illustrate some of the above processes and applications of techniques. Again, there is no such thing as a typical scenario, in this case of a recovery operation, but many recoveries have features in common, and the summaries are intended to depict some of the themes involved, and the breadth of the individual difficulties concerned. As in Chapter 2, the locations and the individuals concerned have been made anonymous. Some of the details have also been changed.

Case 14 The importance of the contextual environment of a recovery

This case exemplifies the importance of the area around the grave for understanding the sequence of events, and a terminus, at a site. On a very hot summer day archaeologists were called to a rural site where a farmer had disturbed human remains while ploughing a field. The journey to the site was slow because of holiday traffic and by the time the archaeologists arrived at the scene SOCOs had begun to 'excavate' the area of the grave. This was done because the pathologist was concerned (rightly) by the fact that the body was clearly decomposing in the excessive heat of the day, and that this could cause a loss of evidence. By the time the archaeologists arrived at the scene, the top of a body was visible, as was the fact that the uppermost levels of the grave cut had been destroyed, and the uppermost level of fill within and around the grave removed. Archaeological work commenced by lightly brushing back loose soil (an alluvial silt) which revealed track marks of a vehicle in the area all around the grave.

117

The ramifications and importance of these tracks were not apparent during the excavation but, as a matter of course, their presence in the vicinity of the grave was recorded. The victim proved difficult to identify and, in the absence of other evidence, establishing a date for the grave became crucial to the investigation. In theory, the date of the grave was recoverable archaeologically because some months earlier, a large mound of gravel had been removed from the field by a tracked vehicle (hence the tracks noticed around the grave). The timeframe of events was such that it was crucial to determine whether or not the grave had cut through, or was overlain by, the track marks. Because the upper levels of the grave fill, its immediate surroundings, and the grave cut had been destroyed without being noticed or recorded, this evidence was lost.

This case also illustrates that because a grave holds diverse potential evidence, there can be conflicting interests in deciding how a recovery operation should proceed. Absence of an archaeological presence clearly inhibited a full discussion and hence favoured the approaches of other forensic specialists. As it happened, the victim was eventually identified via the medium of facial reconstruction and the influence of BBC's *Crime Watch*, but had this not been the case, the loss of archaeological evidence could have been extremely detrimental to the outcome of the investigation.

Case 15 A shallow burial in woodland

A body, partly protruding from the ground surface, had been discovered in woodland by a member of the public. Two of the exposed elements, a foot and the lower end of one arm had been pulled to the surface and had been gnawed away by animals, presumably rats, leaving bones and soft tissue exposed as well as the edges of garments. There was no clear indication of the grave outline. The body had been discovered during the winter and the ground disturbance had been completely overlain by a cover of fallen leaves, indicating that the disposal probably occurred during the previous autumn at the latest. Archaeological excavation took place, initially by clearing half of the general area of the body in order to identify some of the grave or disturbed ground, followed by total clearance of a defined area in order to expose the full extent of the burial. This was achieved leaving a narrow undisturbed baulk across the grave. Subsequent excavation revealed the clothed body of the victim, face down, either side of the baulk. The grave was irregular and uneven with the body barely covered by infill, indicative perhaps of a hurried disposal.

The stratigraphy showed a very simple series of events. The grave had been dug through existing leaf mould into an undisturbed compacted silty soil with the upcast being deposited on the adjacent ground surface. The body had been deposited and the grave then infilled with a mixture of upcast and surface leaf mould. This disturbance was then concealed by dragging looser leaf mould and surface debris across the grave area. All these separate episodes were evident in the retained narrow baulk, including the final leaf fall on top. All were recorded using standard archaeological methodology including plans, sections and context numbers and, when the body was removed, the profile of the grave itself. Sampling for toxins was a standard part of the crime scene process and could be integrated with the archaeological recording – samples being taken from all layers in the baulk, from either side of the body in the fill, above and below the body in the fill, and from undisturbed deposits located below, and to the sides of, the grave itself. A useful feature of this case was that the final section of the burial could therefore identify the sample points and thus integrate the toxin samples spatially and with other archaeological data (notably soil description) in a single exercise.

Case 16 Multiple burials in a terraced house and elsewhere

This case is well known and one of the most horrific examples of serial killing and burial ever to be reported in the UK and occurred at a time when forensic archaeology was beginning to gain impetus (1994). A married couple in Gloucester, Fred and Rose West, had, it seems, systematically abducted young women (including one of their own daughters), abused, tortured and killed them and ultimately buried them in the cellars, gardens and the locality until their crimes came to light. Many of these girls were pregnant at the time of their deaths. The number of victims recovered slowly moved into double figures against a background of sustained media tension. The majority of the investigation took place at the family home, a terraced dwelling in the city. This was a location where recovery was significantly impeded due to instability of buildings and the fact that Fred West, a builder, had allowed domestic sewage to infiltrate the garden soils. Ground-penetrating radar was used to help find the victims, and remains were recovered from both the garden and from the cellar, from the cellar of a previous dwelling used by the Wests, and from a rural site some distance away. This case was probably the most high-profile and media-intensive recovery of buried remains of the twentieth century.

The individuals, as recovered from the house, were partly disarticulated and incomplete largely as a result of the nature of the substrates which provided an unstable physical environment through the infiltration of sewage. This resulted in several of the remains lying not in defined 'grave cuts' as such, but in an amorphous soil environment. The case emphasises the extreme conditions in which clandestine humans burials may be found, and illustrates an unusual process by which partial disarticulation can occur, not to mention problems of taphonomy. Fred West committed suicide in his cell before the trial, but Rose was later convicted of murder.

Case 17 A trussed victim discovered adjacent to a 'grave'

In early spring the trussed body of a teenage girl was discovered in woodland adjacent to a hole in the ground which had been interpreted as a grave. The shape of this 'grave' roughly reflected the cuboid nature of the victim who had been tightly bound, bagged and wrapped in a patterned sheet or duvet cover. No test was conducted to see if this packaged victim could have fitted into the 'grave' and there was little loose soil in the vicinity. A potential offender had been taken into custody and a series of problems began to unfold.

The teenager had disappeared almost a year before the discovery. However, the location of this 'grave' lay along a fairly well-trodden footpath adjacent to a lay-by at the edge of the trees. The person who found the remains asserted that he had found them at the side of the 'grave' as though he had disturbed someone in the actual process of burial. Curious as to what the package might represent, he prodded it with a stick which produced both maggots and an unpleasant smell. The main question pertained as to whether the body was ever buried, and if so for how long, or where (and how) it might otherwise have been kept. This entailed answering a host of subsidiary questions. Was the decay (taphonomic) state of the body commensurate with having been buried in the ground in that particular environment for approximately one year? Was the small amount of soil on the package by the 'grave' from this location or from elsewhere? Was the decay level of the fabric commensurate with having been buried? What were the dyes in the fabric and their durability in the burial process? And did the grave show evidence of root growth and soil erosion indicative of having been dug over a year ago – in fact, how would it be possible to demonstrate archaeologically how long a grave had been dug? However, the defendant confessed to the abduction and killing before these questions could be investigated fully. He was convicted of murder and, under the circumstances, neither the prosecution nor the defence lawyers saw any need to pursue the issues further.

The case illustrates well that a conviction can be obtained without the fullest picture of events necessarily being produced, and that both adversarial parties can opt *not* to use a particular piece of evidence or choose not to follow a line of enquiry if they so wish. From a purely archaeological point of view, this was disappointing as it would have entailed the synthesis of several different areas of research interest. Nevertheless, the case serves as a reminder that no matter how interesting the archaeological dimension may appear to the archaeologist, it will be viewed by the court within a much broader context.

Case 18 *The investigation of a robbed grave*

A rather unusual case demonstrates how important it is to be aware of the destructive nature of archaeological investigation. A victim had been buried in a boggy area, presumably with some difficulty, given the height of the contemporary water table. For reasons which need not be entered into here, the offender later returned, recovered the body and disposed of it elsewhere having first backfilled and concealed the original grave. This primary grave site was later identified by search officers of the investigating police force and it was subsequently excavated by police personnel (but not by archaeologists). Having found it to be empty they filled it in, but later returned with a machine to dig deeper in case anything had been missed. It was subsequently infilled again. Internal problems, it seems, had failed to ensure that adequate records had been maintained throughout this operation: there were no photographs and the observations were not as complete as they might have been. At this point (after the grave had been dug no fewer than four times and had now been obliterated), archaeologists were asked if they could help in any way. The enquiry team was quite open in admitting their mistakes and the archaeologists, by opening a test pit adjacent to the original grave, were able to corroborate statements regarding soil type, depth, harder/softer layers, etc., and add some credibility to the original investigation. Apart from demonstrating the importance of using archaeologists in the first place, the case also highlights the destructive nature of archaeology and difficulties of attempting to replicate situations.

Case 19   The search and recovery of a missing woman
in her own garden

In the summer of 1978 a married woman vanished from her home in the Midlands leaving behind a husband and two children. From all accounts the marriage had been less than faithful on both sides and the woman's departure had been explained away by the husband. The children were told that she had run off with somebody else. She was never formally reported missing. Astonishingly, it was not for some 16 years that one of the next door neighbours thought her absence to have been suspicious and informed the police. Enquiries later showed that the woman in question had indeed 'vanished' from all banking, health, social security and similar records. The neighbour also had some recollection of the husband digging the garden, ostensibly to create a fishpond, at roughly the time she went missing.

As a result of this, a warrant was arranged to search the house and garden, the garden presenting itself as a long, narrow strip of land consisting of lawns, bedding, an ornamental pond and vegetable area. The vegetable area lay away from the house and jutted against a small concrete terrace separating the garden from a tall wall and road at the rear of the garden. The garden was reasonably well secluded in this area and was the point remembered by the neighbour as being the location of the husband's fishpond digging activities.

There was sufficient area of lawn and soil to provide scope for a resistivity survey which was subsequently carried out at 0.5m readings and which showed a small number of low resistance anomalies (for detail, see chapter 3.8.3; Figure 3.4). One of these, measuring c.2.5 × 1m, appeared particularly promising, but was eliminated when a shallow trench placed across it showed undisturbed levels less than 0.4m below the present surface. Another negative anomaly was partially evident projecting from under the edge of the concrete terrace, some 0.5m being exposed. Curiously, when examined on the ground, this disturbance also contained lumps of yellow clay. This was the local bedrock, already tested by exploratory excavation in another part of the garden on arrival. It indicated that the disturbance had been sufficiently deep to enter the clay subsoil, measured at approximately 0.4m below the present surface. As a result, and in order to eliminate this end of the garden fully, the concrete terrace was broken back, exposing the full extent of the disturbance measuring c. 2 × 1m. After due cleaning, this was half-sectioned and was found to be cut deep into the yellow clay with almost clean-cut vertical sides. In the absence of obvious stratigraphy, the infill was removed in coarse 'spits' each c. 10cm deep and a layer of slates found approximately 0.6m below the surface. These appeared to have been carefully placed, several slates thick, across the full area of disturbance. On removal, more fill was taken and some 0.8m below the surface, clothed human lower limbs were discovered. Searching in this manner also had the benefit of indicating the edges of the grave, defining the limits of the available evidence, and illustrating how the grave had been infilled in section. The spoil was maintained for further analysis and sieving.

When excavation resumed, the grave (as it could now be defined), needed to be accessed more easily, and after due recording of the edges the complete end was excavated out into the clay to provide a working platform at the same level as the base of the grave (Figure 4.8; see also case 23). The base of the half-sectioned grave could then be cleaned more easily and carefully and planned. The remainder of the grave

Figure 4.8 Case 19. Improving access to the grave by creating a working platform

was subsequently removed with a small baulk being left, again in 'spits' or layers, with all exhibits being seized in relation to the numbering system of spits/layers employed. One of the layers appeared to have been deliberately added to indicate an artificial bottom to the disturbance (see Chapter 4, Section 4.4 and Figure 4.8). The baulk was later removed and the body totally uncovered *in situ*. The skeleton of the victim appeared to be substantially held together by man-made materials but some soft tissue was still present. The likely manner of death was evident from a rope tight around the victim's neck. Difficulty in removing the body was effected by (1) the state of the remains; and (2) by the glutinous layer of wet clay that had developed at the bottom the grave. It was eventually lifted by sliding a thin metal sheet under the remains and lifting in one piece, a method which effectively (and knowingly) may have caused the removal of any footprints in the grave bottom.

The victim was identified as the 'vanished' wife and the husband subsequently convicted for her manslaughter. Key archaeological elements in the case included the use of resistivity survey for shallow surface detection, the importance of following stratigraphic principles (the layer of slates seem to have been a deliberate attempt to thwart any investigation by suggesting that the disturbance had indeed been a fishpond and that the slates represented the absolute bottom), and the carefully constructed nature of the grave as identified from standard archaeological practice.

Case 20 *The recovery of a teenager from the cellar of a house*

Police were called to a terraced house in the north of England by a paramedic who had been called by the occupant to aid an adult male who had been badly injured in an assault. The victim was reported to have been mugged in the street before stumbling into his friend's house. Noting blood in the living room and the fact that the victim was already dead (in fact, *rigor mortis* had set in), the paramedic sensed that this story was unlikely to have been true. In fact the 'friend' was later convicted of his murder. The two men had indeed been good friends and the police began to look for a motive, and started the long process of interviewing family, friends and work colleagues. During the process of taking statements from other members of the family, it became clear that the surviving man had a 13-year-old step-daughter who could not be found. She had not attended school for three months and there were no other records or sightings. According to the stepfather with whom she lived, the girl had returned to Pakistan to be with her family, but further enquiries revealed no further evidence as to her whereabouts.

During a routine search of the terraced premises, police searched the cellar and noticed mud or soil stains on one of the cellar walls. The cellar measured about 4 × 3m, but the cellar floor, which in other houses in the street were flagged with large paving stones, had a thin skim of cement coarsely brushed across the top. When this was peeled away it became clear that one of the lines of paving stones had been lifted for a length of about 2m and replaced as broken uneven pieces. This had then been disguised by spreading cement across the whole floor.

The disturbed area, which measured about 2 × 0.75m, was treated as a possible burial and excavated accordingly. The disturbance was half-sectioned and one half taken down in 'spits'. It was relatively deep and contained a mixed backfill of wet clay and cinders (the levelling medium for the flags themselves), but no defined layers. The disturbance had been cut into hard undisturbed natural clay and the sides were relatively easy to follow. Excavation was undertaken by trowelling in spits of approximately 10cm each and numbered uniquely in order that any exhibits seized (mostly domestic rubbish including newspapers) could be referred to the appropriate spit. At a depth of about 0.4m the deposits began to become extremely wet, and the water table was encountered at about 0.5m. The main component of the fill was clay and this became glutinous, sticky and impossible to trowel. A pump was eventually introduced and kept on permanently, and although this removed the excess water, the clay infill itself still presented difficulties of removal. At that depth it became very difficult to lean over and remove the wet, sticky fill. Working from within the disturbance was not a viable option as it had the potential to damage any human remains that lay below through the weight of the excavator, and the positioning of an extension access (see case 19) was impossible due to the small size of the cellar and the proximity of foundations. At a depth of almost 0.7m a spherical, wrapped object was uncovered in the sludge located at the very end of the disturbance. This turned out to be a human head. The pathologist was called, and together the pathologist, archaeologist, SIO and crime scene manager reviewed the situation and discussed how best to proceed. The problems were twofold: (1) lack of working space; and (2) the wet, sludge nature of the grave infill.

Once the section had been photographed (it contained no information that merited a detailed plan), the other half of the grave was removed, again using spits until the grave fill was an estimated 10cm above the body. At that point the grave edges and profile were recorded as far as they were exposed and a short wooden platform was made from planks and wedged into the sides of the grave just above the body. This allowed one person at a time to take turns in kneeling on the platform in order to carefully remove the clay from above and around the body until the body was completely exposed. The situation emphasised the difficult circumstances which often occur in forensic archaeology and the need for adaptability. Preservation in the wet clay had favoured preservation of the body itself, the clothes, and even facial features. Once the sides of the body had been cleared, it was possible to pass wide lifting bands underneath and gently raise the body out of the grave to be taken away for post-mortem examination. This then allowed the fill below the body to be removed and the grave cleaned. The base of the grave lay approximately 1m below the floor of the cellar. The whole operation, from removing the broken flags on the cellar floor to the final lifting of the body, took approximately 14 hours.

It later transpired that the girl had been persistently abused by both her stepfather and his friend, and that on one occasion this had resulted in her death. The stepfather, who was a dominant individual, arranged for them to bury her in the cellar of his house. It seems that an argument between the two eventually took place, possibly over responsibility for the death, and this resulted in the murder of the friend in the front room of the house. The stepfather was convicted on two counts of murder.

Case 21 The recovery of a skeletonised individual in a rural environment

A drugs-related murder had involved the search of a number of places throughout the UK until a possible grave was found in a field. The individual in question had been missing for approximately four years. The corner of the field investigated had been used to stack horse manure for purposes of fertilising adjacent crops; it had not been cultivated and was heavily waterlogged during the winter months. Machine stripping had been employed with an archaeological watching brief, and a possible grave outline had been observed dug into the natural clay sub-surface. This was subsequently tested by half-sectioning and the removal of approximately 10cm of upper mixed deposits revealed skeletal remains belonging to the lower half of a human body together with evidence of clothing. Once identified as a human deposit at approximately 11 a.m., the pathologist was contacted, arriving from other cases at approximately 6 p.m. During this interval, appropriate facilities, including a tent, were made available and the necessary equipment and perimeter security set up. This posed a number of minor problems in that the investigation was being carried out by one police force working within the geographical area of another police force (enquiries are handled by the police force within whose area the individual was originally located, irrespective of where they are ultimately found).

By the time of the pathologist's arrival, it was dark and very windy with sporadic rain or sleet. The tent was essential and the pathologist, archaeologists, SIO, and crime scene manager discussed the best way forward. There were two archaeologists present and it was decided that the most effective working method would be to have one archaeologist working at each end of the grave, separated by a narrow (i.e. 10cm) baulk, under the overall supervision of the pathologist. There was no obvious layering of the

Figure 4.9   Case 21. Excavation of the grave showing deposits below body

grave fill and excavation was conducted in spits, each approximately 10cm in depth at each side of the baulk. Separate record (context) cards were made for each side and a running matrix maintained to show the basic relationships and the contexts from which any exhibits had been seized. The body had been dug into clay and the infill was heavily waterlogged. Even the creation of a drainage sump on the downhill side failed to stem the amount of water in the grave, and it was later realised that the original diggers of the grave had accidentally severed a field drain within the grave itself, resulting

125

in persistent waterlogging of the remains. This problem was solved by using the machine to trench the field on the uphill side of the grave, severing the field drain and creating a sump into which the water could be diverted. However, the combination of mixed clay infill and perpetual wetness in the grave should, in theory, have provided a reasonable preservation medium for the remains, but this had clearly not been the case. There was minimal soft tissue surviving and most of the clothing had perished completely. For example, the victim had been wearing jeans but only the leather belt, the leather panel on the pocket, the metal stud at the front and the zip had survived. The upper clothing had survived only partially. This severe degradation of remains in a wet alkaline environment was ascribed to the presence of surface horse manure loosely backfilled into the grave (evident from surviving straw) introducing unusually high levels of bacteria.

The skeletal remains were exposed, the baulk was photographed (it showed no features worthy of detailed planning) and was then removed in order to allow the body to be lifted in its individual elements. This was finally achieved at about 1 a.m., some 7 hours after the excavation commenced. The scene was secured, guarded by local police for the remainder of the night and the fill below the body removed the next day (Figure 4.9). The skull had shown evidence of gunshot wounds and once the grave edges and base had been cleaned by the archaeologists, it was scanned by a metal detector for possible bullets embedded in the natural clay. No evidence was found, but a substantial sample of natural clay lying immediately beneath the skull was sampled for further analysis.

The nature of the grave deposits (sticky wet clay) was such that although large objects might be identified (for example, in this case a wallet, and packet of chewing gum), smaller items may have been missed. Each context or spit was stored separately and later carefully sieved in order to ensure maximum recovery. The fill context below the body yielded three projectiles (bullets) and this gave rise to the question as to whether the victim had been shot in the grave, or had been killed earlier. In archaeological terms it was quite possible that projectiles located within the body might have fallen through the body cavities after decomposition, but this was also a matter for a ballistics expert. Would, for example, point blank execution within the grave have caused the bullets to have penetrated not just the body, and even the loose soil beneath, but also the thick natural clay below? In court, the eventual conclusion was that the shooting had taken place elsewhere, and that the body had been driven to the disposal site and buried during the night.

Case 22 The excavation of a dead animal

Most active forensic archaeologists will have experienced the annoyance (and sometimes relief) of excavating a dead dog, usually a family pet buried in its favourite walking place and carefully concealed in order to evade environment controls. Some of these have been identified as potential human grave sites during the course of search for missing individuals (e.g. Chapter 2, case 2), others have been noticed by members of the public as disturbed ground, or through unpleasant smells. By contrast, a few owners even leave an ostentatious mound of earth, sometimes with a marker. Some of these graves are large enough to accommodate children or small adults. If they need to be investigated, they have to be examined according to normal forensic protocols, but usually their canine nature is apparent before much activity has occurred. However, when any suspicious disturbance is found during the course of an investigation, it is inevitably treated with particular seriousness.

A valuable example occurred during the search for a missing teenager in moorland along a route followed by a likely suspect. A disturbance of appropriate size was discovered in a secluded area some 50m from a lay-by and behind a bank, the turf had been cut in squares and replaced to indicate a disturbance of approximately 1.5 × 0.4m. Loose soil had been used to fill in the gaps and obscure the edges, and large stones had been 'randomly' positioned on top. It had been quite well concealed, and its discovery had been greeted with great acclaim by the search team. The area was secured, support arranged and archaeologists brought in. The disturbance was duly photographed and half-sectioned with the fill being removed in spits (Figure 4.10). A new technique was also employed, namely the taping of individual spit horizons in order to recover fibres from the grave fill. This was both laborious and time-consuming but was deemed worthwhile under the particular circumstances of the case. Approximately 50cm down and on the base of the grave was a large solid decomposing mass tightly wrapped in a printed fabric thought to be similar to one missing from the teenager's house. At this point, with half the grave open, the pathologist was contacted by telephone and the archaeologists asked for permission to remove the other half of the grave fill during the one hour's drive that his journey would take. This was intended to ensure that on the pathologist's arrival the main archaeological work would have been completed, and the body would be fully exposed for examination with minimal delay.

Figure 4.10 Case 22 in which the victim transpired to be a dog

It was only when the other half of the grave was excavated was it realised that the grave was much larger than it needed to have been, and that the remainder of the wrapped body projected only a relatively short way into the other half of the grave. On eventual exposure it was clearly too small to be a teenager and it was also possible to feel the shape of a dog's head and canine teeth through the fabric. This was unfortunately discovered as the pathologist arrived, but he too recognised that the process had been correct and unavoidable. The use of alternative methods would not have been in keeping with the *gravitas* of the situation and this case makes the point well. There was also the question as to why the grave was so large, and if it had any bearing on the missing person, for example, as an earlier grave from which the body was later moved. In any event it proved to be a useful dress rehearsal: the 'real' grave was discovered a week later not far away (see case 28).

Case 23 The recovery of a teenager in a deep grave

A 16-year-old youth had been abducted and murdered by a man who had been formerly married to his sister. It was a revenge killing, exacerbated by the fact that even when convicted, he refused to disclose the location of the disposal. A number of potential sites were searched, working on the basis that the grave was likely to be very deep in view of the offender's known building work history and proven ability to dig deep holes rapidly. However, a partial confession suggested that a particular garden where the offender had worked should be searched. Investigation identified an appropriate

Figure 4.11 Case 23. An unusually deep grave which needed to be accessed by digging an adjacent platform

secluded area in which a group of bricks had been incongruously left, possibly as a grave marker. This transpired to be the case and the outline of the grave was found by careful clearance and trowelling. Excavation identified the body at a depth of about 2m and access for recovery was enabled by digging an area of approach to one side (Figure 4.11; see also case 19). The body could then be cleared in greater detail and examined by the pathologist *in situ* before being lifted. The incident emphasised the tendency for offenders to dispose of victims in areas known to them, the likelihood of totemic grave marking, and the need to create access areas in burials of any significant depth.

Case 24 The excavation of a 'burial' pit in a cellar

Although the majority of graves contain a simple mixed fill, the contents can sometimes be more revealing and open to interpretation. In one case, a pit (initially considered to be a grave) in a stone-flagged cellar was found to contain a layered fill but no human remains (for the case history, see Hunter *et al.* 1996: 53). However, careful examination of the fill in relation to the layers through which the pit had been cut showed some curious features. The pit had been cut through an upper anthropogenic levelling layer of soil, cinders and minor rubble, and then through heavy natural clay. On archaeological examination it was found that clay had been back-filled into the base of the pit, but not up to the level of clay that had been removed. Subsequently, the pit had been infilled to the top with soil, cinders and heavier rubble, quite unlike the material likely to have been in the original upcast. Furthermore, the upper fill also contained paper wrappers from sweet and soap products exhibiting batch numbers which could provide important dating evidence demonstrating the *terminus post quem* (time after which) for the infilling of the pit.

The archaeological interpretation given in court was that the clay had been separated out from the remainder of the upcast when the pit was originally dug, some was replaced at the bottom of the pit (in fact to conceal various significant items as well as a pool of body fluid), and the rest, together with the soil, cinders and small rubble, removed from the site. It seems likely that the pit was then used for the storage of dismembered body parts before their ultimate removal, with infill material brought in from elsewhere. The incident demonstrates the importance of considering not only the nature of the infilling of a suspicious feature, but also how it might be interpreted.

Case 25 The recovery of skeletal remains on an embankment

Human remains were found in a hilly area of derelict wasteland by a group of youths. The discovery was fortunate considering the location was difficult to access, lay on a steep embankment, and was covered with brambles. The body, which turned out to be completely skeletonised, lay approximately halfway down the slope and was hidden from view by undergrowth. On inspection, it was clear that the remains were partially covered by soil and partly exposed, the question being whether this was a burial brought to light by animal scavenging or, conversely, whether soil cover was the result of a natural formation process over a body lying, or deposited on, the ground surface. The former almost certainly indicates suspicious circumstances, the latter less so. There were also other options, for example, in situations of hypothermia, individuals can experience a sense of high temperature, have a tendency to remove clothing ('paradoxical undressing'), and are known to create rapid movement which can cause 'pedalling' with the feet and partial burial.

Fortunately, the SIO had the presence of mind to request archaeological support before physical investigation occurred, and it was rapidly clear that there was no grave cut and that the soil cover was the result of hillwash. The remains were subsequently viewed *in situ* by the pathologist, and recovered by an archaeologist and anthropologist. The individual was later identified by DNA. It transpired that he was a patient with a history of disorientation at a nearby hospital who had discharged himself and wandered away. The inquest found no suspicious circumstances surrounding his death. However, without simple archaeological input, the question over 'burial' may never have been resolved.

Case 26 *Scattered human remains found in woodland*

A young boy, playing truant from school, had been abducted and murdered. A few months later after exhaustive searching, part of a skull bearing his dental features together with fragments of other bones were discovered in woodland. Their discovery was made through a careful process of 'winthroping' from a point where some of his clothes had been found, but the issue here was to ascertain whether they belonged to a burial or whether they reflected a surface deposition. Archaeological examination of the area could find no disturbance of the ground, but other parts of the skeleton were discovered by careful searching of the immediate vicinity. These were mostly vertebrae

Figure 4.12 Case 26. Careful clearance of undergrowth in order to expose scattered skeletal fragments

which had become scattered and partly buried through natural formation processes, probably as a result of local water coursing from an adjacent stream. Animals had been at work, almost certainly badgers, and none of the larger skeletal elements could be found. Cadaver dogs were brought in, but little further material was forthcoming (Figure 4.12). The practical issues related to the difficulties of terrain and undergrowth in the search, the definition of boundaries for searching, and the problem of animal scavenging. The main archaeological role was in demonstrating that there was no burial as such, and in examining in detail an agreed area within which the scattered remains and disarticulation pattern might lie according to research (e.g. Morse 1983: Table 6.1; Haglund *et al.* 1989: 589). The search was concluded when no further skeletal elements could be found in a wider area, including the investigation of nearby badger setts. By this time the boy's identity had been confirmed and a man was later convicted of his murder.

The case contrasts with that of Stephen Jennings (see Hunter *et al.* 1996: 54ff) whose remains were discovered over 26 years after his disappearance. His was also a surface disposal, but in his case the skeleton was virtually complete. Both disposals were in predominantly rural environments, but in the case of Jennings the body may have been wrapped in the first instance and had remained relatively secure during the process of natural soil formation which eventually concealed it.

Case 27 Human remains found during building work

A major redevelopment programme was being undertaken in a large northern city and heavy plant was being used to create an underground car park. The main excavation had been completed using large machinery, and a smaller machine with a back-hoe was being used to regularise the edges. During this process the driver spotted what he considered to be part of a human skull. He stopped the machine and noticed other bones scattered in the soil. The police were called and the remains left *in situ*, thus preserving the integrity of the burial, until archaeologists could attend the scene. Clearance of the surrounding loose soil produced further skeletal elements including the remains of at least four individual skulls. However, investigation of the associated buried profile which had been undisturbed by machine work identified a brick and mortar base together with sections of brick walling within which other human remains were contained (Figure 4.13). Furthermore, the same area also contained thin black vertical staining recognisable as decayed coffin sides. The human remains appeared to be legitimate burials interred in a vault and part of a defined burial ground which had escaped the notice of both developers and planning officials. Straightforward archaeological investigation and recovery methods had enabled the problem to be resolved rapidly and cost-effectively. Any other investigative method which might have failed to define the contextual relationship between the human remains and the brick structure could only have produced the partial recovery of several disarticulated and uncontexted individuals – a result which would have caused a host of other problems, not to mention increased delay in the building programme.

Preserving the contextual integrity of the remains was a significant feature of the process and can be compared to a case on another building site in the same town where the integrity of the remains was not retained. There, building workers had discovered a human femur but had not notified the authorities immediately, instead

Figure 4.13 Case 27. Cleaning of an area of disturbed skeletal remains identifies a mortar and brick structure

using the femur as a cricket bat during tea breaks for several days. When the police, and subsequently the archaeologists, were eventually brought in, the building workers were remarkably vague regarding its location of recovery. The place pointed out contained no other remains and, as an undisturbed cellar floor, was almost certainly not the original site at all. A fear of undue delay in the building programme may have underlain a reluctance to point out the real location. The net effect, however, was that the femur had no genuine context and the problem was never resolved.

On another occasion archaeologists were called out to examine a potential scene where a human lower mandible (jaw) had been discovered in the outbuilding of a rural house. The location of discovery had been clearly pinpointed but, despite intensive investigation, no other remains were recorded. It had been spotted amid the general rubbish lying inside a shed by a prospective purchaser of the property. There had been no disturbance to the ground surface and all the other items in the rubbish – old clothing, pieces of timber, rusty garden tools and furniture – had clearly lain undisturbed for some time and were covered in grime and dust. By contrast, the mandible was clean and dust-free with a surface that had a polished effect and exhibited none of the grime of the other material in the shed. It was from a mature adult but showed no evidence of dentition, and the elderly house owner was at a loss to explain its presence. However, further investigation by the police, and subsequent discussion, provided a tenable explanation. It transpired that the person who had discovered the remains had already visited the house on an earlier occasion with a view to purchasing the property and had shown considerable enthusiasm. The mandible was discovered during a second visit, in advance of a sale by auction. There was a strong feeling that the remains may have been 'planted' during this second visit in a possible attempt to create unhealthy publicity and thus to reduce competition for the property. The location of the mandible, its cleanliness and dentition, were all in favour of this interpretation, although it was not provable. To all intents and purposes the mandible needed to be viewed as a 'stray' find rather than one in context. Ultimately, no action was taken by the police and hence no publicity was generated. The outcome of the auction is unknown.

Case 28 The discovery and excavation of a teenager in woodland

A young girl had gone missing from home and her stepfather was considered the most likely suspect. The SIO in this case was aware of the value of the early involvement of the Forensic Search Advisory Group (FSAG) and from a very early stage a forensic archaeologist and cadaver dog handlers were in close liaison with the POLSA team. The suspect's known movements were checked and the routes that he frequently used to drive in the locality were searched. During the earlier part of the search a partly concealed grave was detected near vehicle access but, after careful excavation, was later discovered to be that of a dog (see case 22).

Continued searching identified disturbed ground in woodland adjacent to a lay-by, next to the remains of a derelict stone building, on one of his known routes. An initial careful examination of the area was undertaken and a small shallow disturbance (approximately 0.9 × 0.6m) was observed by the archaeologist. This was clearly too small to be a grave, but potentially an attempt at constructing one. The remainder of the site (approximately 20 × 20m) was awash with water from springs flowing in the vicinity, and the surface was covered with old masonry blocks which had been removed from a nearby building, and covered by sticks and old branches. The branches themselves were suspicious in that they were located away from the trees growing in this area. The site was subsequently identified by the suspect as being the general location of the disposal.

The forensic archaeologist now had two foci of interest: the indeterminate area beneath the branches and stones, and the potential 'trial grave' which lay approximately 3m away. After discussion with the Crime Scene Manager, the latter was taped off for later attention and examination commenced on the area of branches and stones. Together with the branches, some 30 pieces of masonry were removed, having been surveyed and recorded individually. The ground surface was waterlogged and muddy and required the construction of drainage channels and the presence of a fire engine and crew for pumping. Eventually the grave cut was located by undertaking a half-section using a new sterile trowel. This area was then extended to reveal a shallow burial containing the lower body of the missing teenager. The grave was excavated in arbitrary 10cm spits, with the fill being retained and sealed for further examination and sieving. This sieving led to the discovery of a small number of stones bearing visible traces of green paint.

Following the removal of the body the archaeologist then examined the potential 'trial grave' but using a different set of implements. This was found to be only 20cm in depth, as digging had been restricted by a tree root. The root had clearly been damaged in the digging process and was recovered for examination in the laboratory for potential trace evidence. Laboratory examination revealed that this root had traces of green paint which was identical to the green paint observed on the stones recovered from within the fill of the main grave, thus providing a forensic link between the two occurrences. Finally, both the recovered paint samples were able to be matched to the type of paint used by the manufacturer of a specific type of shovel, one of which had been purchased by the suspect shortly after the teenager's initial disappearance.

This case emphasises the value of careful recovery during an excavation, the importance of continuity of evidence, and the need to consider the potential of cross-contamination from one part of a scene to another irrespective of the prevailing conditions. The case also provides a classic example of Locard's Principle in the transfer of trace material by contact.

Case 29 The discovery of human remains in the vicinity of an ancient monument

An unusual case with legal implications occurred when a forensic archaeologist was asked to assist in establishing whether juvenile skeletal remains ejected from a rabbit burrow and found by a local dog walker were of forensic concern or could be confirmed to be of 'only' archaeological interest. The bones were found on top of Race Down earthen long barrow situated within a military camp at Pimperene (Dorset). This Neolithic monument dates to between 3000 and 3500 BC. The remains were considered as potentially forensic because the mound had been tree-covered until just before their discovery and the mound is situated a short distance from the site of the large annual Dorset Steam Fair that attracts thousands of visitors annually. The investigation was further complicated because the remains were found on military land that was under the jurisdiction of the military police, but the local police were also involved as a member of the public had reported the discovery. The barrow was a Scheduled Ancient Monument and thus without Scheduled Monument Consent, it was illegal to interfere with it. As a result of this situation, consent was quickly made available and an English Heritage inspector assigned to the scene to monitor the work. Limited excavation around the rabbit hole quickly revealed a grave containing *in situ* skeletal remains with the stratigraphy indicating that grave was not recent enough to be of forensic interest.

A year later, the remains were fully excavated to avoid further disturbance and damage by the rabbits. A highly corroded iron knife was the only object found with the extended inhumation. The assemblage suggested that an early Saxon burial of the late fifth to early sixth century AD had been inserted into the earlier mound. If the source of the remains had not been obvious, then a search that included geophysical survey may have been requested. In this situation an application for a Section 42 Licence would have been required before undertaking the geophysical survey on a Scheduled Ancient Monument.

The application normally requires details of the names of the individuals who will undertake the work, the techniques and methodology to be used and the objectives of the survey. Consent to such a licence usually contains conditions requiring the deposition of the survey results and copy of the report with the Inspector and the Archaeometry Branch of the Ancient Monuments Laboratory normally within three to six months of the completion of the survey (David 1995: 34). However, in a forensic case, *sub judice* may require such a report to remain confidential for a much longer period and hence such conditions would have to be waived. In the example quoted, a Section 42

Licence was indeed obtained so that the excavated grave could be put into the context of other archaeological features of the mound. Even though twin-electrode earth resistivity, GPR, EM and caesium magnetometry were used (see Chapter 3), no other burials were defined by the surveys although various other subsurface anomalies that were detected have subsequently added to our understanding of the monument. As the objective was to provide a general survey of the structure of the barrow mound, quarry ditches and surrounding area, a 1m traverse interval was employed (except for the magnetometry for which it was 0.5m), and so the failure to detect any further burials was not unexpected.

References

Brothwell, D. and Gill-Robertson H. 2002. 'Taphonomic and forensic aspects of bog bodies', in Haglund, W.D. and Sorg, M.H (eds) *Advances in Forensic Taphonomy*, Boca Raton, FL: CRC Press, pp. 119–132.

Cole, M. 2000. 'An investigation into the type and nature of post mortem change to *sus scrofa* exposed over winter in the UK', unpublished MSc dissertation, School of Conservation Sciences, Bournemouth University, UK.

Connor, M. and Scott, D.D. 2001. 'Paradigms and perpetrators', *Journal of Historical Archaeology* 35:1, 1–6.

Cox, M. and Bell, L. 1999. 'Recovery of human skeletal elements from a recent UK murder enquiry: preservational signatures', *Journal of Forensic Sciences* 44:5, 945–950.

Crist, T.A.J. 2001. 'Bad to the bone? Historical archaeologists in the practice of forensic science', *Journal of Historical Archaeology* 35:1, 39–56.

David, A. 1995. *Geophysical Survey in Archaeological Field Evaluation*. English Heritage Research and Professional Guidelines, No. 1, London: English Heritage.

Galloway, A. and Snodgrass, J.J. 1998. 'Biological and chemical hazards of forensic skeletal analysis', *Journal of Forensic Science*. 43: 940–948.

Greenberg, B. and Kunich, J.C. 2002. *Entomology and the Law: Flies as Forensic Indicators*, Cambridge: Cambridge University Press.

Haglund, W.D. 2001. 'Archaeology and forensic death investigation', *Journal of Historical Archaeology* 35:1, 26–34.

Haglund, W.D., Reay, D.T. and Swindler, D.R. 1989. 'Canid scavenging/disarticulation sequence of human remains in the Pacific Northwest', *J. Forensic Science*, 34:3, 587–606.

Haglund, W.D. and Sorg, M.H. (eds) 1997. *Forensic Taphonomy: The Post-mortem Fate of Human Remains*, Boca Raton, FL: CRC Press.

Haglund, W.D and Sorg, M.H. (eds) 2002. *Advances in Forensic Taphonomy: Method, Theory, and Archaeological Perspectives* Boca Raton, FL: CRC Press.

Hall, D.W. 1997. 'Forensic botany', in Haglund, W.D. and Sorg, M.H. (eds) *Forensic Taphonomy*, Boca Raton, FL: CRC Press, pp. 353–363.

Hochrein, M. J. 1997. 'The dirty dozen: the recognition and collection of toolmarks in the forensic geotaphonomic record', *Journal of Forensic Identification* 47:2, 171–198.

Hochrein, M. J. 2002. 'An autopsy of the grave: recognising, collecting and preserving forensic geotaphonomic evidence', in Haglund, W.D. and Sorg, M.H (eds) *Advances in Forensic Taphonomy*, Boca Raton, FL: CRC Press, pp. 45–70.

Hopkins, D.W., Wiltshire, P.E.J. and Turner, B.D. 2000. 'Microbial characteristics of soil from graves: an investigation at the interface of soil microbiology and forensic science', *Applied Soil Ecology* 14, 283–288.

Hoshower, L.M. 1998. 'Forensic archaeology and the need for flexible excavation strategies: a case study', *Journal of Forensic Sciences*. 43: 53–6.

Humphrey, J.H. and Hutchinson, D.L. 2001. 'Macroscopic characteristics of hacking trauma', *Journal of Forensic Science* 46:2, 228–233.

Hunter, J., Roberts, C. and Martin, A. 1996. *Studies in Crime: An Introduction to Forensic Archaeology*, London: Batsford.

Hutter, T. 2001. 'Palynology: a new tool for the forensic investigator', in Godwin, G.M. (ed.), *Criminal Psychology and Forensic Technology*, Boca Raton, FL: CRC Press, pp. 15–28.

Jackson, R. 2001. 'An investigation into the forensic potential of soft contact lenses as an identification tool for victims of crime', unpublished MSc dissertation, School of Conservation Sciences, Bournemouth University, UK.

Janaway, R. 2002. 'Degradation of clothing and other dress materials associated with buried bodies of both archaeological and forensic interest', in Haglund, W.D and Sorg, M.H. (eds) *Advances in Forensic Taphonomy: Method, Theory, and Archaeological Perspectives*, Boca Raton, FL: CRC Press, pp. 379–402.

Johnson, D.L. and Watson-Stegner, D. 1990. 'The soil evolution model as a framework for evaluating pedoturbation in archaeological site formation', in Lasca, N. and Donahue, J. (eds) *Archaeological Geology of North America* 4, 541–560.

Kneller, P. 1998. 'Health and safety in church and funerary archaeology', in Cox. M. (ed.) *Grave Concerns: Death and Burial in England 1700–1850*. York: CBA, pp. 181–189.

Melbye, J. and Jimenez, S.B. (1997) 'Chain of custody from the field to the courtroom', in Haglund, W.D. and Sorg, M.H. (eds) *Forensic Taphonomy: The Post-mortem Fate of Human Remains*, Boca Raton, FL: CRC Press, pp. 65–75.

Morse, D. 1983. 'The time of death', in Morse, D., Duncan, J. and Stoutamire, J. (eds) *Handbook of Forensic Archaeology and Anthropology*, Tallahassee FL: Rose Printing, pp. 124–144.

Pollard, A.M. 1996. 'Dating the time of death', in Hunter, J.R., Roberts, C.A. and Martin, A. (eds), *Studies in Crime*, London: Batsford, pp. 139–155.

Sigler-Eisenberg, B. 1985. 'Forensic research: Explaining the concept of applied archaeology', *American Antiquity* 50, 650–55.

Skinner, M.F., York, H.P. and Connor, M.A. 2002. 'Postburial disturbance of graves in Bosnia-Herzegovina', in Haglund, W.D. and Sorg, M.H (eds) *Advances in Forensic Taphonomy*, Boca Raton, FL: CRC Press, pp. 293–308.

Swift, B., Lauder, I., Black, S. and Norris, J. 2001. 'An estimation of the post-mortem interval in human skeletal remains: a radionuclide and trace element approach', *Forensic Science International* 117:1–2, 73–87.

Ubelaker, D.H. 2001 'Artificial radiocarbon as an indicator of recent origin of organic remains in forensic cases', *Journal of Forensic Sciences* 46:6, 1285–1287.

Wells, M.R. 2002. 'Surface retrieval of fibres at recent interment sites: a possible means of assisting forensic evidence gathering', unpublished MSc Dissertation, School of Conservation Sciences, University of Bournemouth.

Willey, P. and Heilman, A. 1987. 'Estimating time since death using plant roots and stems', *Journal of Forensic Sciences*, 32:5, 1264–1270.

Young, S.E.J. 1998. 'Archaeology and smallpox', in Cox, M. (ed.) *Grave Concerns: Death and Burial in England 1700–1850* York: CBA, pp. 190–196.

5

THE ARCHAEOLOGY OF MASS GRAVES

R. Wright, I. Hanson and J. Sterenberg

5.1 Introduction

This chapter is about the archaeology of mass graves. There are various types of mass grave (for example, plague pits and battlefield burials) but this chapter deals with mass graves that are excavated for forensic and evidential reasons or to identify victims and not just to satisfy a desire for knowledge about the past (for a definition of mass graves, see Skinner 1987). These mass graves are likely to be of recent age due to the nature of the legal process and statutes of limitation, and their recency generates problems that are more challenging than those offered by historical mass graves. Among these enhanced problems is the unpleasantness of excavating putrefying soft tissue, coping with grieving relatives, and securing the excavation team from attack by perpetrators or supporters of the killings.

There are now several published works on the archaeology of mass graves (see Connor and Scott 2001; also Chapter 1, Section 1.2), but this chapter is specifically designed as a guide for archaeologists already experienced in fieldwork who may find themselves for the first time asked to participate in, or lead, the excavation of a mass grave. It therefore deals with the special requirements of mass graves, and generally takes for granted that the archaeologist will know how to excavate, manage earth-moving machinery, and survey and record finds. The views expressed here are derived from several years of experience with mass graves in Ukraine (RW) and Bosnia (IH, JS and RW, Serbia (JS), Sierra Leone (JS), Iraq (JS and IH), Guatemala, and the Congo (IH). They are personal views and must not be taken as expressing the opinion of the investigating organisations for which the authors worked. In Ukraine and Bosnia these investigating organisations put archaeologists in charge of the examination of mass graves.[1] It was their job to find the graves, conduct the exposure or exhumation of the bodies and hand the bodies over, together with field notes and observations, to pathologists. This chapter is underpinned by the considerable experience accumulated in this process and presents the opportunity to consider how archaeologists can be involved most effectively in finding and excavating mass graves.

The chief justifications for employing archaeologists in mass graves are that they possess expertise in a range of skills, in:

- recognition of disturbed soil;
- removing soil and identifying safety issues of soil stability;

- evaluating the usefulness and pitfalls of heavy earth-moving machinery;
- finding and recovering objects in soil, often quite tiny and fragile objects that need conservation;
- recording the location of objects in 2-D and 3-D, and representing them in plans and computerised images;
- recognising when they need other experts, such as soil scientists and dating expertise;
- managing large teams of people, with disparate experience and disparate egos, and managing them under stress.[2]

Moreover, suitable archaeologists will:

- have extensive excavation and recording experience;
- be familiar with the interpretation of stratigraphic features;
- be able to distinguish between stratigraphic features and the results of natural soil development;
- have a high degree of anthropological knowledge, since bodies may have been burned, smashed or pulled apart by machinery, making it necessary, before lifting, to associate elements of the same body and separate elements of different bodies;
- know how to keep to schedule and get the job completed within the time available and to the standard required by the end user of the work, for example an investigating magistrate or a prosecutor;
- know about evidentiary requirements and protocols at crime scenes, although these aspects are normally directly handled by a Crime Scene Manager (CSM) to whom the archaeologist defers on evidentiary matters.

It should be clear that a person without archaeological field experience could not possibly satisfy these conditions by merely taking a crash course in excavation methodology. Although hardly 'rocket science', successful archaeological excavation of a mass grave will draw from the wells of varied field experience in the same way that a successful general physician calls not on shining research expertise, but instead on deep experience in distinguishing the normal from the abnormal, in being alert to a potential crisis, and knowing how to deal with people. Broad and detailed archaeological field experience is an important background to the specifics of investigating mass graves (see also Chapter 1, Section 1.5).

5.2 Organisation of a mass grave

Within the overall investigation of a mass grave, the archaeologist's role may appear under one of three broad headings:

1   In charge of the excavation and everything else – logistics, evidence and security.
2   In charge of the excavation 'within the tapes', and liaising with other managers in charge of such matters as logistics, evidence and security.[3]
3   Not in charge 'within the tapes', but given authority to observe.

Case (1) is unsatisfactory because archaeologists are normally unfamiliar in varying degrees with logistics, evidence and security. Trying to cope may rob the archaeologist of sufficient time to attend to the excavation. Case (2) is considered to be productive and is the structure that was set in place in Ukraine and Bosnia, whereas case (3) is an arrangement sometimes forced by considerations of money and politics, although an adaptable and helpful archaeologist may well be able take more control than originally envisaged.

Overall, there is no doubt that the examination of mass graves is well vested within the hands of an experienced field archaeologist who can consult with, but not be controlled by others at the scene such as the Crime Scene Manager. This is an optimum arrangement for the simple reason that the archaeologist, as an expert witness, must be able to carry out an archaeological investigation according to methods that are customary in professionally executed archaeology. The work at the excavation is like the professional analytical work done in the morgue, a soils laboratory, a radiocarbon dating facility or a DNA laboratory, but with the critical difference that the archaeologist works at the scene of crime itself and has responsibility for the recovery and integrity of the primary data. By contrast, anthropologists and pathologists are primarily geared towards the body rather than its buried context and are necessarily less familiar with the overall picture of events.

The principles applied to setting up a conventional excavation can be extended to the excavation of a mass grave. However, in recruitment, it will be necessary to think about psychological matters, not just about technical expertise, and the team should be selected on the basis of individual personalities as well as field competence. The size of the team will depend on the number of bodies to be removed and the time available. Very roughly, and under favourable soil and groundwater conditions, about two bodies can be removed by one person per day. This rate of removal assumes that the bodies are cleaned, photographed and surveyed before removal. In addition to excavators, the team will need the services of staff experienced in archaeological surveying and an understanding of crime scene photography. Each body needs to be photographed, with appropriate documentation, at the critical point between cleaning and lifting. Evidentiary considerations may affect the medium used for photography, and it is important to find out whether images from digital cameras are acceptable in the jurisdiction relevant to the work being carried out.

It is also difficult to imagine a team working efficiently and safely without using earth-moving machinery. The ideal general-purpose machine is one on tracks, weighing three to five tonnes, and with a 360 degree capability. Equipped with an earth-moving blade and range of buckets, including a toothless ditching or grading bucket, it can fulfil most tasks: it can clean horizontally without subsequently running over the cleaned area, and reach down into the grave to remove soil. Also, a larger bulldozer may be required to shift tonnes of unwanted overburden and can be used to define roughly disturbed and undisturbed areas of the overall site. It will normally be required only at the start of the excavation, and at the end for restoration of the site (the team must not depart the scene leaving an unstable hole full of putrid water). The 360° machine will take over for the final stripping and precise definition of the edge of a grave.

Once the excavation has started, there are two enemies for the excavators and the material excavated: rain and sun. A tent with roll-up sides will provide protection over a whole or part of the grave, for example, portable 'cabanas' which are increasingly used for providing shade for campers and cafés can be opportunistically placed over a more dispersed site. Cabanas are usually made of permeable plastic cloth and can be readily made rainproof by stretching a small poly-tarp over the top. The most suitable types are those with metal brackets for the poles, as plastic brackets can soften in high temperatures and cause the frame to collapse. Many mass graves penetrate to below the watertable and virtually all retain water that has fallen, or flowed into the grave following rainfall. Bucketing out water is strenuous and time-wasting and water pumps are therefore necessary, ideally using a '4-inch' submersible sludge pump driven by a diesel or petrol motor. Once the major pumping has been done a smaller '2-inch' submersible electric water pump can be employed, preferably one with an electric switch fitted to allow the pump to activate automatically should the water level rise above a certain level. There are many cheap submersible pumps that run off a motor vehicle's 12V power system, if mains power is not available. The electric pump may also need to be able to cope with fine sediment in suspension.

Laptop computers, and batteries to drive survey equipment, require recharging even if the site is located nowhere near mains power. A small portable generator (perhaps with 2,000 watts output) will therefore be required if mains power is not available for recharging of equipment at the living quarters. Alternatively the recently available 12V to 240 V inverters will prove useful. These can be plugged into a car's cigarette lighter to undertake many low consumption tasks.

Powering all the electrical paraphernalia necessary for modern life tends to get overlooked in advance, with the result that many critical items become white elephants when the work starts at the grave. For example, most specialised electronic equipment, unlike transistor radios, runs off proprietary batteries, not off standard AA cells. Although survey is best carried out with an EDM, a backup system using a dumpy level and staff is a necessary substitute when the EDM stops working for one of many possible reasons (excessive heat, circuitry failure, or lack of power for recharging its batteries). Archaeology is a very specialist area of field activity and it is important to ensure that those who order equipment (such as an institutional procurement officer) only do so according to precise specifications provided by the archaeologists themselves. The authors' experience has included altered specifications leading to refrigerated vans whose doors could not be opened when they were mounted on their trailers, a dumpy level that swung on a 400 unit base instead of the 360 degree base that the polar to rectangular coordinates converting software required; trowels that had blades the size of an A4 sheet of paper (chosen perhaps from an armchair notion that it would allow the archaeologists to shift more soil than the conventional 10cm blade). All these deviations were unfortunately discovered once the archaeologists were in the mission area.

Where soft tissue survives, if autopsy is not to be done at the grave itself, and bodies immediately reburied, then a refrigerated van is needed. Excavation exposes the bodies to oxygen, thereby causing accelerated putrefaction, and without refrigeration, safe storage until autopsy is impossible. Moreover, experience has shown that putrefying bodies, even when placed in a refrigerated van, will generate destructive heat if poorly stacked, insulating each other from the circulating cold air. There are even known instances of body bags melting in such circumstances. If autopsy on site means that a van is not required, then a small refrigerator will be useful for preventing the decay of items of evidence such as damp identification papers. However, the refrigerator will also need a source of power.

5.3 The excavation environment

It is assumed that the organiser of the excavation will be familiar with the general needs of an excavation environment, and with health and safety procedures relating to digging holes and using machinery. However, at a mass grave there are enhanced responsibilities towards the physical and psychological well-being of staff. For example, on more traditional excavations archaeologists are free to move between the site and the living quarters, but in the case of mass graves there must be a rule that protective clothing and boots stay at the site, and that people shower and change into ordinary clothes before returning to their accommodation. Washing facilities, with hot water, are therefore required at the excavation itself. The unpleasantness of the excavation environment should be completely isolated from living quarters: hosts and camp managers look unfavourably on putrid mud being brought back to residences on boots and clothes (see also Chapter 4, Section 4.2.1).

If there have been military actions in the area, and if hostile persons could have placed booby traps, it is essential to obtain an *explosive ordnance disposal* (EOD) expert to check the site. This person may be needed throughout the excavation to check suspicious objects found at depth. In the authors' experience other dangers and health hazards at mass graves are not as serious as might be imagined, although this can very much depend on individual circumstances. Excavators need to adopt the normal precautions taken by archaeologists and be protected against tetanus and hepatitis but the authors have not, however, experienced infections deriving from contact with bodies, even when an excavator's skin was accidentally pierced through a protective glove. It is, nevertheless, important to check beforehand that the employing organisation does not have health and safety protocols that impose impossible working conditions, for example, by demanding the wearing of impermeable protective clothing (as opposed to disposable, and partly permeable, plasticised paper suits), inflexible reinforced gauntlets and enveloping face masks. If these are stated requirements, it will normally not be possible to do any work in a mass grave, due to the severe heat stress that such outfits induce.

Paradoxically then, mass graves have empirically proved to be a relatively healthy working environment for teams in which the authors have been involved, and the dangers to health have proved to be nothing compared with those faced by archaeologists working in crypts with lead coffins (for further detail, see Kneller 1998 and Cox 2001). This is not to say that all possible circumstances relevant to health have been encountered, and workers need to be on their guard – particularly when the grave is associated with local garbage that may contain noxious chemicals and medical waste. As always, a health and safety risk assessment will need to be undertaken and appropriate mitigation applied to reduce the risk factors. All personnel should be drawn into the identification of risk, made aware of health and safety policy and, wherever possible, inducted into the tactics of management. In locations such as a garbage site, a site contamination audit is essential well before work starts. In fact it is more likely that the excavators will be dressing up in protective clothing to protect themselves from industrial chemicals rather than to protect themselves from the bodies.

Psychological risks of mass graves are more difficult to evaluate for the simple reason that psychological trauma is not normally as visible as physical trauma. In general, the authors have found it preferable to recruit people who have already had experience

141

with handling soft tissue, although research also shows that longer-term exposure need not protect from high levels of stress (e.g. Thompson 1993; McCarroll *et al.* 2001). At the very least the person recruited should have worked closely with skeletal remains, so that they have already overcome the sometimes disturbing intimations of mortality that close contact with any human remains can induce. It is also important to favour people with tolerant international experience – that is people who have worked and lived comfortably with people from a culture other than their own. At greatest psychological risk are workers who live socially isolated lives in the homes they return to when the excavation is over. While they are working in mass graves, workers will not require crisis counselling (in the strict sense), for the reason that they approach the work slowly and with anticipation. The work is not shocking in the manner that suddenly having to help at a catastrophic road accident is shocking. Nevertheless, nobody can expect to be psychologically unscathed if they are uncovering children and the remains of the tortured and cruelly murdered. In the authors' experience the best remediation at the site is an informally supportive team environment, in which people can talk things over after hours. Disruptively unsupportive people may need to be sent home.

Where possible, it is desirable to let people accommodate themselves in an *ad hoc* way in village or town accommodation, rather than establish a barrack-type setting. If people can accommodate themselves as they wish then they can form congenial groups among themselves and get away from people whose company they find uncongenial. People living entirely alone is normally discouraged. During excavation, monitoring can take place to ensure that selection of the individuals was appropriate, including tactfully enquiry as to the kind of home environment the excavators are returning to. It is important to retain a watchful contact with those who live on their own and have no friends.

5.4 Locating the grave

There may be problems finding the grave itself, unless it can be pointed out by a witness (see also Chapter 2, Section 2.1). Aerial images (whether from aircraft or satellites) may be needed, and if the grave is recent the normal archaeological subtleties of oblique shadows and differential vegetation growth may not be needed. The disturbed soil itself may be readily apparent in the image. In most cases, especially when machinery is used, the exposure of fresh soil is much larger than the area of the grave itself. Machinery used originally to dig the grave damages or destroys vegetation on the grave surroundings and spreads the spoil around a wide area, hence even if the general area of the grave can be located, the spread of soil may disguise its exact position. It may even be that the area of the grave has been deliberately covered by landscaping. For example, at Brcko in Bosnia, the authors found some 25,000 tonnes of demolished buildings and soil had been dumped on the mass graves.

It may not be possible to find the grave until the area is visited, but moving from aerial images to the ground also raises the question of permission. Will the authorities need to be persuaded to allow the area to be examined? Is it wise to visit the area and alert the authorities to the place of interest before excavation starts? The lengths that perpetrators will go to disguise their crimes should never be underestimated. Somewhere in Bosnia there is an as yet undiscovered tertiary grave. Forensic interest in a primary grave caused the bodies to be moved to a secondary grave (see also Skinner *et al.* 2002). Forensic interest in that secondary grave caused the bodies to be removed to a tertiary grave. Is it possible, as it was in Bosnia, to go to the site without local permission but backed by an authorisation such as a UN Security Council resolution and at the point of a gun? All this needs to be thought through before interest in an aerial image is transferred to the ground itself. Only after this is it possible to walk over the area (if necessary, after it has been checked by an EOD expert for unexploded ordnance) and try to identify the precise location of the grave within a disturbed wider area. Differential vegetation growth may be evident, for example, in Bosnia, in June, the authors noted that *Artemesia vulgaris* (wormwood) grew prolifically within the precise area of the grave. Often a grave retains water, leading to a local growth of aquatic plants such as sedge. It is unusual for the grave, its surroundings, and the undisturbed ground beyond to manifest the same combination of plants.

Why do plants show things up? The reasons are varied, and according to circumstance produce paradoxically opposite results (see also Chapter 2, Section 2.2). Sometimes the digging of the grave brings poor soil (e.g. subsoil rich in salts and low in humus) to the surface. This poor soil encourages opportunistic weed growth and discourages the return of the climax vegetation. Sometimes the digging of the grave penetrates a band of water that is under slight artesian pressure. The water rises through the porous filling of the grave, becomes charged with organic products of the putrefying bodies, and encourages lusher growth of herbs and grasses.

It may be necessary to call in experts in remote sensing (ground-penetrating radar, fluxgate gradiometry or resistivity measuring equipment). One of the authors (JS) has had some success with resistivity at a cemetery site close to Belgrade. It yielded important information about the depth of the graves themselves and, more importantly, indicated that there were no further disturbances beneath those grave cuts. This information proved to the various commissions interested in the site that there was no need to dig up the whole neighbourhood, and most importantly put an end to much gossip about the scale of events. For some of the larger sites fluxgate gradiometry may be useful for locating the overall shape in plan, and resistivity to give some idea of depth and location of body mass (see Chapter 3). These techniques will only work in the right conditions but should help to narrow down the search area during initial investigations and without disturbing the surface. The results may also help guide the excavation timetable and team size. If a backhoe is available, rapid definitive results may be obtained by using a toothless ditching bucket to clean a line or lines across the suspect area, although it may be necessary to check for shell-cases first to identify execution points. Cleaning by machine scraping of the surface, not trenching, is emphasised. Trenching is less effective and can be damaging. Up to 500 metres can be carried out by machine scraping in an hour. If cleaning by hand is necessary, then it is probably better to spend money on more staff so that an unambiguously positive or negative result can be guaranteed within a short time. The purpose of such cleaning is to find the surface edge of the grave in plan with minimal disturbance (Figure 5.1).

The machine bucket can be followed with a trowel for finer clarification, and the edges can be found by differences in colour or texture, or a combination of both. The differences are manifest because the digging of a grave brings up subsoil which is normally finer (richer in clay) and coloured differently (has more salts such as carbonates, manganese and iron) from the topsoil. Furthermore, the original topsoil is often

Figure 5.1(a) Finding two edges of the 1942 grave at Serniki (Ukraine) in plan and without disturbance to the contents of the grave. The fill is mottled. The pine tree growing in the fill of the grave was used for dendrochronology.

Figure 5.1(c) Excavation completed. The mass grave contained the bodies of some 550 Jews, mainly women and children. They had been made to lie face down on the base of the grave and were then shot in the back of the head. The killing was organised by a mobile Nazi *insatzgruppe*, assisted by a local Ukrainian.

Figure 5.1(b) Proving, in section, the existence of the grave that was first seen in plan (Figure 5.1a). The stratified natural soil is to the left, the mottled refilling of the grave to the right.

dark with humus, and a break in its continuity is highly visible. Even if it is not possible to spot the actual edge of the cut, any sign of mottling in the freshly cleaned plan is suspicious. Mottling is a strong indicator of soil mixed by refilling of a grave.

In general, mass graves are dug by people who know where they can readily dig a deep hole in relatively soft sediments. Such environments include river terraces and deposits of loess (a windblown accumulation of silty clay). Over thousands of years soil profiles developed on these deposits, leading to the development of a humic horizon on top (the 'A' horizon), the eluviation of salts and clays down the profile to concentrate at lower levels (the 'B' horizon) and the unaltered parent material below that (the 'C' horizon). Graves are relatively easy to find in such soils, but harder to find in immature man-made ground, such as dumps of sand or dredged soil where the archaeologist is without the advantage of the mixing of humic horizons and lower subsoil. Nevertheless an experienced archaeologist should be able to find some traces of a cut, since even 'made' ground is rarely homogeneous from top to bottom in colour and texture.

Where graves are found in a clay containing iron, the general area of the grave tends to be defined by a clay that is altered from brown to a greenish colour, sometimes even to a vivid blue. The change of colour is due to reduction of the iron from a ferric to a ferrous state. The same processes occur naturally in waterlogged clays, and lead to what are known as gley soils. In the case of mass graves the reduction of iron is probably due to anaerobic putrefying bacteria (such as the ubiquitous *Shewanella putrifaciens*) that scavenge the oxygen atoms from the ferric iron instead of 'breathing' (Kostka *et al.* 1996; Dhawan *et al.* 1998).

Although reduction of iron to a greenish colour may indicate the general area of the grave, it offers stratigraphic traps for the unwary, the problem being that the boundaries of the interface between green and brown do not correlate properly with the actual boundaries of the grave. Parts of graves that are empty of bodies do not show as green, and can only be discovered by scraping for differences in texture and colour. In parts of graves with bodies the reduction of iron may extend beyond the actual boundaries of the grave. It is particularly dangerous to rely on a green to brown change to identify the base of a grave, since reduction of iron will extend down below the base into the undisturbed natural soil, falsely suggesting that the grave is deeper than it really is. To find the base of a grave it is necessary to rely on textural differences or signs of tracks and tooth marks from machinery that dug the grave originally. With these provisos, searching for green clay is a powerful tool for locating graves. It may even occur patchily in graves that have been completely robbed of their bodies and then refilled.

5.5 The excavation

5.5.1 The excavation brief

Any examination of a mass grave will require excavation, but not all excavations will require exhumation. The archaeological examination is just one step in the process of determining the cause and manner of death, or other forensic issues including dating, or identity. The pathologists may require all, or merely some, of the bodies to be removed to a morgue, and may even be happy to examine the bodies within the grave itself. An example of this occurred in a mass grave at Serniki in Ukraine where, in 1942, the victims were stripped and made to lie down on their faces like sardines. They were then shot in the back of the head. The bodies rarely lay more than two deep. The pathologist worked in the grave itself after the bodies had been uncovered and only a few problematical bodies needed exhumation. This lack of disturbance accorded with the wishes of the villagers who wanted to erect a memorial at the grave. Compared with total exhumation, the archaeologists' need for time and equipment at Serniki were markedly reduced by the *modus operandi* of the pathologist. It is therefore important that the archaeologist gets a clear brief about what is required of excavation work within the grave. The brief the archaeologist gets will affect the way in which the work is done, the amount of time that is required and the equipment that must be obtained.

The mandate will almost invariably include a requirement on dating of the grave using means independent of the statements of eyewitnesses and the opinions of crime investigators. This can include identifying indicators of lapsed time between the digging of the grave, the placing of the bodies within the grave, and the filling of the grave with soil; there is also the importance of observed insect activity. A further dating possibility that frequently offers itself, but is easily overlooked, involves the shrubs or trees that grow on top of the filling of the grave. If they show annual growth rings they will provide a powerful indication of a date younger than the grave. In one case, at the grave of Serniki, it was suggested that the investigators had been the victim of a KGB plot – that the grave had been manufactured to deceive the archaeologist. Preposterous as this claim might seem, it could be formally refuted by showing that the pine trees growing on the grave were some 20 years old. At the very least, it was a very old KGB plot!

Nor is it unusual for bodies within a single grave to show radically different states of preservation at different points within the grave (for detail, see Haglund and Sorg 2002). Such differential preservation is not necessarily an indication of some bodies being chronologically older than others. It is commonly found that bodies dumped in a single event can become skeletonised at the edge of the distribution but preserved in the centre of the mass so well that even features with such delicate tissues as eyelids were present. Some chronological indicators can be unexpectedly powerful when found in the numbers that only mass graves can reveal, for example, in Bosnia the authors found, in one year, ten mechanical automatic watches. These selfwinding watches stop within 36 to 48 hours of their last movement, but have a day/date window. It was alleged that executions took place on a Friday 14th July, and eight out of ten watches had stopped on either Saturday 15th or Sunday 16th. One watch, found in a single grave, does not offer the statistical power that a collection of watches offered. It is worth noting that most of these watches were watertight and still working when excavated and that further movement restarted their actions. Had their dials not been photographed at the time of discovery, but left everything to subsequent examination, the critical day/date combinations would have been lost.

Regardless of the wishes of pathologists and investigators, it is possible that the archaeologist finds, on first investigating the grave, that only an attenuated project is possible within the time and resources available. In this case, it is important not to let things slide towards incompleteness but to discuss the problems and possible solutions with the pathologists and investigators. They may be content with systematic sampling of areas of the grave. Sampling can be a more rigorous approach than starting a full-scale excavation at one end of the grave, and then running out of time with the other half totally unexcavated. In order to ensure that an excavation brief is manageable, it is important for the archaeologist, at first contact with the grave, to model its size and content. It is not only the pathologists and investigators who need to be kept informed of what is feasible within the time available. This has implications for others, for example, the teams responsible for security may have to pull out if the excavation inconsiderately drifts over the time originally indicated.

5.5.2 Preparatory procedures at the grave

Having located the grave, the site must be evaluated as a whole. The site is more than just the grave itself, since there may be such features as execution areas around the grave. The archaeologist now needs to formulate a coherent strategy of work to ensure adequate evidence can be recovered and recorded within the time and resources that are available. Some steps to consider are:

- Identifying grave edges by finding the exact limits of the grave by cleaning around its perimeter, bearing in mind the need to observe the evidential properties of the surfaces adjacent to the grave.
- Digging a control trench well away from the grave in order to identify the natural soils and evaluate the depth of possibly troublesome groundwater. The section of this trench is useful for briefing workers, some of whom may have had an archaeological career restricted to culturally derived deposits and who may be unfamiliar with both the dramatic pseudo-stratigraphy evident in natural soil profiles and the false appearance of disturbance that naturally buried humic horizons present.
- Probing, once the perimeter of the grave has been defined, by using a steel probe to detect whether there are bodies, and roughly where they concentrate. Probing may be necessary in several areas, since not all mass graves contain an even coverage of bodies (e.g. at Gnivan, Figure 5.2). If the soil is stony, or contains wood, probing may prove ineffective. Systematic probing is blindly destructive, and only justified if information is urgently required for working out the logistics of the forthcoming work. Probed holes should be kept to a minimum, surveyed, and the pathologist warned about which bodies, subsequently excavated, might show penetration by the probe.
- Establishing a system of description of soils in terms of colour and texture before starting excavation by making use of the stratigraphic control trench dug outside the area of the grave and using consistent definitions (e.g. Munsell colours). One person's informal description of a 'brown silt' may be a 'red clay' to somebody else. Such discrepancies in description may encourage a lawyer to argue in cross-examination that the archaeologists were confused in what they were looking at. It is particularly important to have consistency of description if the grave transpires to be a secondary grave, containing soils brought in with bodies originally buried elsewhere.[4]

Part of the evaluation of the job ahead depends on knowing not only the 2-D surface extent of the grave, but also how deep the bodies lie within the grave and the thickness of the deposit. This knowledge may be required for predicting the size of the labour force needed and the expected time that the excavation will take. One method of

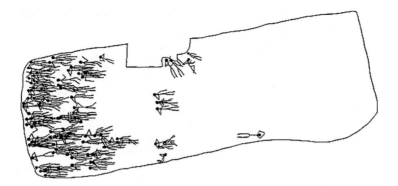

Figure 5.2 The distribution of all the bodies in the 1942 mass grave of Gnivan (Ukraine). Such uneven distributions are a potential source of mistaken extrapolation of numbers if the grave is merely probed or sampled.

determining the 3-D distribution of bodies is by digging a narrow exploratory trench perpendicular to the line of the grave and exposing the pile of bodies at the margins of the grave. The trench needs to be narrow to minimise the risk of destabilising the body mass. These exploratory trenches should be refilled once they have revealed relevant information.

Alternatively, a marginal trench may provide the answers, but the excavation of such a trench can pose a number of implications and requires careful thought. One extreme action is to dig a perimeter trench that destroys the walls of the original grave, while the other extreme is to excavate entirely within the confines of the original grave and avoid the use of trenches at all. Trenches of varying lengths and location take the middle ground of possible action. If it is decided to dig a trench, then it is important not to create one that is so deep that it destabilises the mass of bodies. It is safer to keep the depth of the trench just slightly deeper than the surface of the bodies being currently excavated. Furthermore, it is important to remember to survey the sides of the grave progressively as the depth increases before the grave profile becomes destroyed. In that way, a contour diagram showing the original 3-D outline of the grave can be created. The authors have sometimes disagreed in the field about the best course of action at a particular site. However, what they do agree about is that it is possible to characterise the problem as akin to a factor in factor analysis – the factor being *the need to dig a trench*. Various independent variables are weighted on this factor. The factor has polar opposites and these are listed below, together with the independent variables.

A trench is needed if there are:

- unstable deposits (e.g. sand);
- problems of surface water control (inability to channel all surface water away from grave in rainstorm);
- groundwater problems (penetration of aquifer);
- deep deposits;
- many workers (who need to get better access to bodies to prevent people idly standing around);

- opportunities only for a short excavation period (generating a need to get better access to bodies to meet deadlines);
- no requirements to preserve original grave cut, or if infeasible to do so.

A trench is not needed if there are:

- stable deposits (e.g. clay);
- no surface water control problems (guaranteed ability to channel surface water away from grave in rainstorm);
- dry deposits;
- shallow deposits;
- few workers (who can comfortably work within area of grave);
- adequate opportunities and time to complete excavation in manner desired (e.g. bodies can be removed in correct reverse order of deposition to assist in identification of possible depositional events such as discrete episodes of dumping);
- requirements to preserve the original grave, or if feasible to do so (preservation might show tooth marks of digging machines that identify equipment used).

Whether or not to adopt one of the extreme courses of action, or to find some compromise such as partial trenching, depends on the professional expertise and experience of the director. Some sort of sump may be required for drainage of the active surface of the excavation, irrespective as to whether a marginal trench is used or not. If there is no marginal trench, then the sump can be judiciously placed within the area of the grave itself, but where a marginal trench has been used, then it may be preferable to dig a deep sump outside the line of the marginal trench, but connected to it. This sump will accept both groundwater and surface water that flows into the grave. Water should be pumped out of the sump, since pumping water directly out of the grave or marginal trench can collapse the walls due to pressure of water in the soil behind. Getting drainage wrong invites disastrous flooding of the grave and potential collapse of the walls during pumping out of the flood. Using shoring to secure the original walls of a small grave is possible, but in most mass graves shoring is either impractical or grossly expensive and requires specialist engineering knowledge.

5.5.3 Methods of soil removal

As with conventional excavation, soil can be removed with implements that range in power from backhoes to paint brushes, but where to put the soil can be more of a problem than how to remove it if the precise location of the grave is not known (see also Chapter 2, Section 2.3.5). However, if the perimeter of the grave has already been defined, there should be no problem in finding a place where it can be safely dumped without fear of having to move it later.

The extent to which soil is sieved depends on the excavation protocols. There may be occasions when sieving has a specific purpose, for example recovering bullets from soil under bodies. Alternatively, it may be decided to sieve only samples of the grave fill according to strategy. Protocols which require all the fill to be sieved may leave little time left to do anything else. Material which can be recovered from sieving includes small body parts, objects that directly bear on the manner and cause of death (such as bullets and shell cases), and objects that bear on the identification of the perpetrators. Moreover, there is a strong argument in favour of collecting all artefacts, since it is not necessarily known what objects might bear on the case. Total collection is common practice at the forensic investigation of individual criminal graves (see Chapter 4, Section 4.4) since it is not known what may become evidence. Unfortunately, as with total sieving, such a policy may be unmanageable, for example, with a grave dug into a town waste dump containing an infill almost entirely of artefacts. Time and storage will preclude total collection, but observation of the surrounding waste will serve to identify objects which are out of character lying within the waste in the grave itself. At one site in the former Yugoslavia there was considerable 'noise' from dumped artefacts among the bodies. However, on close inspection of the filling not only were discarded surgical gloves noticed but also the packets from which the gloves came. Such things are not commonly found in town waste. They were taken as signs that the bodies might have been dumped after some autopsies had been carried out. Obviously these gloves and packets were retained.

In summary, some process of selection is normally necessary, based on knowledge of the case and on judgment of what might be important; and it may be possible to retain samples of each type of artefact. For example, at one Bosnian secondary grave, the bodies were mixed up with thousands of pieces of broken green bottles. Collecting all of them was out of the question. It was soon noticed, however, that many of these unlabelled broken bottles had their rusting crown seals still in place, leading the team to suspect (correctly, as it turned out) that the source of the bottles was originally a dump of bottles broken in a major accident at a bottling factory. It was concluded that the accident took place after filling, but before labelling. It would have been irresponsible not to have retained a sample of these glass fragments, but impossible to have retained all. From a pile of unused labels also found within the grave it was learned that there was indeed a bottling factory in the nearest town, and examination of the town dump (where the factory dumped its waste) led to the discovery of an execution site and an 'unrobbed' section of the original primary grave. Excavations at the primary site later showed that the victims had been forced down a slope made up of thousands of broken bottles and then shot. Attempts had been made to hide the evidence by taking some of the bodies away to the secondary grave where we first noticed the green glass.

It is also important to look carefully at what lies under the lowest bodies that lie on the base of the grave, for example, shell-cases that represent execution at the side of the grave before the bodies fell, or were pushed, into the grave. It is important also to look carefully under the lowest bodies where the grave is not dug as such, but consists of soil bulldozed over a heap of bodies that lie on an original surface. The dampness, coupled with the deficiency of oxygen, immediately under a body may have preserved the vegetation that was growing before the body fell into place. At one Bosnian execution site, where dirt had been bulldozed over bodies, it was possible to recover from the execution surface five species of whole flowering plants, whose state of flowering indicated a grave that dated from high summer.

The job of inspection is not finished when the filling of the grave has been removed along with the last body. Inspection of impressions in the base and sides of the grave may determine whether the grave was dug by hand (with pick and shovel) or dug by machinery. If the latter, marks may indicate whether the machine had wheels or tracks, and these may indicate the breadth of the bucket and how many teeth it had. These

Figure 5.3(a) The murdered children at Ustinovka (Ukraine) lie on a 'false' base to the mass grave. In 1942 adults were killed first, then the grave was partly refilled. The children were brought to the grave and thrown in on top of the refill. Then the grave was filled to the surface.

Figure 5.3(b) The 'false' base in section. A mottled partial refill of the grave lies between the children and the adults below (just being revealed by the brush). This section was a critical vindication of the statement of witnesses, who said that children were killed after the adults.

tell-tale signs will survive in the base of the grave because the action of machine digging compresses the natural subsoil, and the subsequent filling of the grave remains relatively uncompacted allowing the compacted marks to be revealed by expert trowelling. Finally, it is essential to ensure that the bottom of the grave has been reached. In both Ukraine and Bosnia the authors have found graves that were partly filled after some bodies were deposited on the real bottom with more bodies being subsequently added to the fill. Tooth marks from machinery usually guarantee that excavation has reached the true bottom of the grave, but features rarely show up in graves dug by hand. One cautionary example comes from the grave at Ustinovka in Ukraine. The grave dates from 1942. Figure 5.3 shows a mass of children lying on what was provisionally taken as the bottom of the grave. However, this surface looked suspiciously mottled, and unlike the soils at that level in the natural deposit to the side. Digging into the surface below the children revealed that the children were lying on a pseudo-base, caused by partial refilling of the grave after the execution and burial of adults and before the

151

killing of the children. Where ordinary observation proves inconclusive, geophysical techniques may help to show whether there is anything below what is believed to be the natural base of the grave.

5.5.4 Procedures applied to bodies

Removing bodies is easy in sand and difficult in clay, but whatever the nature of the deposit several points need to be taken into account. These are sufficiently general to allow flexibility in view of the likely distasteful and uncomfortable working conditions, but usually it will be necessary to do the following:

- work out the distribution of the limbs of the body which may be drastically contorted if bulldozed or thrown into the grave;
- free as much as possible of the body from the soil and from surrounding bodies – this can be difficult if the bodies are intertwined;
- clean the body for a photograph, to reveal clothing and suspected injury;
- survey points on the body to tie its location into the site grid system and possibly to provide 3-D information on the body that can be represented in rotatable diagrams of the bodies in the grave;
- fill out a recording sheet with information about the properties of the body and associated artefacts such as clothing, prostheses and jewellery;
- remove the body.

Within this process, particular attention needs to be paid to the position of the body. Bodies that lie in all directions are an indication of lack of respect for the dead: chaotic arrangement of limbs usually shows that bodies were thrown into a grave, whereas gross contortion of bodies, breakage, and intertwining of limbs are indications that bodies may have been bulldozed. In recording these positions photographs are a more unambiguous descriptive medium than the interpretation that goes into a drawing, although some sketching may well be added to the body sheet. Photographs, in addition to showing the general configuration of the body, can also be used to show easily disarranged evidence such as blindfolds (which may end up as inconspicuous and displaced dirty rags in the body bag delivered to the pathologist). In many cases the unambiguous representation of blindfolds and ligatures is important because it undercuts a defence that killings took place 'in the heat of battle'.

Some method of consolidating this type of evidence, such as 'cling film' around the head or hands, may be required but also needs to be noted on the body sheet to prevent a pathologist having to consider whether death was due to suffocation! Standardised recording sheets, such as those used to record the properties of each body and its associated artefacts, are valuable, but they need to be formatted in a way that will allow the recording of unexpected observations not to be constrained. There needs to be space on the sheets for additional comment, and each sheet should always contain a signed statement by the person who filled it in (Figure 5.4).

The surveyed points on the body, when used to generate a rotatable 3-D image of the bodies within the grave, may show discrete dumps of bodies which have gone unnoticed because of the method of piecemeal removal forced on the excavators as a result of the difficulties of putrefaction. It may be necessary to remove each body immediately on discovery, for example, to avoid scavenging of wild dogs, and this may

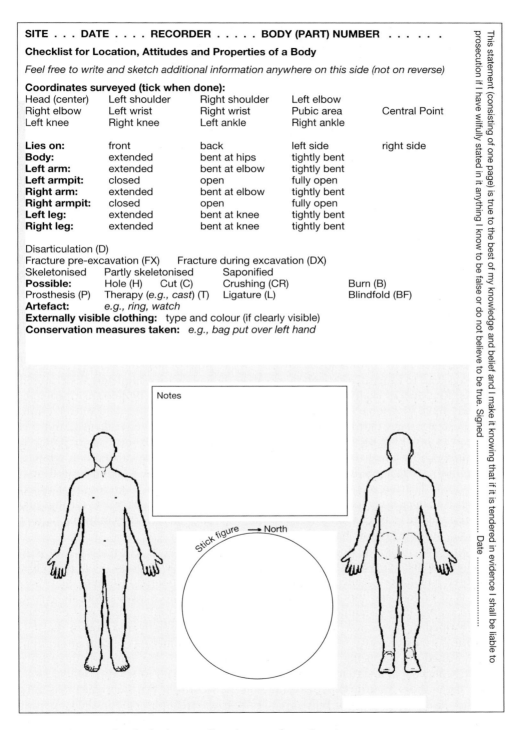

Figure 5.4 Example of a body recording sheet used at a Bosnian mass grave

prevent an immediate overview of the arrangement of bodies within the grave. Equally, where soft tissues are well preserved, it may be desirable to remove bodies immediately to avoid further putrefaction vitiating examination by pathologists. However, where bodies are relatively mummified, or skeletonised, it may be decided to leave them exposed to reveal the distribution of bodies in the grave. Such photos have great impact. It is difficult, if impossible, to predict the state the bodies may be in as decay conditions will vary even within the same grave, depending on the location of each individual in relation to the mass (see Haglund 2002).

Nevertheless, even if several bodies are left in place for a photograph, the record is essentially still a 2-D representation. A 3-D reconstruction with depth parameter requires the use of the survey of points on the bodies and allows them all to be viewed as a structure within the grave. It then becomes possible to rotate an image to see whether there are clusters of bodies, and also allows a vivid portrayal of the disposition of bullets in relation to the bodies, assuming the bullets are also recorded by XYZ coordinates. The authors have developed software (Rotate)[5] that assists in the creation of rotatable 3D images of bodies in mass graves based on the XYZ coordinates for 13 anatomical points – the cranium, shoulders, elbows, wrists, left and right ilium on the pelvis, knees and ankles, the bodies being represented as stick figures.

Several methods of interim storage of the body are possible, but not all are feasible. The ideal method would perhaps use thick foam mounted on a plywood base, the foam being specially cut out to receive the particular body in the posture that it adopted in the mass grave. In that way there would be minimum disturbance to the body before it was delivered to the pathologist. However, for reasons of cost and storage, standard body bags tend to be used, although these can be damaging for completely skeletonised remains. Removal of skeletonised bodies is simple, but fleshed bodies are a problem: they may have lost some of their live weight due to dehydration and putrefaction; the periosteal tissues that hold the body together may also have weakened, and this may lead to breaking off of parts if the body is stressed by lifting. Ease of lifting is a measure of how effectively cleaning around the body has been carried out, without leaving body parts stuck in the matrix, torn off or left behind. Having to pull on a body is an indication of poor preparation. A complete body is therefore best rolled gently into an open body bag for storage in a refrigerated van for delivery to the morgue. Where bodies are to be examined in an on-site mortuary facility, they may just require temporary storage in body bags after lifting.

As an aside, it is worth commenting on the appearance of vivianite (an iron phosphate) in mass graves. Sometimes excavators will suddenly notice what looks like a fine blue powder on cleaned up skin or clothing and be tempted to think the obser-vation is of evidentiary importance. They may, for example, suppose that the person brushed against blue distemper *perimortem*. Vivianite is entirely natural in occurrence and is formed by a reaction between phosphates from the body and iron in the soil. It has the curious property of being invisible when the surface of the skin or clothing is first cleaned off, but being altered to a vivid blue within a few minutes of exposure to light. Contrary to a statement that it takes 15 to 20 years to form (Holland *et al.* 1997), the authors have observed vivianite on the victims of the Srebrenica massacre after they had been buried for only three years. It was also observed in the garden of 23 Cromwell Street (Gloucester, UK), where many of the victims of Fred and Rosemary West were interred for varying periods (see Cox and Bell 1999).

5.5.5 Recording procedures

Survey and 3-D recording of bodies and objects will ideally be carried out with an EDM (keeping the dumpy level as a back-up). The EDM is a surreptitious recorder of information and, unlike working with other instrumentation on a site gridded with pegs and strings, keeps the surveying procedures out of the way of the excavators. The EDM, and its baseline, can be placed well away from the area of activity in and around the grave.[6]

Recording necessitates a suitable numbering system for both bodies and artefacts (see also Schmitt 2002). An optimum system involves a single log for all recovered objects (bodies, body parts and artefacts) with numbers allocated sequentially (e.g. 0001, 0002, 0003, etc.) and suffixed by *B* for body, *BP* for body part and *A* for artefact. The activity of recording can generate considerable noise within and around the grave and there can be chaos if excavators are individually calling for sequence numbers, for surveying to be done, for photography, and for assistance in removing the body over and above the noise from wind, pumps, backhoes and generators. To avoid confusion it is therefore useful to have one person appointed as the supervisor within the grave through whom excavators, photographer, Crime Scene Manager/Scene of Crime Officer, surveyor and EOD expert can channel their requests for service.

The primary log is written on paper sheets designed as a spreadsheet. This information should be continuously transferred to a computerised spreadsheet with identical information in its columns and rows where it can, if required, be sorted by rows so that bodies, body parts and artefacts are grouped together (see Figure 5.4). The employing organisation may require data to be entered into a prepared database. If this is the case, it is important to try and ensure that the data can be output as a spreadsheet, since this is the most accessible medium for comparison with the paper log.

Experienced field archaeologists will already be familiar with the routine recording procedures applied at mass graves. However evidential requirements must be added to customary recording procedures, particularly the requirements of chain of custody. Ideally, all such matters should left to the scene of crime officer to administer. In forensic work, protocols are necessarily much more formal than those used in research excavations (see Chapter 4, Section 4.5). They also need to be included in the induction process of new team members. These protocols should be carefully worded, be minimalist in concept, and not unrealistically burdensome. There is the temptation, in the comfort of an office, to draw up protocols that are so complex that they lead to a fall in standards due to the workload that the protocols themselves manufacture. Deviation from protocols might not matter in a research environment, but in an evidentiary environment deviation could be damaging to the prosecution case. Any such deviation might be used in cross-examination as evidence of a chaotic and careless approach to the work. Protocols are best drawn up by experienced staff familiar with the coal-face of archaeological excavations.

The director (and only the director) should keep a field notebook in which the day to day events can be recorded together with information not catered for in the prepared recording sheets. This narrative is a more flexible account of what is going on than any *proforma* and will be an invaluable aid to writing up the official report on the excavation. The reason for restricting the keeping of a notebook to the director is an evidentiary one and assumes all documents will have to be disclosed to the court.

The director will be giving evidence in court and the director can speak to her/his own notebook, but not to the notebooks of others.

Photographs taken of the state of work at the end of each day can assist in the writing of the report, and it is also important to photograph the state of the site at the start of each day's work, to prove that no tampering with the evidence has taken place during the team's absence overnight and at weekends. Finally, the director should think about the evidence that may be required to be given in court. It is important to witness frequently, and get close to, the day-to-day activities within the grave. In a trial in South Australia relating to the Serniki grave, the defence wrongly assumed that the Australian experts had merely been spectators of the Soviet experts uncovering the bodies in the mass grave. In the first few days of the work that was indeed the position: the archaeologists were not actually kept out of the grave, but the local experts were so busy trying to do everything that the evidence was 'contaminated' from the point of view of the archaeologists presenting it as their own. Fortunately only one end of the grave had been exposed. The compromise proposed was that the Australian team should reveal and excavate the other end of the grave. This was accepted by the Soviets and solved the potential evidentiary problem of the archaeologists being only eyewitnesses, not expert collectors of actual evidence.

5.5.6 Security

In certain environments there may be a clear need to consider the potential for hostile or over-curious parties stealing the log at the site or, as is more likely, at the team's living quarters. Disks need to be backed up at the end of every day's work and copies distributed to more than one person rather than simply retained as a single disk stored vulnerably in the carrying case of the laptop. It may be worthwhile periodically mailing somebody unconnected with the work an encrypted version of the log and field notes, written to a CD or flash disk. In some socially hostile environments evidence itself may also be at risk. Security advisers will need to protect not only the individuals in the team but also the bodies and artefacts. It may be necessary to take special precautions to maintain a contingency sample of critical evidence for fear of theft or destruction of the container holding the main body of site evidence. The authors, for example, used to open wallets and immediately photograph any information that appeared on the inside. An ID, such as a driving licence or bank card, is often displayed on top of other contents in a wallet, so critical information can be retrieved without probing any deeper into the damp contents. The wallet was then closed, without further probing, and put it in a sealed plastic bag in the refrigerated van to slow down decay. The wallet, with its documents, was properly examined later in the morgue, but by photographing the essential information there was a contingency sample of information that would have mitigated the physical loss of the wallet itself.

Evidentiary requirements may preclude media contact and this may cause conflict or tension between, on the one hand, legal considerations and, on the other, sponsoring institutions that may require some publicity for their input. It is important to work out a media plan with interested parties and ensure that everyone is briefed at the outset. Unfortunately, most mass graves will be near a public highway and it is normally not possible to prevent the press getting some photographs and film even if the excavators decline to speak to them. The team needs to be warned about journalists posing as tourists and there should be a policy of not discussing work in bars and restaurants. Additionally, there is the problem of allowing photographers from the media to hang around a visually unshielded excavation. Their intentions may not be to portray the work in a sympathetic light and shots of excavators chatting or even laughing during prolonged filming can deliberately distort the customary demeanour of excavation when cut and pasted into a brief broadcast. Even minimal precautions, for example, pegs, with 'keep-out' style plastic tape strung between them can have the valuable psychological effect of stopping all but the most brazen in their tracks. The grave can be screened from exterior view as an additional precaution, and the site may lend itself to post-supported sheeting of hessian or poly-tarps. Conversely, a tent may be erected over a single or small multiple grave.

It is also important to consider the question of the interaction between media publicity and personal security. Publicity can reduce security if work takes place in an environment where hostile locals are aware of an archaeological presence and the nature of the work being done. However, they may choose to ignore them entirely so long as their noses are not rubbed into what is happening. However, if the activities are splashed over international satellite TV, they may decide to employ violent means to shut the operation down. Publicity has to be considered as a security issue, as well as an evidentiary one.

5.6 Concluding advice

Excavating a mass grave is a bizarre experience. Because it is bizarre does not mean the required methodology should be out of the ordinary. The archaeologist should do what comes naturally in a professional sense. He/she must remember that it is as an archaeologist that her/his expert testimony will be given. A touchstone of expert testimony is that the archaeologist did at the mass grave what would normally be done on an excavation.

Acknowledgements

The authors would like to acknowledge the contribution of dozens of team members with whom they have discussed, on site and over the years, the best way of doing things. Peter Douglas and Sonia Wright made helpful comments on early drafts of this chapter.

Notes

1   The work in Ukraine was carried out by the Australian Government's Special Investigations Unit (SIU) following charges that three men then living in South Australia had assisted in the murder of hundreds of Jews in Ukraine in 1942. The work in Bosnia was conducted by the International Criminal Tribunal for the Former Yugoslavia (ICTY).
2   Some professions are hierarchically ordered, with attendant hierarchically ordered privileges and comforts. This culture does not transfer productively to the more egalitarian fieldwork scene. Making sense of the novel properties of each mass grave favours a seminar environment at the site rather than an unquestioning command structure, although a protocol for decision-making is still essential.
3   The authors are grateful to Steve Garner, one time Project Manager for ICTY's Bosnian fieldwork, for this felicitous phase.
4   Descriptive standards should be established with the knowledge of all the team. Aids such as a *Munsell Soil Color Chart* should be used, and the informal determination of texture that

squeezes a moist ball of soil in the hand. Sandy soil feels gritty and forms no balls; silty soil is smooth, sticky and forms a ball – but one that disintegrates easily; clay soil is sticky and is plastic enough to form ribbons between the fingers. These procedures are simple and commonplace but it is depressingly easy to get an excavation off to a bad start by not carrying out these procedures as controls on the team's vocabulary.

5 Wright 2003.

6 It is worth noting that the proper type of backup dumpy level (one with tachaeometric hairlines and a (360 degree base) can mimic an EDM by using polar instead of rectangular coordinates. The polar coordinates can be simply converted by computer to rectangular for the purpose of description.

References

Connor, M. and Scott, D.D. 2001. 'Paradigms and perpetrators', *Journal of Historical Archaeology* 35:1, 1–6.

Cox M.J. 2001. *Crypt Archaeology: An Approach*, IFA Technical Publication, available at http://www.archaeologists.net/pubs.html.

Cox M.J. and Bell L.S. 1999. 'The recovery of human skeletal elements from a recent murder inquiry: preservational signatures', *Journal of Forensic Sciences* 44:5, 945–950.

Dhawan B., Chaudhry R., Mishra B.M. and Agarwal, R. 1998. 'Isolation of *Shewanella putrefaciens* from a rheumatic heart disease patient with infective endocarditis', *Journal of Clinical Microbiology*, 36, 2394.

Haglund, W.D. 2002. 'Recent mass graves, an introduction', in Haglund, W.D. and Sorg, M.H. (eds), *Advances in Forensic Taphonomy*, Boca Raton, FL: CRC Press, pp. 243–261.

Haglund, W.D. and Sorg, M.H. (eds) 1997. *Forensic Taphonomy: The Postmortem Fate of Human Remains*, Boca Raton, FL: CRC Press.

Haglund, W.D. and Sorg, M.H. (eds) 2002. *Advances in Forensic Taphonomy. Method, Theory and Archaeological Perspectives*, Boca Raton, FL: CRC Press.

Holland, T.D., Anderson, B.E. and Mann, R.W. 1997. 'Human variables in the postmortem alteration of human bone: examples from U.S. War Casualties', in Haglund, W.D. and Sorg, M.H. (eds), *Forensic Taphonomy*, Boca Raton, FL: CRC Press, pp. 263–274.

Kneller P. 1998. 'Health and safety in church and funerary archaeology', in Cox, M.J. (ed.) *Grave Concerns: Death and Burial in England 1700–1850*. York: Council for British Archaeology, pp. 181–189.

Kostka J.E., Stucki J.W., Nealson K.H. and Wu, J. 1996. 'Reduction of structural Fe(III) in smectite by a pure culture of Shewanella putrefaciens strain MR-1'. *Clays and Clay Minerals* 44, 522–529.

McCarroll, J.E, Ursano, R.J., Fullerton, C.S., Liu, X, and Lundy, A. 2001. 'Effects of exposure to death in a war mortuary on post-traumatic stress disorder: symptoms of intrusion and avoidance', *Journal of Nervous and Mental Disease* 189:1, 44–48.

Schmitt, S. 2002. 'Mass graves and the collection of forensic evidence: genocide, war crimes, and crimes against humanity', in Haglund, W.D. and Sorg, M.H. (eds), *Advances in Forensic Taphonomy*, Boca Raton, FL: CRC Press, pp. 277–292.

Skinner, M. 1987. 'Planning the archaeological recovery of evidence from recent mass graves', *Forensic Science International*, 34, 267–287.

Skinner, M.F., York, H.P and Connor, M.A. 2002. 'Postburial disturbance of graves in Bosnia-Herzegovina', in Haglund, W.D. and Sorg, M.H. (eds), *Advances in Forensic Taphonomy*, Boca Raton, FL: CRC Press, pp. 293–308.

Thompson, J. 1993. 'Psychological impact of body recovery duties', *Journal of the Royal Society of Medicine* 86:11, 629–9.

Wright, Richard (2003) 'Aids to the display of bodies from mass graces represented in 3D: Program BODROT'. Retrieved from http://box.net/public/richwrig/dfiles/BodyRotation.ZIP

6

ANTHROPOLOGY IN A FORENSIC CONTEXT

Tal Simmons and William D. Haglund

6.1 Background

Forensic anthropology is that branch of applied physical anthropology concerned with the identification of human remains and associated skeletal trauma related to manner of death in a legal context (Reichs 1998). In the United States, the past two decades have witnessed the medico-legal community embracing forensic anthropology as a forensic specialty. The traditional role of the anthropologist has been to determine sex, race, age, and stature of skeletal material to assist in human identification. More recently, this niche has expanded via a major evolution into the realm of fleshed, decomposing, burnt, and dismembered remains. Today, anthropologists provide expertise in the recovery of remains, assist with identification of decomposed or burnt remains, interpret trauma to bone, assist with multiple fatality incidents, and provide court testimony. Auxiliary techniques, such as creation of visages from the skull and photo-superimposition often fall within the expertise of the forensic anthropologist in the USA (Haglund and Rodriguez 1998), though not in the UK where it remains a separate specialism. Unfortunately, there has been a lag in the acceptance of archaeologists/ anthropologists in other parts of the world, including the UK, where they have barely begun their adolescent entry into the forensic community (Hunter *et al.* 1996; see also Chapter 1, Section 1.3). Thus, while this chapter has wide application, much of the casework and experience is derived from US sources.

The acceptance of forensic anthropology in an international setting has, in contrast, a relatively long history, beginning with the 1984 investigations of Eric Stover and a team of forensic scientists from the American Association for the Advancement of Science (AAAS), who began the exhumation of mass graves in a search for the disappeared in Argentina (Stover and Ryan 2001). This work is ongoing and has also led to the use of mtDNA comparisons of the deceased and living relatives for purposes of identification (Boles *et al.* 1995) and has included the creation of a voluntary National Genetic Data Bank for this purpose (Stover and Ryan 2001). In Guatemala the use of forensic anthropology became established in 1991 and has continued to the present where only relatively recently (since 1998) have individuals been brought to trial and the anthropological evidence heard in court. Both Argentina and Guatemala have established permanent national forensic teams as a result of the early training they received during these investigations. Stover, Clyde Snow and other international forensic and human rights experts were also involved in investigations in Iraqi Kurdistan in 1991.

The date that hallmarks a burgeoning of activity for anthropologists/archeologists in the arena of international forensic investigations was 1996. This evolution was spearheaded by the employment of forensic specialists by the international criminal tribunals for Rwanda (ICTR) and the Former Yugoslavia (ICTY; see also Chapter 1, Section 1.7 and Chapter 7, Section 7.7). In 1996, over 1,200 bodies in Rwanda, Croatia, and the Republika Serbska area of Bosnia in Herzegovenia were exhumed by teams from Physicians for Human Rights (PHR), under the auspices of the ICTR and ICTY (Haglund 2002). A recently published example of the use of forensic archaeology examines excavations carried out by experts provided by the PHR (Connor and Scott 2001). Connor and Scott discuss the Kibuye (Rwanda) case in some detail. Other chapters in the same volume (Stover and Ryan 2001; Connor and Scott 2001) briefly mention cases in the former Yugoslavia.

As forensic anthropologists, the authors have been involved in the exhumation and identification of victims of war, ethnic cleansing and/or genocide in the former Yugoslavia, Sri Lanka, Cyprus, Guatemala, Rwanda, and many other countries. No individual forensic anthropologist acts alone in this type of investigation; rather it necessitates the cooperation of multiple agencies and organizations – many of which have competing agendas or mandates. The work is by definition multidisciplinary and it integrates all four fields of anthropology (biological, cultural and linguistic, and archaeological) as well as a variety of other disciplines including pathology, odontology, criminalistics and the law. The political environment in which all of this takes place has, for better or worse, a great influence on the process of investigation and, ultimately on the identification of victims. There are numerous responsibilities accorded to the forensic anthropologist involved in this process: to maintain the scientific integrity of the investigation; to maintain and conform to the appropriate legal conventions of the investigation; and to fulfill his/her responsibility to the local community affected by the events. All three aspects are important and in many cases unique to each location and investigation, often requiring the application of different guidelines, protocols and standards and invoking new and different pressures from various agencies and individuals.

In recent years, the role of the forensic anthropologist has expanded in scope within the boundaries of the USA in the context of medico-legal investigations. It has also developed within the increasing number of international human rights forensic projects with which the anthropological community has become inextricably involved. While the same basic techniques are useful in both contexts, flexibility is prerequisite to conducting most investigations. An experienced forensic anthropologist must know how to cope with situations where the ideal protocol and methodology are both followed. However, in situations where they are either not pragmatic or unavailable in a given situation, he/she must know what of the 'ideal' may be eliminated without losing necessary information. This chapter discusses aspects of a minimum examination protocol. It is not meant to be a manual of anthropological techniques, as it is assumed that personnel responsible for these tasks will have adequate training in the field of forensic anthropology.

6.2 The analysis

6.2.1 The skeletal inventory

The first phase of the analysis begins with a skeletal inventory of the presence/absence of each element, as well as any duplication of elements that might be present (indicating that there is more than one individual represented). Placing the remains in anatomical order also allows ease of completion of skeletal inventory, which is critical to documenting and maintaining chain of custody (Figure 6.1). This inventory should also indicate fragmentary bones; yet these should not be expressed numerically as these may subsequently disintegrate into smaller fragments and the 'number' becomes problematic because the numbers change. The inventory must also note the condition of the remains at this stage of the analysis, including a taphonomic assessment of post-mortem damage (e.g. staining, carnivore or rodent gnawing, breakage, weathering, root etching, etc.). The condition of each element should be noted. It is recommended that the anthropologist prepares in advance a list of post-mortem damage likely to be seen in forensic cases. Anticipating what is probably going to be encountered allows the anthropologist to predetermine how things will be described. While not a defining factor in most single-case forensic work, the standardization of descriptive terminology and its recording becomes essential in mass disasters and international human rights and humanitarian projects which require the processing and documentation of hundreds of remains (below). Likewise, standardized views of the skeleton should be taken as well. Such photographs should include the following: a skeletal overview of the individual in anatomical order; the maxillary and mandibular dentition; all elements used to estimate the age of an individual; all ante-mortem trauma or pathology, and all peri-mortem trauma.

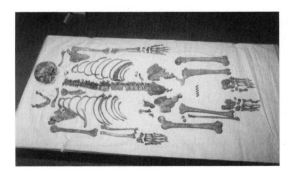

Figure 6.1 A forensic case laid out anatomically

6.2.2 The biological profile

The second phase of the analysis is concerned with creating a basic *biological profile* of the individual skeleton: determining sex, ancestry (if relevant to the identification of individuals for repatriation and/or judicial needs), age, and stature during life. It is not the intention to repeat what is widely understood about basic anthropological methods but to stress issues of key concern in forensic applications. It is, however, necessary to review aspects of methodology that are generally not well reviewed in standard osteological texts.

6.2.2.1 Sex

Sex (not gender) must be assessed first, as it will prescribe the methods used for the estimation of both age and stature. When a biological anthropologist examines a skeleton, he/she is determining the individual's sex, not his or her gender. Sex is a biological consequence of chromosomal inheritance; gender is a social construct based on how the individual self-identified, was classified by his/her culture, and behaved during life. While gender may be inferred from the context in which the skeleton appears (clothing, personal effects, etc.), the anthropologist needs to assess the skeleton independently of these features first to determine biological sex.

Methods for determining sex are discussed in standard texts such as White (2000), and France (1998), and critically reviewed by many others such as Mays and Cox (2000). Sex differences may be observed in the human skeleton after the onset of puberty and no attempt should be made to appraise the sex of an individual whose innominate is not fully fused at the acetabulum, nor of an individual who displays a complete lack of epiphyseal union of the long bones. DNA can be used to determine the sex of infants and juveniles. Caution must be applied when transferring anthropological techniques from one population to the next until the anthropologist becomes familiar with the normal range of variation between males and females within any given population.

In certain populations, most notably the United States, it is also possible to assess sex osteometrically from the cranium by employing a discriminant function. Several notes of caution are warranted. The features applicable to US populations may not be appropriate if applied to the remains of individuals derived from other geographic regions. For example, the crania of Japanese males are extremely gracile by American standards (Bass 1983; Sledzik and Ousley 1991) and may be classified incorrectly using US metric and visual cues. (A more reliable, if subtle, indicator in these cases is the extended suprameatal crest present in Japanese males, Bass 1983.) In another example, if the population to which an individual belongs is unknown, osteometrically based discriminant functions may classify the individual incorrectly because ancestry cannot be taken into consideration. Newer formulae (e.g. FORDISC 2.0; Ousley and Jantz 1996) calculated from cranial measurements obtained from a broad geographic sample allow one to input a single series of measurements and receive an output providing information of both sex and ancestry simultaneously. However, caution is warranted in applying this method as well; like all statistical packages, the program will always classify the data input into the categories available to it – and only into those categories known to it. It must also be noted that, as with morphological assessment, metric methods are also population specific and cannot be applied indiscriminately.

Only if the pelvis (or even a single innominate or pubic bone) and cranium are not available, should the anthropologist turn to other skeletal elements to determine sex. While osteometric standards for many postcranial elements exist and provide a reasonable degree of accuracy (most classify an individual correctly approximately 80 per cent of the time), their reliability is less than that of the pelvis and cranium. Many of these formulae are based on measurement of bony landmarks that correlate strongly to size differences between males and females, such as femoral or humeral head diameter. They are, however, like all studies in human variation, population specific. So the same precautions about cross-population applicability apply as regarding the non-metric observations discussed above. Sex determination should always be done using as many features of the skeleton as possible. No single indicator is as accurate as an assessment of the whole.

6.2.2.2 Ancestry

The estimation of ancestry, or the biological and geographic origins of the individual according to their genetic history is an integral part of the biological profile. While most medico-legal agencies ask for a determination of the *race* of the individual remains in order to search missing persons files, it is not possible to precisely correlate *social race* and biogeographic *ancestry*. The former is primarily based on external differences perceived to exist among populations or ethnic groups (and definitions may differ greatly from country to country) as well as individual self-identification during life. The latter is based on population biological variability as maintained via genetic drift and marriage patterns and preferences (non-random mating). Human variation results from relative genetic isolation (endogamy) of populations for long periods of time, which accentuated particular characteristics in each population. While some variability is adaptively based, much of it is simply the result of the perpetuation of particular morphology due to breeding within a restricted area. This is all relative, as people living in the *centre* of a population area will most resemble the 'norm' for that population, while people on the *edges* of the population will share characteristics and 'blend' with those of other adjacent populations. Because more variation exists *within* some populations than exists *between* them, race as a biological concept is untenable.

The ability of most forensic anthropologists in the USA to estimate ancestry so that it does, in fact, correspond with a social race category is no mystery (Sauer 1992). Most of the formulae and morphological criteria for separating 'whites' from 'blacks' were established based on collections of individuals of *known* 'race' who had donated their bodies to science, such as those that make up the Terry Collection at the National Museum of Natural History at the Smithsonian Institution. In other words, the individual cadavers were assessed for sex and race while they were still fleshed by an anthropologist who assigned a social race category to them. Then, when anthropologists later measured the remains in these collections to derive formulae for estimating race, their race categories were those designated by someone who had already established their 'social' race based on their external appearance. It is no wonder, then, that these skeletally based estimates often appear to coincide with socially prescribed categories that are, however, biologically meaningless.

An anthropologist is able, nonetheless, to be fairly accurate in estimating the ancestry of individuals. Ancestry is most accurately assessed through the observation of morphological and osteometric craniofacial variation (see, for example, Gill 1998; Howells 1973, 1989). Because, however, the majority of forensically-oriented craniofacial studies have been based on skeletons of known social race categories, our applied categories of ancestry are themselves rather limited (for example, African, European, Native American, and Asian). Few crania are likely to exhibit all the characteristics typical of a given population; the anthropologist makes these determinations based on the presence of a majority of characteristics that typify a particular ancestral population. In the event that character states are truly mixed, the anthropologist should indicate that the ancestry of the individual is mixed. A cranium that displays an equivalence of European and Native American features should simply be reported as such, with no concession to a social race category as this can be very misleading. For example, the skeleton of a young woman whose cranium displayed such a mix of features was examined; when identified, it became known that her father was 'white' but her mother was a Blackfoot Indian. In another incident, the cranium of a young male displayed a similar suite of features; when identified, the individual was a migrant farm worker of Mexican ancestry. His social race category would have been 'Hispanic' or 'Latino,' but such a category is really a linguistic grouping fraught with implications that have no biological population basis.

A word of further caution is appropriate here. In many international investigations of human rights abuses, ethnic cleansing and genocide, the assessment of ancestry can be highly inflammatory. These situations are created when one group of people accentuate the differences (religious, ethnic, cultural, historical, visual, etc.) between themselves and another group. While this process may be initiated by political leaders with a nationalistic agenda, the idea quickly spreads via propaganda throughout the population at large. The consequences are readily apparent throughout the twentieth century – the (alleged) Armenian genocide, the Holocaust, the Rwandan genocide, the war in the former Yugoslavia, etc. Therefore, it is necessary for the anthropologist to consider whether assessment of ancestry is truly necessary to either the identification process or the judicial process. If it is not, it is recommended that ancestry assessment should not be undertaken The potential ability of a 'scientist' to differentiate individuals on the basis of their cranial shape may be adding fuel to the fire by appearing to legitimize the very practices the consequences of which they are investigating.

6.2.2.3 Age at death

Estimating the age at death from the human skeleton is arguably the most important and the most difficult portion of the analysis (for a critical review of this subject, see Cox 2000). The importance of age estimation is that it allows the investigator to narrow the search through missing person's records (for all females, for example) to a specific range (e.g. females between the ages of 25 and 35 years). Despite the methodological problems inherent with available techniques, the anthropologist must always provide a range of age, as none of the techniques for estimation can account for variation in growth and degenerative changes across sex and population differences (see, for example, Brkic *et al.* 2000; Simmons *et al.* 1999). With experience, an anthropologist will be able to provide an age range estimate with reasonable accuracy, but not with precision (he or she will never report that 'the individual was 22 years of age' but rather that 'the individual was 20–25 years of age'). The anthropologist should always examine all available skeletal markers of age, and not rely on a single age indicator. The final age estimate must be broad and inclusive; it should incorporate the age ranges for all indicators. For example: the epiphyseal age for a skeleton is ≥ 17 and ≤ 30 years; the pubic symphysis provides a range of 19–34 years; the auricular surface of the ilium suggests 20–24 years; and the sternal rib morphology indicates 24–28 years (see Figure 6.2). An age estimate of 20–30 years might be rather broad, but not inappropriate. Margins of error should always be stated. It should be remembered that most ageing methods (juvenile and adult) available to anthropologists are also *population specific* and they may only be applied to other populations with caution. In juveniles, nutrition, disease, altitude, and other environmental factors have been demonstrated

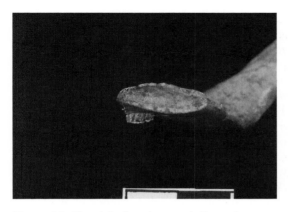

Figure 6.2 The right fourth sternal rib used to estimate age in a forensic case

to affect both growth and maturation rates (Frisancho 1993; Scheuer and Black 2000). Skeletal and dental ages are not always in agreement within the same individual (Ubelaker 1987); as dental development appears to be less susceptible to periodic environmental stressors, dental estimates should be regarded as the more reliable age indicator. If the individual suffered from nutritional stress or disease, it is not unusual for skeletal growth to be retarded by several months or years relative to dental maturation. Dental development in sub-adults is the most important means of age estimation. Both the deciduous and permanent dentition develop through well-defined stages of formation and eruption (Garn *et al.* 1959). The best means of evaluating dental age is radiographic, although a visual inspection is sometimes adequate for a rough estimate. Standards for dental eruption exist for several populations, but the variability should not be underestimated. It should be remembered that the sequence of development and eruption may be regarded as more fixed than the *timing* of eruption.

6.2.2.4 *Stature*

If the remains contain any complete long bones, stature estimation can be accomplished for USA and some other populations with both ease and accuracy. It must be remembered, however, that as discussed above for other aspects of the biological profile, stature formulae are population specific to geographic area and time period. Nutrition, disease, altitude, and other environmental factors all affect both growth rate and trajectory, and hence they impact upon population target height (and average height). Most stature formulae are based on the assumption that a long bone is proportionally related to the overall stature of the individual. Stature estimation can be quite accurate (if not precise) when the individual is compared to a population with established growth curves, known average statures and stature distributions, and one which is contemporary with the individual. This is particularly important since secular trends regarding proportionality and stature estimation factor into the accuracy of prediction. Jantz and Meadows (1995) and Simmons *et al.* (1990) both discuss the secular trends in femur:tibia ratio over time in the USA, based on data from the Terry and UT-K collections. Tibia length is seen to have increased over the past 50–60 years, and now accounts, proportionally, more for total stature than does femur length. Similar trends have been observed in stature and body proportions among the Japanese (Ohyama *et al.* 1987) and in other populations. Obviously, this renders the accuracy of stature estimates for recent leg bones, when using the Trotter and Gleser (1952) formulae, subject to question. If an individual in the USA died prior to the 1960s, for example, the Trotter and Gleser formulae are probably the appropriate ones to use; if on the other hand, the individual died within the past 20 years, then Ousley's (1995) equations based on a modern forensic sample are probably better. Certainly the original observer's measurements must be accurate and replicable for any stature estimation method to be reliable. Jantz *et al.* (1994) recently pointed out discrepancies in Trotter's measurements of the tibia as used in her 1952 and 1958 formulae (Trotter and Glaser 1958). These articles recommend that if the *1952 formulae* is used, the maximum tibial length *without the malleolus* should be measured, if the *1958 formulae* is used, the maximum tibial length *including the malleolus* should be measured. Furthermore, they recommend that the 1958 formulae be avoided, as Trotter's original measurements cannot be assessed for accuracy.

Estimating stature from fragmentary long bones (i.e. Steele 1970) presents some unique problems concerning the ability to replicate measurements. The Steele formulae covered all long bones, but the landmarks were particularly difficult to locate, and hence measurement reliability and repeatability were compromised. Simmons *et al.* (1990) attempted a revision of the Steele method (for the femur only) by proposing more clearly defined skeletal landmarks. Their results actually bettered Steele's, albeit to a small degree, but still require the estimation of bone length first, prior to the estimation of stature. This compounds measurement error, as two formulae are used, both with standard errors of estimated. With both the Steele and Simmons, *et al.* formulae, however, the estimates are quite broad, and may serve as exclusionary evidence but only for professional basketball players and jockeys!

As in estimating age, it is vital to provide a stature range, not a precise estimate of an individual's height. Some individuals (e.g. Ousley 1995) advocate using two standard deviations for estimating stature, thus insuring that the individual's height in life will fall within the low and high ends of the range. While this may be the statistically correct procedure, most stature estimates using one standard deviation usually estimate an individual's height with excellent results. It should also be noted that while stature estimation is a necessary portion of the biological profile of an individual, and is often useful in single case-work in the USA, it is not a particularly dependable criterion for identification in an international setting (Komar 2003). In the USA the stature estimate may help to eliminate a range of missing persons (e.g. those under 170cm and over 180cm in height) from the pool of possible victims. However, in places such as Rwanda or Bosnia where ante-mortem stature measurements are not routinely recorded (e.g. no medical or driver's license statures available), the information is of equivocal value. Relatives may be able to estimate the stature of a missing person, but as yet no standards exist for correlating 'recollected stature' with estimated skeletal stature. In addition, applying any stature formulae consistently to the Srebrenica population revealed that the vast majority of the 4,500 individuals exhumed were of similar stature, between 170–180cm.

6.2.3 Trauma, cause and manner of death

The next phase of the analysis is identifying any evidence of ante-mortem trauma or pathology on the skeleton that may aid in the identification of the individual, and the final phase is identifying any indications of peri-mortem trauma that may indicate how the individual died. With the latter, the anthropologist must be able to distinguish peri- from post-mortem trauma to bone. As with the taphonomic inventory discussed above, it is recommended that the laboratory protocols contain a comprehensive listing of potential ante-mortem conditions and peri-mortem trauma that is anticipated to be encountered. This allows the conditions to be coded for ease of data retrieval for both identification and judicial proceedings, respectively.

6.2.3.1 Ante-mortem trauma and pathology

The forensic anthropologist must assess the skeleton for congenital abnormalities or any signs of disease or trauma that the individual suffered during life (Figure 6.3). Mainly, the anthropologist is searching for evidence of diseases that alter bone (hypertrophy or atrophy) on local or systemic levels. In both cases, certain neoplastic, infectious, and metabolic diseases can be the causal agents. In the case of trauma, the anthropologist is searching for evidence of past injury to bones or joints (fractures, dislocations, etc.), which may be healed or active. This also applies to the dentition for which disease as well as its treatment (dental restorations, crowns, etc.) should be recorded. Ante-mortem and post-mortem radiographic comparison is the best means of positive identification, whether dental or skeletal. If radiographs are not available for comparison, only a presumptive identification can be made on the basis of injury (or disease) location and type. If present, prosthetic implants are another key factor in identification as most produced within recent decades contain maker's marks as well as serial numbers that allow them to be traced to the manufacturer and/or the hospital where the surgical procedure was performed (Ubelaker and Jacobs 1995).

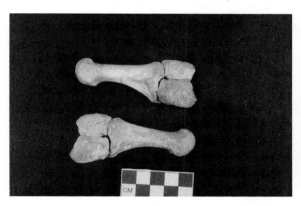

Figure 6.3 A bilateral congenital abnormality of the medial cuneiform in a forensic case

6.2.3.2 Peri-mortem trauma

A careful evaluation of all peri-mortem trauma to the skeleton is critical to a forensic anthropology examination. Signs of injury may not only suggest manner and cause of death (traditionally the realm of the forensic pathologist), but they may also provide insight into the treatment of the body around the time of death, and its disposal. Peri-mortem injuries are those that occur around the time of death. As bone retains its organic component for some time after death (though this is variable dependent upon taphonomic factors), it is extremely difficult to differentiate between damage inflicted to living bone, or to bone shortly after death. This can, however, be undertaken using scanning electron microscopy (when it can be detected after about 12 hours – Jones and Boyde 1993). The first change that can be detected macroscopically is often a localized periosteal reaction.

(a)

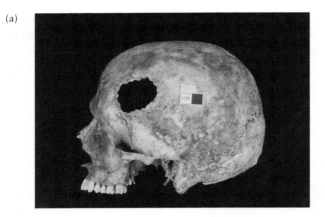

(b)

Figure 6.4 (a), (b) Peri-mortem surgical trauma to the left parietal resulting from the removal of shrapnel from a blast injury in a forensic case

A forensic anthropologist is generally concerned with three types of peri-mortem trauma: blunt force, sharp force, and projectile (gunshot and fragmentation injuries, e.g. Figure 6.4). As in all things, a great deal of experience is necessary to evaluate each of these types with authority. Unfortunately, given the events of the past decade in Rwanda, Bosnia, Kosovo, Sri Lanka, Indonesia and other places, these types of injuries are frequently being seen on a large scale by forensic anthropologists working for such organisations as human rights organisations and war crimes tribunals. The literature on blunt force, sharp force, and projectile trauma to the skeleton is still in its infancy, but includes work by Maples (1998) on trauma analysis in general, Smith *et al.* (1987) on gunshots to the cranium, Sauer (1984) on blunt and sharp force trauma, Galloway (2000) on blunt force trauma, and Kerley (1978) on battered-infant syndrome. Surgical trauma may also be recorded as peri-mortem, if the individual did not survive the procedure long enough for skeletal healing to be evident (Figure 6.4).

6.2.4 Identification

One of the most challenging issues in investigations of genocide and crimes against humanity is that of victim identification. Identification has critical meaning for survivors, for courts, and to the expert. For the latter, the status of an identification can be expressed as tentative, presumptive, or positive, on the basis of how the identification will stand up to objective criteria and second opinion scrutiny. The majority of identifications done both in the USA and abroad are presumptive identifications, based on good faith acceptance of the dead person's identity. This is generally not questioned. In homicides and insurance cases, the identifications are generally held to a higher standard and must therefore be positive. The identification of victims in mass fatality events, war, ethnic cleansing, genocide, etc. is often seen as a more complicated issue.

6.2.4.1 Identification in the USA

Identifications in the US are the result of predominantly circumstantial and visual means. These consist of recognition of facial features, or based on circumstantial evidence such as personal effects, documents associated with the body, or unchallenged testimony to the effect that a person is who s/he is presumed to be. Technically, these are presumptive means of identifications and are common practice when there are no questionable circumstances that would call the identification into question. For example, a body is removed from the wreckage of a car after an accident. The wallet in the individual's trouser pocket indicates a white male, aged 35, 5' 10'' in height by the name of John Smith. The car from which the body comes was registered to a John Smith. The body conforms reasonably well to that of a male about 5' 10'' in height in his thirties. The body is therefore identified as John Smith. As long as John Smith does not appear, and assuming that the family, insurance company, or others do not dispute the identification, then the identification is accepted. In the vast majority of cases such as this one, an anthropologist and/or odontologist is not involved in examination of the remains.

Deviations from this practice in the USA occur when: (1) there is no means of visual identification possible; e.g. bodies that are disfigured, decomposed or skeletonized; (2) in all cases of homicides; (3) when there are perceived questionable circumstances surrounding the death; and (4) in the event of a mass fatality situation (e.g. a plane crash, bombing, fire). It is at this point that objective, scientific means of identification are pursued by way of fingerprints, dental identification (Figure 6.5) medical radiographs, or genetic (DNA) identifications. Where none are initially available, the stage is set for methodologies that will document lead-generating information, and it is here that disciplines like anthropology may become involved. As anyone who has ever

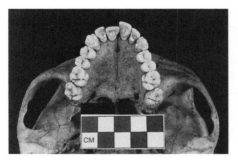
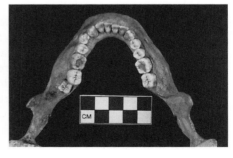

(a)   (b)

Figure 6.5 The maxillary (a) and mandibular (b) dentition can aid identification where dental records exist

worked on a mass fatality incident knows, there is tremendous pressure to insure the rapid identification of all victims. Sometimes this is due to political pressure. Primarily, however, such pressure comes from the families of victims. They desire the return of their loved ones' remains with all due speed so that the death can be authenticated and the more ritualized and formalized mourning period can begin (and that probate and other financial matters can be settled). In the USA and developed countries with relatively sophisticated infrastructures, most victims can be identified with relative rapidity owing to the ubiquitous presence of, and ease of access to, independent documentation such as medical and dental records, or fingerprints. This is particularly so for certain segments of society (e.g. military and other employees previously screened for security clearances, etc.). DNA is utilized more and more to effect such identifications.

What is perhaps of most interest in the context of this discussion, is that the issue of positive identification becomes paramount in mass fatality events. This is for two reasons. First, multiple victims are involved for whom there is no reliable manifest (e.g. passenger and crew manifest, documentation of employees present in a building on a given day, etc.). Second, there is often fragmentation of the victims – or delay in recovery of remains with subsequent decomposition. In either case, recognition of individuals and ready association of all parts of an individual obstructs the identification process. There is extreme reluctance in US mass fatality events to issue a death certificate reliant upon 'circumstantial', or presumptive identifications (although the events of 11 September 2001 were an exception, although all identifications are being confirmed by DNA). Experience has shown that even in passenger manifests there are falsities, hence, plane tickets and even personal identifying documents found on the body are susceptible to question and a death certificate may not be issued.

There are of course, exceptions, but these do not come quickly to the certifying authorities. Such an example is a plane crash with one individual to be identified. No dentition for this female was recovered, she had no tattoos, she had never been fingerprinted, and the family could not provide any ante-mortem radiographs for comparison to the body in question. The biological profile for the body matched and the woman was wearing copious amounts of gold and diamond jewelry on every appendage, which the family jeweler had designed for her alone – and kept photographic records of each piece. Despite this, the Medical Examiner was reluctant to declare that the female body was passenger X, because there was no means of positive identification. This was despite the unlikely possibility that this woman had boarded the plane and had elected to voluntarily exchange every piece of her highly unique and expensive jewelry in mid-flight with another woman. Ultimately, as she was the only unidentified (by positive means) individual recovered from the complement of victims, she was presumptively identified on the basis of the biological profile and her documented unique personal effects alone. A death certificate was ultimately issued for her as it had been for all other positively identified passengers.

The families and agencies involved in mass fatalities attain resolution to the deaths via identification and are able, with the aid of the existing infrastructure of various social services, the government, religious and cultural institutions to resume their day-to-day lives. Things will never be the same for the family members, but the reality of the death as attested by positive identification is not in doubt and is rarely questioned.

6.2.4.2 Identifications after war, genocide and crimes against humanity

People's attitudes toward the exhumation and identification process are varied and, to a certain extent controlled by the political climate. For example, the identification of people killed in 1992–95 in Bosnia is a complex process that has different meanings for different people. For some relatives of the missing, it is a relief, providing the end of uncertainty regarding the fate of their loved ones. For others, it is undesirable, forcing them to confront the death of an individual for whom they held out hope of life. Several families of Greek Cypriot and Greek victims of the 1974 conflict have long been activists lobbying for identification of the missing. On the personal level, differences in people's acceptance of the exhumation and identification process often reflect the political perspective because it gives them hope, however false, that their loved one is alive. Some people want to know if their loved one is dead and to be able to bury them. They seek resolution to their questions so that they can move on with their lives. They will accept the identification. Some survivors are so desperate for resolution to their pain and uncertainty that they have tried to persuade experts to attribute an identification for which there is no scientific basis.

The establishment of the identification of the victim is most crucial both to proving charges of homicide and directing the inquiry into the cause and manner of death, leading to an identification of the perpetrator (Geberth 1995). While this dictum forms the basis of localized and individual homicide investigations within most developed countries, there is frequently less emphasis on personal identification than one would expect from the prosecutors in current International Criminal Tribunal investigations of deaths related to war crimes and genocide (Haglund 2002). For their purposes, it is often considered sufficient to 'categorically' identify the victims by their ethnicity or their religion, whether they were men, women or children, civilians or combatants, or soldiers incapacitated by bindings or blindfolds. This does not imply that positive personal identification would not lend deeper support to indictments or to the international criminal tribunal's investigations. Nor does it imply that personnel connected with the tribunals do not feel that personal positive identification is important to the families of the victims. It is simply that a pursuit of this level of identification has not been a primary issue to the prosecution. It is arguable that the changing nature of international forensic projects (including the growing sophistication of the families of the missing and their awareness of the possibility of identification through DNA, etc.) necessitates the inclusion of a provision for the identification of the victims for humanitarian reasons. This provision will, of course, extend not only the budget, but the duration of cases as well as the number and expertise of personnel required. This is true regardless of whether presumptive or positive identifications are sought. Personnel, expertise and resources are needed to conduct interviews gathering ante-mortem information about the missing, collect DNA samples from the relatives, and compile databases. Community education is also a necessary component of such work in order to educate the families of the missing about the process of identification and the length of time it is projected to take. The issue of 'capacity building' within the local, established forensic community also bears consideration wherever practical.

6.3 Laboratory resources

Undertaking analysis of human remains requires a secure examination and storage area. A secure area means that only authorized people have access to the area, room or building, which is kept locked and/or guarded at all times. A detailed inventory of what evidence enters the facility is kept and the chain of custody is maintained. The safety of laboratory personnel is of paramount concern and all individuals should use universal precautions when dealing with human remains. As a minimum, everyone should wear latex examination gloves if dealing with fleshed remains. Protective clothing and masks should be worn when necessary. All personnel who are certified to work in the laboratory should also have been vaccinated for tetanus and hepatitis B. A first aid kit should be available and all personnel aware of its location and its contents. Contents should inventoried and re-supplied regularly. All personnel should be knowledgeable about biohazards and necessary safety measures (Galloway and Snodgrass 1998) and briefed on any unique potential hazards relative to a particular project.

The laboratory should ideally have running water, electricity and an examination table large enough to place an adult human skeleton in the anatomical position (see also Table 6.1). If the remains are skeletal, the table or other examination surface should be padded (foam rubber or bubble-wrap work well) so that the bones are not damaged by contact with a hard surface. If the remains contain soft tissue, then the table should be metal (plastic/fiberglass trays are an option) and the availability of water becomes essential. When handling skeletal remains, the anthropologist must ensure that the bones are clean prior to examination in order to observe morphological features, analyze trauma or pathological conditions, conduct osteometric analyses, and facilitate storage. To remove loose dry extraneous material, it is best to simply brush bones with a soft bristled brush of natural or nylon fibre. If the bones are more encrusted, washing them in plain water with the aid of a soft brush may also be appropriate. Bones should never be allowed to 'soak' in water. Care must be taken during the drying process. Bones must not be allowed to dry too quickly, and exposure to heat, direct sun, or blowing air should be avoided as these may cause surface fissuring and breakage. A drying rack of wire or plastic mesh that allows air to reach all surfaces of the wet bones evenly is ideal for this purpose and easily constructed. When absolutely essential to deflesh selected elements (i.e. age, sex, etc. cannot be determined without doing so), it may be necessary to remove certain elements (pubic symphyses, sternal rib ends, medial clavicles, etc.) from the body and remove soft tissue from them prior to examination for determining the individual's biological profile. Surgical saws, either electric or hand-powered, and clippers are necessary to this task and dissecting equipment may be needed to expose the bony landmarks prior to their removal.

Defleshing remains, whether in whole or in part, is an integral part of laboratory analysis. Removal of tissue from remains brings up several issues to be considered. It is not uncommon that remains will not be identified for a long period following their examination. Removed soft tissue should be considered a part of the remains and thus should not be simply discarded. Unfortunately, unlike bones, which are relatively simple to store, soft tissue decomposes in the absence of preservatives or proper refrigeration. When faced with this challenge, alternatives need to be explored. An often utilised measure is to bury the remains as a storage measure. It is necessary that burial occurs in an identified grave from which remains can later be retrieved. While this

Table 6.1 Basic laboratory equipment for anthropological analysis

Secure storage area
Laboratory protocols
Recording forms (paper or computerized)

Latex examination gloves
Face/eye shields
Cloth or disposable protective clothing

Examination tables
Evidence bags and boxes
Metal tags
Case labels/tags (paper or plastic)

Spreading calipers
Sliding calipers
Osteometric board

Comparative age estimation casts (Rib, Pubic Symphysis
– males and females, and epiphyseal union)
Study skeleton (both articulated/hanging and boxed)

Selected reference texts

Drying rack

Sand box
Glues (both water soluble and acetone soluble) and solvents

Basic photographic equipment (SLR 35mm, digital and video cameras)
Darkroom equipment
Photo stand, tripod and ladder
Measuring scales

Dissecting microscope

Thin section equipment

X-ray machine and radiographic developing equipment

Computers, scanners, printers, and various software, programs such as FORDISC 2.0

does not forestall nature taking its course as far as decomposition is concerned, it does reduce potential liability from having discarded the material and may satisfy religious customs (e.g. Islam, Judaism) that prescribe the burial of all body parts.

The ideal way to deflesh is by use of a dermestid beetle colony in which beetles eat away the flesh without damaging the skeletal elements. However, the beetles consume the flesh at a rate that is usually too slow for most forensic cases, and relatively few laboratory facilities are able to maintain these insects (a colony must have a constant 'food' source in order to perpetuate itself). Thus, in order to expedite the cleaning of remains, as much excess soft tissue as possible should be first removed, taking care not to use sharp-edged implements near the bone surface itself (marks left might potentially be confused with peri-mortem injuries). Following this, the skeletal elements should be simmered, at a low boil in a weak solution of water and a commercial enzyme detergent (Fenton *et al.* 2003). Adding potassium hydroxide to this solution also acts as a catalyst to the reaction, but vigilance is necessary to ensure that the water level remains high enough that the bones do not char and/or that erosion and bleaching does not occur. A hot plate and commercial aluminum pots of considerable size may be employed; this process should ideally be conducted under a fume hood. It is helpful that the material be suspended in the water, rather than resting on the pan surface in order to eliminate the possibility of the contact surface of the bone with metal. A variety of materials may be used for this, including screening material (plastic or metal) and mesh laundry bags. With small sections of bone, the same process can be accomplished more quickly with the aid of a microwave oven. In either case, the bones should be removed from the water at frequent intervals and additional loosened soft tissue removed until the process is complete.

6.4 Conclusion

Forensic anthropology has expanded rapidly during the past decade. The case-load of forensic anthropologists has risen markedly in the United States (Reichs 1998) and begun to develop in the UK. It has grown to include fleshed and burnt remains, led to an increase in courtroom testimony regarding the interpretation of trauma, as well as involvement in civil suits concerning accidents and other issues to which our subject may be relevant (Galloway 1999). The expertise of forensic anthropologists has also become integral to investigations of genocide, war-crimes and crimes against humanity in many parts of the world. This may be through the auspices of non-government human rights organizations, the United Nations and the *ad hoc* international criminal tribunals. With their participation in international projects the role of the forensic anthropologist has also changed, necessitating changes in training and perspective relevant to this context. The focus of forensic anthropology has shifted. From the creation of biological profiles providing leads to identification in individual cases, it is predominantly the interpretation of peri-mortem trauma, and the demonstration of patterns in large-scale events, that demonstrate criminal intent by the perpetrators of mass murder.

The roles the forensic anthropologist is expected to fulfill have multiplied in international missions and a new training, beyond mere competence in technique, is needed for those entering the field. Today's forensic anthropologist must be expected to be well versed in anthropological techniques, law, aspects of crime scene investigation, and issues involving human rights, and humanitarian and diplomatic aspects of international projects. Too few individuals hoping to gain entry to the field are aware of the complex nature of the work, its context, and the multiplicity of functions that they must fulfill. It is this that the providers of graduate and post-graduate education and continuing professional development must address.

References

Bass, W.M. 1983. *Human Osteology: Laboratory and Field Manual*, Columbia, MO: Missouri Archaeological society.
Bass, W.M. 1995. 'The Occurrence of Japanese trophy skulls in the United States', *Journal of Forensic Sciences* 28:3, 800–803.

Boles, T., Snow, C. and Stover, E. 1995. 'Forensic DNA testing on skeletal remains from mass graves: a pilot project from Guatemala', *Journal of Forensic Sciences* 40:3, 349–355.

Brkic, H., Strinovic, D., Kubat, M. and Petrovecki, V. 2000. 'Odonotological identification of human remains form mass graves in Croatia', *International Journal of Legal Medicine* 114, 19–22.

Connor, M. and Scott, D. 2001. 'Paradigms and perpetrators', *Society for Historical Archaeology* 35:1, 1–6.

Cox, M. 2000. 'Ageing human skeletal material', in Cox, M. and Mays, S. (eds) *Human Osteology in Archaeology and Forensic Science*, London: Greenwich Medical Media Ltd, pp. 61–82.

Fenton, T., Birkby, W. and Cornelius, J. 2003. 'A fast and safe non-bleaching method for forensic skeletal preparation', *Journal of Forensic Sciences* 48:2, 274–6.

France, D. 1998. 'Observational and metric analysis of sex in the skeleton' in Reichs, K. (ed.) *Forensic Osteology: Advances in the Identification of Human Remains*, Springfield, IL: Charles C. Thomas, pp. 163–186.

Frisancho, R. 1993. *Human Adaptation and Accommodation*. Ann Arbor, MI: University of Michigan Press.

Galloway, A. (ed.) 1999. *Broken Bones: Anthropological Analysis of Blunt Force Trauma*, Springfield: Charles C. Thomas.

Galloway, A. (ed.) 2000. *Broken Bones: Anthropological Analysis of Blunt Force Trauma*, Springfield, IL: Charles C. Thomas.

Galloway, A. and Snodgrass, J. 1998. 'Biological and chemical hazards of forensic skeletal analysis', *Journal of Forensic Sciences* 43:5, 940–948.

Garn, S., Christabel, G., Rohmann, G. and Silverman, F. 1959. 'Variability of tooth formation', *Journal of Dental Research* 43, 243–258.

Geberth, V. J. 1995. *Practical Homicide Investigation: Tactics, Procedures, and Forensic Techniques*, New York: Elsevier.

Gill, G.W. 1998. 'Craniofacial criteria in the skeletal attribution of race', in Reichs, K. (ed.) *Forensic Osteology*, Springfield, IL: Charles S. Thomas, pp. 293–317.

Haglund, W.D. 2002. 'Recent mass graves, an introduction', in Haglund, W.D and Sorg, M. (eds) *Advances in Forensic Taphonomy: Method, Theory, and Archaeological Perspectives*, Boca Raton, FL: CRC Press, pp. 243–262.

Haglund, W.D. and Rodriguez, W.C. 1998. 'Forensic anthropology', in Fierro, M and Schachowa, I. L.L. (eds) *CAP Handbook for Postmortem Examination of Unidentified Remains: Developing Identification of Well-preserved, Decomposed, Burned, and Skeletonized Remains*, Skokie, IL: College of American Pathologists, 2nd edn, pp. 107–132.

Howells, W.W. 1973. *Cranial Variation in Man: A Study by Multivariate Analysis of Patterns of Difference among Recent Human Populations*, Cambridge, MA: Papers of the Peabody Museum of Archaeology and Ethnology, vol. 79, Harvard University Press.

Howells, W.W. 1989, *Skull Shapes and the Map: Craniometric Analyses in the Dispersion of Modern Homo*, Cambridge, MA: Papers of the Peabody Museum of Archaeology and Ethnology, vol. 67, Harvard University Press.

Hunter, J., Roberts, C.A. and Martin, A. 1996. *Studies in Crime: An Introduction to Forensic Archaeology*, London: Routledge.

Jantz, R., Hunt, D. and Meadows, L. 1994. 'Maximum length of the tibia: how did Trotter measure it?', *American Journal of Physical Anthropology* 93, 525–528.

Jantz, R. and Meadows, L. 1995 'Secular change in long bone length and proportion in the United States, 1800–1970', *American Journal of Physical Anthropology* 110, 57–67.

Jones, S.J. and Boyde, A. 1993. 'Histomorphometry of Howship's lacunae formed in vivo and in vitro: depths and volumes measured by scanning electron and confocal microscopy', *Bone* 1:3, 455.

Kerley, E. 1978. 'The identification of battered-infant skeletons', *Journal of Forensic Sciences* 23:1, 163–168.

Komar, D. 2003. 'Lessons from Srebrenica: the contributions and limitations of physical anthropology in identifying victims of war crimes', *Journal of Forensic Sciences* 48:4, 713–16.

Maples, W. R. 1998. 'Trauma Analysis by the Forensic Anthropologist' in Reichs, K. (ed.), *Forensic Osteology*, Springfield, IL: Charles S. Thomas, pp. 218–228.

Mays, S. and Cox, M.J. 2000. 'Sex determination in skeletal remains' in Cox, M. and Mays, S. (eds), *Human Osteology in Archaeology and Forensic Science*, London: Greenwich Medical Media Ltd, pp. 117–130.

Ohyama, S., Hisanaga, A., Inmasu, T., Yamamoto, A., Hirata, M. and Ishinishi, N. 1987. 'Some secular changes in body height and proportion of Japanese medical students', *American Journal of Physical Anthropology* 73:2, 179–184.

Ousley, S. 1995. 'Should we estimate biological or forensic stature?', *Journal of Forensic Sciences* 40:5, 768–773.

Ousley, S. and Jantz, R. 1996. *FORDISC 2.0*. Knoxville, TN: Forensic Anthropology Center, University of Tennessee.

Reichs, K. 1998. *Forensic Osteology: Advances in the Identification of Human Remains.* Springfield, IL: Charles C. Thomas Publishers.

Sauer, N. 1984. 'Manner of death: skeletal evidence of blunt and sharp instrument wounds', in Buikstra, J. and Rathbun, T. (eds) *Human Identification: Case Studies in Forensic Anthropology*, Springfield, IL: Charles C. Thomas, pp. 176–184.

Sauer, N. 1992. 'Forensic anthropology and the concept of race: if races don't exist, why are forensic anthropologists so good at identifying them?', *Social Science and Medicine* 34:2, 107–111.

Scheuer, L. and Black, S. 2000. *Developmental Juvenile Osteology.* San Diego: Academic Press.

Simmons, T., Jantz, R., and Bass, W.M. 1990. 'Stature estimation from fragmentary femora: a revision of the Steele method', *Journal of Forensic Sciences* 35:3, 628–636.

Simmons, T., Tuco, V., Kesetovic, R. and Cihlarz, Z. 1999. 'Evaluating age estimation in a Bosnia forensic population: "Age-at-Stage" via Probit Analysis', paper presented at the American Academy of Forensic Sciences. February, Orlando.

Sledig, P.S. and Ousley, S. 1991. 'Analysis of six Vietnamese trophy skulls', *Journal of Forensic Sciences*, 36: 2, 520–30.

Smith, O.C., Berryman, H., and Lahren, C. 1987. 'Cranial fracture patterns and estimate of direction from low velocity gunshot wounds', *Journal of Forensic Sciences* 32:5, 1416–1421.

Steele, G. D. 1970. 'Estimation of stature from fragments of long limb bones', in Stewart, T.D. (ed.), *Personal Identification in Mass Disasters*, Washington, DC: National Museum of Natural History, pp. 85–97.

Stover, E. and Ryan, M. 2001. 'Breaking bread with the dead', *Society for Historical Archaeology* 35:1, 7–25.

Trotter, M. and Gleser, G. 1952. 'Estimation of stature from long bones of American whites and negroes', *American Journal of Physical Anthropology* 10, 463–514.

Trotter, M. and Gleser, G.C. 1958. 'A re-evaluation of estimation based on measurements of stature taken during life and long bones after death', *American Journal of Physical Anthropology* 16, 79–123.

Ubelaker, D. H. 1987. 'Estimating age of death from immature human skeletons: an overview', *Journal of Forensic Sciences* 32:5, 1254–1263.

Ubelaker, D. H. and Jacobs, C. 1995. 'Identification of orthopedic device manufacturer', *Journal of Forensic Sciences* 40:2, 168–170.

White, T. D. 2000. *Human Osteology*, 2nd edn. San Diego: Academic Press.

7

LEGAL MATTERS

Robert Dilley

7.1 Introduction: the forensic archaeologist and the law

One of the aims of this book is to explore archaeology's role in the detection and prosecution of crime within the constraints imposed by law. Archaeological evidence can be used in court, but only if it can be considered relevant and appropriate to the legal issue. In a criminal case these issues will be directed towards bringing individuals to justice by imposing a criminal penalty.

Perhaps surprisingly, there are some significant similarities between the disciplines of archaeology and law. First, both are concerned with reconstructing the past. This is self-evident for archaeology, but perhaps less obvious for law where practical legal problems also involve an investigation into the facts of an event – a process which lawyers refer to as reaching 'findings of fact'. Second, both disciplines are susceptible to comparable scientific processes and methods, each being concerned with collecting facts, separating relevant facts from those which are not relevant, analysing them by logical reasoning, and then drawing a conclusion. In each discipline, the available evidence is critically interpreted and its value assessed according to accepted and objective standards.

Forensic archaeology is a relatively new discipline. The key to its meaning is the word 'forensic' which means 'of, or used, in a court of law'. In other words, forensic archaeology is concerned with the presentation of archaeological evidence in a court of law in instances where such evidence may be relevant to issues arising in litigation in criminal or civil cases. The difference between the two is that criminal cases are concerned with the prosecution by the State of offending behaviour classified as criminal, whereas civil cases are concerned essentially with private disputes between individuals or between individuals and the State.

This chapter is concerned primarily with interaction between the courts of England and Wales and the forensic archaeologist. In this interaction the forensic archaeologist is likely to be recognised by the court as an expert in his or her field, and the court will expect in return not only a high standard of competence and independence, but also a willingness to assist the court in achieving the right conclusion. This is why forensic archaeologists can, if they wish, be certified according to criteria drawn up by the Council for the Registration of Forensic Practitioners (see Chapter 1, Section 1.5).

The distinctions between the civil and the criminal law are reflected in different and separate court systems Each has a structured hierarchical system of courts in which

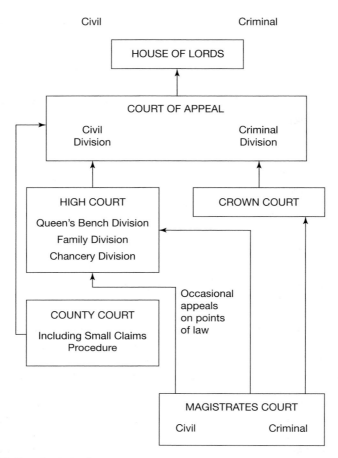

Figure 7.1 Civil and criminal court structures

cases are generally first heard in a 'lower court' and may then progress to a 'higher court' either by way of appeal in civil cases, or by committal or appeal in criminal cases. The civil and criminal court system in England is outlined in Figure 7.1. Broadly speaking, civil cases are heard either in the County Court or the High Court and go by way of appeal to the Court of Appeal (Civil Division), thence to the House of Lords. Criminal cases are first tried either in the Magistrates Court or the Crown Court and go from there by way of appeal to the Court of Appeal (Criminal Division), thence also to the House of Lords. In fact, relatively few cases find their way that far, partly because the House of Lords will not hear an appeal unless there is a matter of general public importance at stake. The operation of the courts is a political responsibility of the Lord Chancellor, but the day-to-day detailed administration is carried out by an Executive Agency known as the Court Service.

In the English and Welsh legal system which is a combined legal system, all criminal offences are classified as one of three types – 'summary', 'indictable', or 'either way'. Summary offences are not discussed further here because they relate only to relatively minor criminal offences and are heard and disposed of by the Magistrates Court.

Indictable offences are the most serious and will be tried in the Crown Court before a judge and jury. Depending on their seriousness 'either way' offences will be heard either in the Magistrates Court or the Crown Court. The choice depends on two factors: first, whether the Magistrates consider the offence too serious to exercise their own jurisdiction, or second, whether the defendant elects his or her right to trial by judge and jury in the Crown Court. Since forensic archaeologists will be dealing almost exclusively with crimes of homicide, and since those crimes are indictable, this chapter is focused mainly on procedures of the Crown Court.

Mention may be made here of the office of the coroner, an institution dating back to the twelfth century. The Coroner's Act 1988 requires an inquest to be held when there is a reasonable cause to suspect that the deceased died an unnatural death (or a sudden death) of which the cause is unknown. The inquest is intended to ascertain principally who the deceased was, and how, when and where death occurred.

The coroner is entitled to empanel a jury who will sit with the coroner to determine these matters. The jury no longer has power to nominate an individual as responsible for the death. A coroner's court will hear evidence which will be partly oral and partly by way of written statements. Generally, if there are criminal proceedings pending or contemplated, the coroner will adjourn the inquest to await the outcome of those proceedings.

The forensic archaeologist will be working as an expert witness, as part of a team of professionals in the conduct of a particular case. He or she will not be directly appointed by the court but will be instructed on behalf of one or more of the parties in the case. In a criminal case, it is far more likely that a forensic archaeologist will be instructed by the prosecution than by the defence. However, it is quite possible that the prosecution and the defence may instruct separate experts, although it is highly unlikely that one will only be instructed by the defence. Difficulties caused by these arrangements are examined below. As a member of the team, an expert witness needs to understand the roles of other individuals involved in the legal process as well as their own (see Chapter 1, Section 1.3). They should also be aware that lawyers, whether acting for the prosecution or the defence, are bound by rules of etiquette and conduct and owe professional obligations to each other and to the Court. If the case proceeds to trial, the archaeologist will come into contact with the following professionals:

- *The judiciary.* There is a hierarchy of judges, of varying degrees of seniority, who will be assigned to hear a particular case. Generally speaking, the more important or complex the case the more senior the judge will be assigned to hear it. An indictable offence will be heard in the Crown Court before a Circuit Judge or a High Court Judge who will try a defended case with the assistance of a jury if the defendant is pleading 'not guilty'. If the defendant is pleading 'guilty', it will not be necessary to empanel a jury and the judge will proceed to sentence. In cases of homicide the Judge is obliged, in the case of murder, to impose a mandatory life sentence, whereas in the (lesser) offence of manslaughter, the judge has the full range of sentences available from a discharge of the defendant up to a life sentence.
- *The legal profession.* Unlike most other jurisdictions, the legal profession in England and Wales is a dual system consisting of both solicitors and barristers. Solicitors are regarded as the general practitioners of the law: they usually work in partnership and offer a full range of legal services direct to the public. Solicitors have limited

rights of advocacy, and in a homicide case will be obliged to instruct a barrister to handle the case in court. Barristers act mainly as specialists in advocacy and in advising on complex cases in both civil and criminal matters. They do not provide their services directly to the public and must generally be instructed by a solicitor acting on behalf of one of the parties. Barristers who have attained the required level of competency and reputation in their particular field can apply for an appointment as 'Queens Counsel' and are entitled to the designation of QC after their name.

- *Magistrates*. The appointment of Magistrates dates back to the *Justices of the Peace Act 1361*. There are now some 30,000 magistrates who hear cases exclusively in the Magistrates Court, trying some 95 per cent of all criminal cases. These consist of summary or 'either way' offences which are not tried in the Crown Court. However, in indictable cases the Magistrates must hold a preliminary, or committal, hearing to decide whether there is sufficient evidence to justify transfer of the case to the Crown Court.

- *The police*. In most instances the forensic archaeologist will have been brought into the investigation by the police. This is the group of professionals with whom the archaeologist is likely to have the closest working relationship (see Chapter 7, Section 7.2).

- *Experts*. Various experts may be involved in the forensic examination of a crime (see Chapter 1, Section 1.3), some may be members of professional bodies, and all will expect to be paid fees for their professional services. In most cases, experts in court are paid from central government funds (prosecution costs) or by the Criminal Defence Service (defence costs). Forensic archaeologists should, at the outset of a case, clarify the basis on which they are to be paid, irrespective as to whether they are instructed by the prosecution or by the defence.

7.2 The investigation of crime

The *Police Act 1996* consolidated earlier legislation and dealt with the organisation and supervision of the police, as well as ancillary matters (for background, see Hunter and Knupfer 1996). Britain has no national police force as such, but there are currently 43 police areas in England and Wales, together with a further 8 in Scotland, each of which is responsible to its own police authority (mainly through Local Authority election). The 1996 Act imposed a duty on every police authority to secure and maintain an efficient police force for its area. Police authorities are empowered to set local police objectives after consulting the Chief Constable (or in the case of the Metropolitan Police Force, the Commissioner) and by considering the views of the community on policing in the area. Each force has the responsibility for controlling its own budget, deciding on appropriate levels of manpower and recruitment, and allocating priorities. Although policing is carried out on a local basis, there is also a National Criminal Intelligence Service (NCIS) whose function is to gather and distribute intelligence to police forces, and a National Crime Squad (NCS) whose function is to prevent and detect serious crime which spreads across local and regional boundaries. Furthermore, the Home Secretary exercises overall responsibility for many of the functions under the Act.

The legal basis of police powers formerly rested on a variety of common law and statutory provisions which have been reviewed over recent years by various commissions and enquiries. The *Royal Commission on Criminal Procedure 1978* (reporting in 1981) led to major changes in police powers which were enacted in the *Police and Criminal Evidence Act 1984* (uniformly known as PACE). *The Prosecution of Offences Act 1985* saw the establishment of the Crown Prosecution Service (CPS). The purpose of the latter was to separate the investigative functions of the police from their prosecuting responsibilities. Henceforth, the role of the police was to investigate and that of the CPS to prosecute. The police and the CPS became independent bodies with different functions.

In reaching a decision as to whether to prosecute, the CPS must have regard to two tests stipulated in the *Code for Crown Prosecutors* (DPS 2002). First, the CPS must be satisfied that there is sufficient evidence to support 'a realistic prospect of conviction' in respect of each charge against a defendant (ibid.: s. 5.1). In applying this objective test, the CPS will have regard to the admissibility and reliability of the evidence. Second, and only if the evidence test is satisfied, should the CPS consider whether prosecution in the particular circumstances would serve the public interest (ibid.: s. 6.1). Should the case satisfy both tests, the CPS has discretion either to take no further action, or return the case to the police so that they may caution the offender; or initiate a prosecution. The legal basis of the police investigatory function is now largely codified in PACE (Figure 7.2).

Importantly, the Home Office has issued five codes of practice (HMSO 1997) under the authority of PACE which contains detailed rules governing the following matters:

Code A. Code of Practice for the exercise by police officers of statutory powers of stop and search.
Code B. Code of Practice for the searching of premises by police officers and the seizure of property found by police officers on persons or premises.
Code C. Code of Practice for the detention treatment and questioning of persons by police officers.
Code D. Code of Practice for the identification of persons by police officers.
Code E. Code of Practice on tape recording of interviews with suspects.

The Act and the Codes together not only provide a comprehensive set of powers and duties for the police but also have implications for the archaeologist involved in the search and recovery of buried human remains within a forensic context (Code B).

The police will be in charge of any crime scene and will have taken steps, including the limitation of access, to ensure that the scene is not contaminated. The investigation of a 'serious crime' (e.g. homicide) is co-ordinated by a Senior Investigating Officer (SIO) who works in conjunction with a Crime Scene Manager (CSM) and other scene personnel. The CSM and the scene officers will advise the SIO on the need and availability of specialist facilities, services, or experts. An expert such as a forensic archaeologist has no independent legal powers and therefore works under the control of, and within the powers of, the police. Forensic archaeologists must understand the function and responsibilities of other police investigators, some of whom may be sensitive to the appointment of an outside expert. They must be aware that any decisions to instruct them, and to continue to do so, will depend on a number of crucial factors including cost (since the expenditure will be charged to the police budget). These decisions may also be influenced by the likelihood of success or failure in using outside

POLICE AND CRIMINAL EVIDENCE ACT

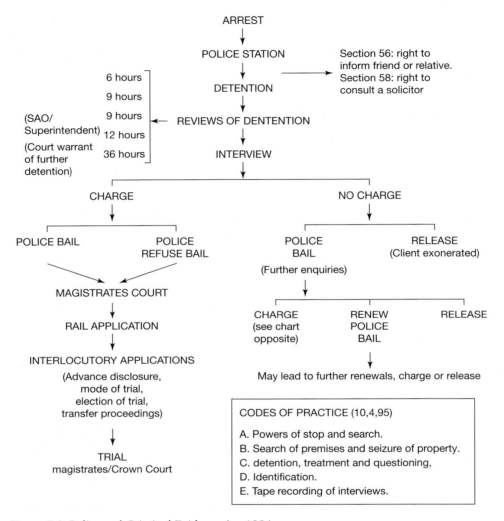

Figure 7.2 Police and Criminal Evidence Act 1984

support, or by the strength of other evidence against a defendant, especially if a confession has been made (see Chapter 1, Section 1.2). The stronger the prosecution case, the less likely the police are to spend from their predetermined budget on the costs of expert assistance. However, in 'major incidents' (and homicides normally fall within this category), additional resources are likely to be available from the Home Office.

In investigations which involve the extensive search of premises, for example, to locate the whereabouts of buried remains, the police will probably obtain a search warrant issued under the authority of a Magistrates Court. This is allowable under Section 8 of PACE, and a constable may seize and retain anything for which a search has been authorised (under sub-section 1) if there are reasonable grounds for believing:

- that a serious arrestable offence (PACE 1984, Schedule 5) has been committed; and
- that there is material on premises specified in the application which is likely to be of substantial value in an investigation; and
- that the material is likely to be relevant evidence.

Furthermore, Section 22 of PACE contains the following provisions:

Subject to sub section 4 below, anything which has been seized by a constable or taken away by a constable following a requirement made by virtue of Section 19 or 20 above may be retained so long as is necessary in all the circumstances.

Without prejudice to the generality of sub section 1 above, anything seized for the purposes of a criminal investigation may be retained:

i) for use as evidence at a trial for an offence;
ii) for forensic examination or for investigation in connection with an offence.

Code of Practice B, paragraphs 1–8, sets out detailed provisions as to the application and execution of these powers of search and seizure – powers which are clearly wide enough to justify the removal of buried remains for forensic examination.

A Code of Practice made under the *Criminal Procedure and Investigations Act 1996* (CPIA 1996) specifically requires that certain material, as far as relevant to the investigation be retained, namely:

Communications between the police and experts such as forensic scientists, reports of work carried out by experts, and schedules of scientific material prepared by the expert for the investigator, for the purpose of criminal proceedings.

(paragraph 5.4)

Where a custodial sentence is imposed, relevant material must be retained until the date of release. Where a custodial sentence is not imposed, material is to be retained for six months from the date of conviction. However, the Code contains no specific requirements for the safe keeping of materials in an environment appropriate for preservation. It could be argued that failure to do this might prejudice the outcome of any appeal.

PACE also confers on the police the power to detain a suspect against his or her will provided that they have been lawfully arrested. Section 30 provides that if a suspect is not arrested at a police station, he or she must be taken there 'as soon as practicable' while enquiries are made. The suspect can then be formally interrogated (unless released before interrogation). PACE provides strict procedures to be observed as to the grounds and time limits for which a suspect may be detained. Detention must be authorised by the designated custody officer, i.e. a police officer who is not involved in the investigation of the case and who will normally authorise detention on the grounds that it is necessary 'to secure or preserve evidence' or 'to obtain such evidence by questioning the suspect' (PACE 1984: s. 37). There are provisions for regular review by an Inspector or by the Custody Officer (PACE 1984: s. 40) of the grounds on which a suspect is detained.

Provided that the above conditions continue to exist in England and Wales the police may detain the suspect for up to 24 hours without charge. In England and Wales, detention beyond a period of 24 hours requires the authority of a Police Superintendent for a further 12 hours. If the police wish to detain the suspect beyond that total period of 36 hours, they must apply to the Magistrates Court for a Warrant of Further Detention. A Magistrates Court may initially authorise detention for up to 36 hours (bringing the total to 72 hours) and on further application extend that total period of 72 hours up to a maximum of 96 hours. The suspect cannot be detained for a period longer than this without being charged or released. This is the maximum time available in England and Wales during which premises can be searched or surveyed without interference by the suspect.

These time limits mean that the forensic archaeologist may be under pressure to produce enough preliminary information to assist the police in their gathering of evidence and in the conduct of their interrogation of the suspect. In those circumstances forensic archaeologists may have to discuss with their professional colleagues from the police and other disciplines which procedures should be carried out as a matter of priority in order to give the best support to the investigating officer in his interview of the suspect and to resolve any alleged crime. Under Code C, paragraph 16.1 of PACE, the police should charge the suspect as soon as the CPS consider that there is sufficient evidence to prosecute. Under paragraph 16.5, questions relating to an offence may not generally be put to a suspect after he or she has been charged with that offence (Figure 7.3).

The most significant of recent scientific developments in the prosecution of crime is the advances made in the establishment of a DNA database. The police have powers under Sections 62 and 65 of PACE to take bodily samples from a suspect for the purpose of analysis and comparison with any samples found at the scene of the crime. It is now possible to match body fluid traces left by a suspect at (e.g. semen, blood, or saliva) with samples taken from a suspect pursuant to the provisions of PACE (above). Furthermore, the police have been granted new powers under PACE which were designed to enable them to build up a national DNA database containing the genetic details of individuals. For a full explanation of the scientific basis of DNA fingerprinting and profiling, including crucial legal and ethical issues (see Krawczak and Schmidtke 1998).

The broad effect of the new powers is that if the police are able to obtain a bodily sample from a suspect, it may be possible to confirm a match between that sample and a crime stain left by the offender at the scene of a crime. Furthermore, a suspect may be identified by undertaking a speculative search to confirm whether there is a match between a crime stain and details already held on the DNA database of a previously convicted individual. A match will be expressed in terms of a mathematical probability of coincidence between the crime stain and the bodily sample of the suspect. This can be powerful, if not conclusive, forensic evidence establishing a case against the suspect. Indeed, it should be noted that a suspect may be convicted solely on DNA evidence even if there is no other supporting evidence (see *R v Adams* 1996).

THE CUSTODY CLOCK (HRS)	PAGE (SECTION)	CONDITIONS	
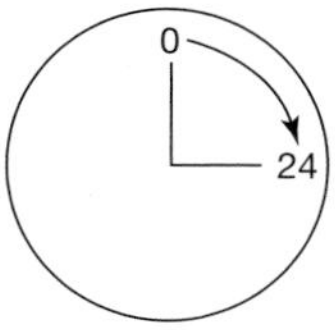	41(2)	1	Custody clock starts from time of suspect arrival at Police Station.
	37	2	Custody officers responsibility to authorise initial detention
	37(2)	3	Custody officer must be satisfied that statutory grounds exist.
	40(3)	4	Periodic reviews of detention: 6 hours, then at 9 hour intervals (from time of initial authorisation to detain).
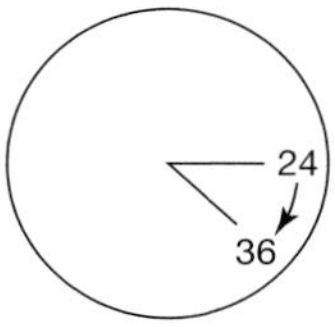	42(1)	1	Further detention can only be authorised by superintendent or higher rank.
	42(1)	2	Offence must be a serious arrestable offence (SAO).
	42(1)	3	Superintendent must be satisfied that statutory grounds exist.
	40(3)	4	Periodic reviews of detention.
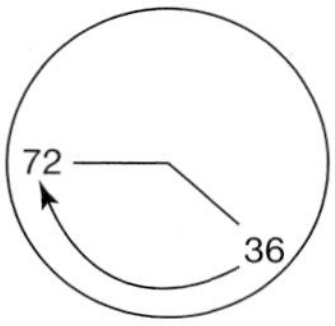	43(1)	1	Police must apply to Magistrates Court and obtain warrant of further detention.
	43(4)	2	Magistrates court must be satisfied grounds exist.
	43(3)	3	Suspect may be legally represented.
	40(3)	4	Periodic reviews of detention.
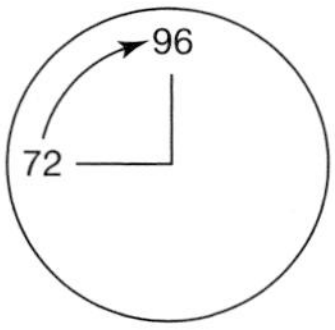	44(1)	1	Police must apply to Magistrates Court and obtain extension of warrant of further detention.
	44(6)	2	Suspect may be legally represented.
	44(7)	3	If application refused, suspect must be charged or released.
	40(3)	4	Periodic reviews of detention.

Figure 7.3 The custody clock

In the case of *R v Doheny* (1997) the Court of Appeal gave guidance as to how DNA evidence should be dealt with. The Court drew attention to three main factors as follows:

* that the testing should be rigorously conducted;
* that the method of analysis and statistical calculation should be transparent to the defence;
* and that the conclusion should be accurately and fairly explained to the jury.

Although this case deals only with DNA evidence, the observations must apply to the submission of all scientific evidence, including the results of any archaeological survey or excavation.

7.3 The expert's report

As discussed above, a forensic archaeologist is most likely to come into contact with the courts and the criminal justice system in the role of an expert witness. However, the attitude of the courts towards expert evidence has often been ambivalent. On one hand, the courts have recognised that in technical and complex cases expert evidence may be invaluable to the court in circumstances where the court has no expertise of its own. However, on the other hand, there has been criticism that the impartiality of expert testimony may be biased towards the party which provides the instruction and the funding, and furthermore, that some expert witnesses have strayed beyond their remit in reaching conclusions which the court has traditionally regarded as its own responsibility.

Nevertheless, the evidence of experts is now being increasingly sought and relied on by lawyers. This may be due to the following factors:

- increased recognition of the importance of expert evidence in some kinds of case;
- the development of new techniques (e.g. DNA);
- more accurate and reliable testing procedures;
- the development of new disciplines (including forensic archaeology).

Expert evidence may be relevant in both criminal and civil legal procedures, both of which are based on the adversarial principle in England, Wales and Scotland. This means that a case is regarded as a contest between two opposing sides, in civil cases between the claimant and the defendant and in criminal cases between the State and the defendant. One of the features of the adversarial system is that the two parties, not the judge, contest the case and decide what evidence to use. The Judge is not there to call witnesses nor to intervene in the conduct of the trial other than to determine whether a particular piece of evidence is or is not admissible, or to give directions to the jury as to what the law is in a particular case. Because neither the judge nor the jury has an investigative function, there is a heavy responsibility on the lawyers representing the opposing parties to ensure that all relevant pieces of evidence are placed before the court.

In criminal cases it is fundamental that the defendant is presumed innocent until proven guilty. The burden of proof is therefore on the prosecution. Defendants are entitled, if they wish, to sit tight, to give no evidence, and to compel the prosecution to prove its case by such evidence as is available. However, if the defendant exercises this right, it is possible that the court may draw an adverse inference, e.g. an innocent defendant would be unlikely to give up his or her opportunity to explain his defence to the court. The prosecution must also meet the required standard of proof, namely, that the case is proved against the defendant beyond all reasonable doubt. The judge will normally direct the jury (in a jury trial) that they must be sure of the defendant's guilt, but that any conviction must be based only on the evidence that they have heard. The defendant is also entitled to the benefit of reasonable doubt. The court cannot convict the defendant if the *only* evidence against him or her is failure to testify at court. There must be adequate supporting evidence from another source, and this supporting evidence may be forensic.

Each side in the adversarial system can decide whether to instruct an expert, and if so, to what purpose. It may be that neither side wishes to obtain expert evidence –

which will be the position in the vast majority of cases. However, it may be that one or more of the parties to the litigation will want to support their case with expert testimony. If each side instructs its own expert, those experts may be in agreement or disagreement (or partial agreement) and in each circumstance the court will have to decide which evidence it prefers to accept. In theory, expert evidence carries no more weight than any other evidence, although it would be perverse for a jury to ignore unchallenged expert opinion without good reason. In common with all other evidence, the reliability of expert evidence will be tested by cross-examination, but obviously the court (and in particular, the jury) is bound to pay special regard to the opinion of an expert in a field which is relevant. However, expert witnesses cannot possibly hope to present effectively the results and conclusions of their investigation to the court unless they are adequately prepared for the trial.

It is a fundamental principle of procedure in relation to expert evidence that each side must disclose to the other *before the trial* any expert evidence on which it intends to rely. In both civil and criminal cases, rules of court have been made to ensure that this procedure is observed. In Crown Court cases these are embodied in the *Crown Court (Advance Notice of Expert Evidence) Rules 1987* (Figure 7.4), and corresponding Rules have been introduced in the Magistrates Court. In practice, this means that before the trial the expert witness must produce a written report which adequately covers his or her proposed testimony in a format suitable for disclosure to the other side. Expert witnesses must ensure that they have been fully briefed by the lawyers instructing them in order to counter suggestions which may be raised at trial that the expert's report has been prepared on the basis of incomplete or misleading information.

In civil and criminal law cases the report will first be sent by the expert to the instructing lawyer. At this stage, the report should be regarded as a draft because the lawyer may have comments to make regarding both its format and content. Furthermore, the draft carries the benefit of legal professional privilege which means that its contents (though not its existence) do not have to be disclosed to the other side. At this stage the lawyer would have to decide whether to instruct his or her own counsel to consider the draft report prior to exchange of reports by the parties. This may involve a conference at counsel's chambers (offices) at which the lawyer and the expert witness will both be present. It is perfectly proper for such conferences to be held but it is not permissible for the lawyer or counsel to seek to persuade the witness to depart from his or her genuine opinion. It is, however, permissible for the lawyer or counsel to comment on issues such as the clarity of the report; whether it covers all the issues on which the expert has been instructed to report; and what issues are likely to be raised at the trial.

Once each side has finalised its draft report, the normal procedure is that the reports of both parties are exchanged simultaneously as this prevents the 'doctoring' of one side's report to take account of the matters raised in the other side's report. At this point the benefit of legal professional privilege ceases and the reports are now open to inspection by all parties. After this exchange, counsel may want a conference to confer with his or her side's expert on possible lines of cross-examination arising from any perceived weaknesses of the other side's report.

Only the final version of the report has to be disclosed to the other side and then only if the lawyer decides to call that expert as a witness at trial. If the lawyer does not like the conclusions in the report, that witness does not need to be called, and it is

---

S.I. 1987 No. 716

1. These Rules may be cited as the Crown Court (Advance Notice of Expert Evidence) Rules 1987 and shall come into force on 15th July 1987.

2. These Rules shall not have effect in relation to any proceedings in which a person has been committed for trial or ordered to be retried before 15th July 1987.

3. — (1) Following the committal for trial of any person, or the making of an order for his retrial, if any party to the proceedings proposes to adduce expert evidence (whether of fact or opinion) in the proceedings (otherwise than in relation to sentence) he shall as soon as practicable, unless in relation to the evidence in question he has already done so —

(a) furnish the other party or parties with a statement in writing of any finding or opinion which he proposes to adduce by way of such evidence; and

(b) Where a request in writing is made to him in that behalf by any other party, provide the party also with a copy of (or if it appears to the party proposing to adduce the evidence to be more practicable, a reasonable opportunity to examine) the record of any observation, test, calculation or other procedure on which such finding or opinion is based and any document or other thing or substance in respect of which any such procedure has been carried out.

(2) A party may by notice in writing waive his right to be furnished with any of the matters mentioned in paragraph (1) above and, in particular, may agree that the statement mentioned in sub-paragraph (a) thereof may be furnished to him orally and not in writing.

(3) In paragraph (1) above, "document" has the same meaning as in Part I of the Civil Evidence Act 1968.

4. — (1) If a party has reasonable grounds for believing that the disclosure of any evidence in compliance with the requirements imposed by rule 3 above might lead to the intimidation, or attempted intimidation, of any person on whose evidence he intends to rely in the proceedings, or otherwise to the course of justice being interfered with, he shall not be obliged to comply with those requirements in relation to that evidence.

(2) Where, in accordance with paragraph (1) above, a party considers that he is not obliged to comply with the requirements imposed by rule 3 above with regard to any evidence in relation to any other party, he shall give notice in writing to that party to the effect that the evidence is being withheld and the grounds therefor.

5. Any party who seeks to adduce expert evidence in any proceedings and who fails to comply with rule 3 above shall not adduce that evidence in those proceedings without the leave of the court.

Figure 7.4 Crown Court (Advance Notice of Expert Evidence) Rules 1987

permissible instead to instruct a further expert in the hope of obtaining a more favourable opinion. In that event, the lawyer may decide to rely solely on the evidence of the second expert in which case, then only the second expert's report will have to be disclosed, and only the second expert will be called to give expert evidence at the trial.

However, in criminal cases, unused reports obtained by the prosecutor would have to be disclosed to the defence if the prosecutor is of the opinion that they might undermine the case against the defendant (CPIA 1996, Section 3). These problems are discussed below.

It is essential that the expert witness's final report is both accurate and complete for the following reasons. First, as a result of the rule requiring prior disclosure (above), the report will be scrutinised before the trial in detail by the other side, and by the other side's expert (if any) with a view to identifying weaknesses which can be exploited in cross examination. Second, it will be difficult, if not impossible, for the expert witness to depart from the contents and conclusion of his or her report at trial without losing substantial credibility. Finally, the trial judge may exercise discretion to disallow evidence to be given at trial if that evidence raises new matters not covered in the report. The reason for this is that to allow such evidence to be given would effectively evade the rules requiring prior disclosure.

In the criminal courts, there are no regulations requiring the report to be set out in a particular manner. However, lawyers normally expect the report to deal with the following matters:

- qualifications and experience of the expert;
- statement of the issues on which the expert has been asked to report;
- background facts and assumptions on which the report is based;
- description of the materials examined;
- methodology adopted;
- sampling procedures, observations, measurements, tests, recording of results;
- analysis of results;
- conclusions;
- evidence dated and signed;
- exhibits: plans, photographs, tables, source references.

It may be useful to contrast the detailed provisions regarding expert witnesses in the civil court with the lack of such provisions in the criminal court. In the civil court no party can call an expert or put in evidence an expert's report without the courts permission. The civil court also has power to direct that evidence is to be given by a single joint expert. In such a civil case, each of the parties may give instructions to the expert and send a copy of those instructions to the other side. Furthermore, expert evidence is to be given in a written report unless the court directs otherwise. Any party may put written questions to the expert before trial providing this is done within 28 days of service of the expert's report. The content of the report must comply with specified requirements and contain a statement that the expert understands the obligation of duty to the court and has complied with that duty. These detailed provisions were enacted on the basis of proposals in the report *Access to Justice* published in 1996 by Lord Woolf's committee appointed to deal with reforms to the civil justice system (Woolf 1996). If these procedures are not complied with the court has the right to debar the expert witness from giving evidence at the trial (see *Stevens* v *Gullis* 1999). It must be emphasised that these provisions apply only to civil law.

The publication of the *Auld Report* (2002) on the workings of the criminal justice system may well lead to legislative proposals to similarly restrict the use and number of experts in the criminal courts. However, it maybe that such provisions, if introduced, would amount to a breach of the *Human Rights Act 1998*, which provides (Article 6.3) that anyone charged with a criminal offence has the following minimum rights:

> to examine or have examined witnesses against him and to obtain the attendance and examination of witnesses on his behalf under the same conditions as witnesses against him.

The Human Rights Act 1998 is important because it has incorporated into English law the fundamental rights in the *European Convention on Human Rights 1953*. On the issue of the admissibility of expert evidence the court would, generally speaking, allow a national court the discretion as to whether certain evidence should be called or not, usually depending on its relevance. However, the exercise of discretion by the court to exclude a defence witness under Article 6 (3) (a) may be in breach of the general fair hearing requirement in Article 6 (1). Furthermore, it has been held unlawful (and in breach of the general European law principle of 'equality of arms') for an expert witness approved by the defence not to be accorded equal treatment with one appointed by the trial court (*Bonisch* v *Austria* 1987). However, in another case, it was decided that concerns regarding impartiality by a court appointed expert were unjustified (*Brandstetter* v *Austria* 1993). Further decisions concerning the application of the Human Rights Act 1998 with regard to the status of expert witnesses may be expected.

7.4 Disclosure and ethics

A forensic archaeologist who accepts instructions to act for one of the parties assumes certain professional obligations not only to that party but to the court itself. These include an obligation to disclose the existence of relevant material to the other parties, and not to mislead the court deliberately, and to observe duties of confidentiality and to avoid conflicts of interest. In this context, 'material' includes both documentary and non-documentary material. The question of what material has to be disclosed to comply with court rules can only be understood in the context of the actual work undertaken by the expert. As far as prosecution work is concerned, this can be broadly summarised in the following four stages which will have the effect of setting scientific parameters for the investigation.

The first stage will be contact between the forensic archaeologist and the police. The forensic archaeologist, at the request of the police, may either advise on a search strategy and its implementation or alternatively may be involved in the search itself. The second stage is the excavation and recovery of buried remains. Excavation is a destructive process and the site of such investigations can never be reconstructed. The importance of this is that the forensic archaeologist must be involved on site at the earliest opportunity and that all records and excavated material should be retained so far as possible in anticipation of the possible involvement of an expert instructed by the defence.

The third stage involves the processing or examination of recovered material. The forensic expert will need to make a decision as to the material which is to be sampled, decide what processes or tests should be applied, carry out or supervise any work, evaluate the results, and draw any conclusions. The fourth stage will be the selection of information to include in the expert's written report. This raises issues as to the extent of the forensic expert's obligation to disclose in the report all, or merely some, of the data recovered. It also raises the issue as to whether the contents of the report adequately cover the matters on which the expert is likely to give evidence.

The role of the forensic expert for the defence will be significantly different. It is highly unlikely that the defence expert will have had the opportunity of attending the examination undertaken at the scene of the crime. The scene will be fast moving as excavations proceed and even if a defence lawyer has been appointed, it is likely to be some time before a defence forensic expert can be arranged. In view of this, it is essential that the prosecution forensic expert retains as much information as possible for making available to the defence. This should cover all relevant material as defined in CPIA Code 5.5 (even material which the prosecution expert may not consider significant) including detailed site records, drawing/plans, context sheets, and results of any processes, as well as any records of any work carried out by an assistant, including those which appear to assist the defence rather than the prosecution. If assistants are involved, the expert should be able to identify the work carried out by an assistant and if necessary that assistant can be summonsed to appear at court.

The forensic expert for the defence will be engaged in four main activities:

1   Checking the terms of the instructions given to the prosecutor's forensic expert.
2   Checking the results and records arising from the work of the prosecution expert and (if necessary) undertaking any further investigation at the scene or on samples.
3   Clarifying and interpreting the prosecution expert's own findings.
4   Advising on and assessing the relevance and significance of the evidence overall.

The quality of the advice and assistance given by the defence expert will depend not only on the qualifications and field experience, but also the extent to which he or she has been able to undertake the tasks described above effectively. The issue of the advance disclosure of an expert's work is at the heart of the ethical issues arising in these cases.

Rules requiring advance notice to be given of expert evidence in both the Magistrates Court and the Crown Court have already been noted (Magistrates Courts (Advance Notice of Expert Evidence) Rules 1997 (SI 1997 No 705)). However, these Rules apply only to findings or opinions of the expert who is being used to provide evidence in court. They do not apply to an expert's findings or opinions that are not to be used in court.

A wider problem that then arises is that during the course of investigation one side or the other may have discovered evidence which it does not intend to rely on in court because it does not assist that side's case. For example, the police and/or the CPS may come into possession of information which would, or might, assist the defence, or obtain the results of forensic work which might support the defence's case rather than that of the prosecution. The question is, to what extent does this material have to be disclosed to the defence, given that it falls outside the disclosure rules referred to above? This has to be considered within the context of the expert's perceived role.

The courts consider that the role of the expert is to:

> furnish the judge or jury with the necessary scientific criteria for testing the accuracy of their conclusions, so as to enable the judge or jury to form their own independent judgement by the application of these criteria to the facts proved in evidence.
>
> (*Davie* v *Edinburgh Magistrates* 1953)

The factors that a judge should refer to in assessing the credibility of the expert witness are well summarised in the case of *Loveday* v *Renton* (1992).

This involves an examination of the reasons given (by the expert witness) for his opinions and the extent to which they are supported by the evidence. The judge also has to decide what weight to attach to a witness's opinion by examining the internal consistency and logic of his evidence. The care with which he has considered the subject and presented his evidence; his precision and accuracy of thought as demonstrated by his answers; how he responds to searching and informed cross-examination, and in particular the extent to which a witness faces up to and accepts the logic of a proposition put in cross-examination or is prepared to concede points that are seen to be correct; the extent to which a witness has conceived an opinion and is reluctant to re-examine it in the light of later evidence, or demonstrates a flexibility of mind which may involve changing or modifying opinions previously held; whether or not a witness is biased or lacks independence.

From time to time, courts have recognised and expressed concern regarding possible conflicts of interest in which an expert witness may be involved. As the Court of Appeal remarked:

For whatever reason, whether consciously or unconsciously, the fact is that expert witnesses instructed on behalf of parties to litigation often tend to espouse the cause of those instructing them to a greater or lesser extent, on occasion becoming more partisan than the parties.

(*Abbey National Mortgages plc* v *Key Surveyors Nationwide Ltd and others* 1996)

In *Autospin (Oil Seals) Ltd* v *Beehive Spinning (A Firm)* (1995), Mr Justice Laddie said that:

The special respect and weight given to expert's evidence carried with it the responsibility to approach the task seriously and an expert should not be surprised if the court expressed strong disapproval if that was not done.

In the case of *Whitehouse* v *Jordan* (1981), the House of Lords considered the nature of ethical responsibilities of expert witnesses. The plaintiffs had instructed two experts who had prepared a joint report on the basis of conferences with counsel. Lord Denning MR in the Court of Appeal criticised this practice in the following terms:

In the first place, their joint report suffers from my mind from the way it was prepared. It was the result of long conferences between two professors and counsel in London and it was actually 'settled' by counsel. In short, it wears the colour of a special pleading rather than an impartial report. Whenever counsel 'settle' i.e. (a draft) we know how it goes. 'We had better put this in', 'We had better leave this out' and so forth. A striking instance is the way in which Professor Tizard's report was 'doctored'. The lawyer blacked out a couple of lines in which he agreed with Professor Strang that there was no negligence.

In the House of Lords, two of the five judges said:

> While some degree of consultation between experts and legal advisors is entirely
> proper, it is necessary that expert evidence presented to the court should be,
> and should be seen to be, uninfluenced as to form or content by the exigencies
> of litigation. To the extent that it is not, the evidence is likely to be not only
> incorrect but self defeating.

This statement of principle in *Whitehouse* v *Jordan* was adopted by Mr Justice Cresswell
in *National Justice Compania Naviera* v *Prudential Assurance Co. Ltd ('The Ikarian
Reefer')* (1993) into a Code to include the following principles:

- Expert evidence presented to a court should be and should be seen to be the independent product of the expert uninfluenced as to form or content by the exigencies
  of litigation (adopting the remarks in *Whitehouse* v *Jordan*);
- Independent assistance should be provided to the court by way of objective,
  unbiased opinion regarding matters within the expertise of the expert witness. An
  expert witness should never assume the role of advocate.
- 'Facts or assumptions upon which the opinion was based should be stated together
  with the material facts, which could detract from the considered opinion.
- An expert witness should make it clear when a question or an issue falls outside
  his expertise.
- If the opinion was not properly researched because it was considered that
  insufficient data were available, then that has to be stated with an indication that
  the opinion is provisional. If the witness cannot assert that the report contains the
  truth, the whole truth and nothing but the truth, then that qualification should be
  stated on the report.
- If after exchange of reports an expert witness changes his mind on a material matter,
  the change of view should be communicated to the other side and, where
  appropriate, to the court.
- Photographs, plans, survey reports and other documents referred to in the expert
  evidence must be provided to the other side at the same time as the exchange of
  reports.

Returning to the problems that have arisen regarding the extent of the material which
has to be disclosed to the defence, these principles raise questions regarding what
material should be disclosed, and by whom it should be disclosed. The importance of
these issues is that a significant number of defendants have been released on appeal
over the years for failure by the prosecution to disclose relevant material to the defence.

Prior to the implementation of the *Criminal Procedure and Investigations Act 1996*,
the test as to whether material should be disclosed in these circumstances was laid down
in *R* v *Keane* 1994. Lord Taylor argued that the prosecution should disclose to the
defence any material

which on a sensible appraisal, is considered:

(i) to be relevant or possibly relevant to an issue in the case;

(ii) to raise or possibly raise a new issue whose existence is not apparent from the evidence that the prosecution proposes to use;

(iii) to hold out a real (as opposed to fanciful) prospect of providing a lead or evidence which goes to (i) or (ii) above.

The test in Keane followed earlier decisions in *R v Ward* 1993 and *R v Maguire* 1992. Both the *Ward* and the *Maguire* cases held that not only was the prosecution under an obligation to disclose relevant evidence but that this obligation extended personally to forensic scientists instructed by the prosecution. The Court said in *Maguire*:

> We are of the opinion that a forensic scientist who is an advisor to the prosecuting authority is under a duty to disclose material of which he knows and which may have some bearing on the offence charged and the surrounding circumstances of the case. The disclosure will be to the authority which retains him and which must, in turn, (subject to sensitivity) disclose the information to the defence. We hold that there is such a duty because we can see no cause to distinguish between members of the prosecuting authority and those advising it in the capacity of a forensic scientist. Such a distinction could involve difficult and contested enquiries as to where knowledge stopped. Most importantly, it would be entirely counter to the desirability of the amelioration of the disparity of scientific resources as between the Crown and the suspect. Accordingly we hold that there can be a material irregularity in the course of trial when a forensic scientist advising the prosecution has not disclosed material of the type to which we have referred.

It will be noted from this decision that the duty of disclosure applies to a forensic scientist who is 'an adviser to the prosecution authority' and that disclosure will be to 'the authority which retains him'. It follows from this that complete disclosure by an expert to their own side will fully discharge their obligation. Under no circumstances should an expert for one side meet the other to discuss the case without informing, and obtaining the consent of, the original instructing lawyer. The potential problem with this suggestion is that either expert may (unwittingly or otherwise) make concessions or enter into agreements without the authority of either of the parties to the litigation.

In criminal matters the Crown Court will normally list a case for a Plea and Directions Hearing (PDH). The court will require counsel for each of the parties to attend at the PDH and will review progress and procedural issues including those relating to expert witnesses. The PDH will identify which matters are agreed and which are in dispute, particularly with regard to the proposed use of expert evidence at the trial. Issues might include, for example, the number of witnesses to be called; whether their evidence will be oral or in writing; whether reports have been exchanged, and the availability of witnesses for the proposed trial date. It may be that at the PDH counsel are able to agree on various disputed matters leading to a change of plea of guilty by the defendant in return from some concession made by the Crown.

The CPIA supported by a Code of Practice sets out detailed requirements and a timetable for disclosure of prosecution evidence to the defence. The CPIA also requires the defence, in cases proceeding in the Crown Court, to give advance disclosure to the prosecution of the nature of the intended defence to be argued at trial.

The main provisions are as follows:

- Specific roles and defined duties are allocated to the police officers involved in the investigation of the case. These are the roles of the '*investigator*', '*the officer in charge of an investigation*', and 'the *disclosure officer*'.
- The investigating officer has the duty of recording and retaining all material which may be relevant to an investigation, defined as meaning that it has some bearing on any offence under investigation or on any person being investigated. This material must be disclosed by the investigation officer to the disclosure officer.
- The disclosure officer must prepare two schedules listing relevant material which he or she believes will not form part of the prosecution case. One schedule lists 'sensitive' material and the other 'non-sensitive'. The code gives examples of what is deemed to be sensitive material. The disclosure officer must then give those schedules to the prosecutor (i.e. the CPS representative).
- The prosecutor is then under a duty to disclose to the defence any previously undisclosed material which, in the prosecutors' opinion, might undermine the case against the prosecutor ('primary prosecution disclosure').
- The defendant must then give to the prosecutor a written defence statement which sets out in general terms the nature of the defendants defence and the materials on which, and the reason why, he or she takes issue with the prosecution.
- The prosecutor is then required to disclose to the defendant any prosecution material which might be reasonably expected to assist the defendant's defence as disclosed by the defence statement ('secondary prosecution disclosure'). (See Figure 7.5.)
- There are provisions whereby the prosecutor may apply to the Court for an order that it is not in the public interest to disclose material which would otherwise be disclosable, or whereby the defendant may apply to the Court requiring the prosecutor to disclose relevant material.
- Failure to comply with these provisions will result in the Court drawing adverse inferences against the party in default.

The effects of these provisions on disclosure remain to be seen in the longer term. On the one hand, it is a matter of subjective judgement as to the meaning of phrases such as 'might undermine the prosecution case' or 'might reasonably be expected to assist' the defence. These subjective decisions will be taken ultimately by the prosecutor without reference to the defence. The requirement that the defence should give a defence statement is new and arguably imposes an obligation on the defence which is at odds with the presumption of innocence. On the other hand, the designation of individuals with defined responsibilities under the Act is to be welcomed, though as with any routine procedures, there is always the danger of complacency. Furthermore, the obligation of the defence to serve a defence statement can be seen as a justifiable *quid per quo* in return for the obligation on the prosecution to make statutory disclosure under the Act.

In any event, the Act does not affect the legal position of the expert beyond their pre-existing obligations. The Act should, however, focus the attention of the expert witness on certain matters: the obligation to prepare a report for the benefit of the court and not the parties; the need to retain unused material so far as possible for inspection by the defence; the ethical duties imposed personally under the case of *R v Ward* (1993),

DISCLOSURE IN THE CROWN COURT

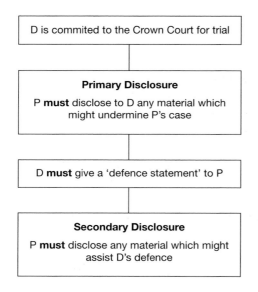

D is commited to the Crown Court for trial

Primary Disclosure

P **must** disclose to D any material which might undermine P's case

D **must** give a 'defence statement' to P

Secondary Disclosure

P **must** disclose any material which might assist D's defence

Figure 7.5 Disclosure in the Crown Court (D = defence, P = prosecution)

and above all the maintenance and improvement of professional standards in acting in these cases.

7.5 The forensic archaeologist in court

In criminal proceedings as serious as homicide, the case will be transferred from the Magistrates Court to the Crown Court for trial (see overview of criminal procedure, in Figure 7.6). What happens next depends on the defendant's plea. If the defendant pleads 'guilty', the prosecution will not be obliged to call any evidence and the expert's report will not be tested in court. However, if the defendant pleads 'not guilty', and on the assumption that the expert evidence is disputed, the expert witness will be called to give evidence. The content of the report and conclusions will be subject to challenge as in the case of any other witness. If the report is not disputed by the other side, it will generally be admitted in evidence without requiring the expert to attend and give evidence personally.

In a criminal case, it is the obligation of the prosecution to present its case before that of the defence (Figure 7.7). The prosecuting counsel will open the case with a short speech indicating what they intend to prove and the nature of the evidence to be given by their witnesses. These witnesses will then give evidence (on oath or affirmation) followed by cross-examination. The prosecution case will have been concluded when all the witnesses have been heard. The defence counsel will then open their case and call their witnesses followed by cross-examination. Witnesses may also be re-examined by the party for whom they are providing the evidence for matters of clarification (below). On conclusion of that evidence, both the prosecution and the defence will make closing speeches, the judge will sum up the case to the jury, and the jury will retire to consider their verdict.

AN OVERVIEW OF CRIMINAL PROCEDURE

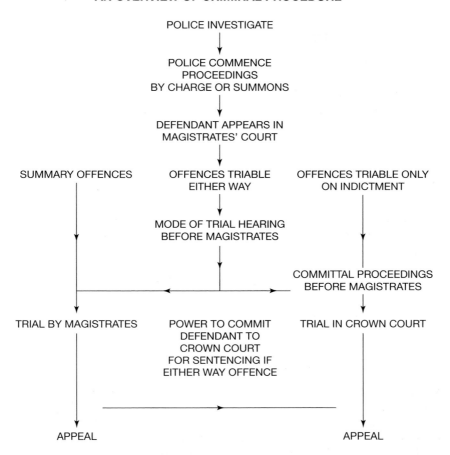

Figure 7.6 Overview of criminal procedure

The manner in which counsel conducts the examination-in-chief will depend on the status of the witness and the circumstances of the case. In a civil case, counsel may deal with this quite shortly by simply presenting the expert's report as their evidence-in-chief and then offering the expert for cross-examination. In a criminal case the jury will not normally be given a copy of the expert's report. It will, therefore, be necessary for counsel to take the expert through their evidence in some detail in order that the jury can appreciate the content of the evidence and form a view as to the credibility of the expert. It is essential that the expert is fully cognisant of the contents of their report because counsel is not permitted in examination-in-chief to 'prompt' the witness by asking leading questions (i.e. questions which are asked in such a form that they convey the required answer to the witness). If there are weaknesses in the report, it may be best for counsel to raise these during the examination-in-chief rather than allow them to have a more substantial impact by being raised for the first time in cross-examination. Experts may, with the court's permission, refer to their report in giving evidence. This

CROWN COURT PROCEDURE – NOT GUILTY PLEA

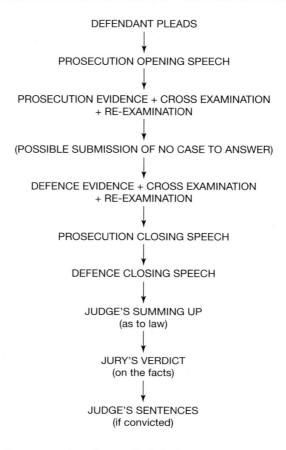

DEFENDANT PLEADS

PROSECUTION OPENING SPEECH

PROSECUTION EVIDENCE + CROSS EXAMINATION
+ RE-EXAMINATION

(POSSIBLE SUBMISSION OF NO CASE TO ANSWER)

DEFENCE EVIDENCE + CROSS EXAMINATION
+ RE-EXAMINATION

PROSECUTION CLOSING SPEECH

DEFENCE CLOSING SPEECH

JUDGE'S SUMMING UP
(as to law)

JURY'S VERDICT
(on the facts)

JUDGE'S SENTENCES
(if convicted)

Figure 7.7 Crown Court procedure ('not guilty' plea)

is normally granted as a formality. Counsel may ask the expert witness to summarise their evidence at the end of the examination-in-chief.

Effective presentation of the expert evidence is vital. The way in which the evidence is presented will differ according to the nature of the court or tribunal hearing the case. In a civil case, it is reasonable to assume that the judge will acquire a quicker understanding of the expert evidence than in a criminal case in which a jury of lay persons will need to have the evidence more fully explained. Furthermore, in most cases the judge will have had the advantage of reading case papers before the trial. The status of an expert witness will normally carry great weight with the jury but a poor presentation of evidence will lose that initial advantage.

Counsel and the expert witness may have met in conference before the trial and discussed the technical issues on which the witness is to give evidence. It is entirely a matter for counsel as to how the case is to be presented in court. In examining an expert witness, counsel may wish to cover the following matters:

- proof of the qualifications of the expert;
- confirmation of authorship of the report and the acceptance by the expert of responsibility for it;
- by whom, and when, the expert was instructed;
- the terms of the instruction including any background information and any assumptions on which the report is to be based;
- whether the expert visited the scene, or whether samples were delivered to the expert;
- the chain of custody procedures in order to prevent unauthorised access to the material. Were established handling procedures followed?
- the responsibility for retention and safe keeping of material and the maintenance of documentary records;
- steps taken to prevent the material from deterioration or contamination so far as possible (in order to afford facilities for defence examination);
- explanation of the experts decisions as to:
  - choice of material to be sampled
  - the scientific tests to be applied
  - the interpretation of the test results.
- a summary of findings in order to close the examination-in-chief.

Once the examination-in-chief of the expert witness has been concluded, opposing counsel is entitled to ask an expert witness questions on their evidence. This procedure is known as cross-examination. The purposes of cross-examination are as follows:

- to challenge those parts of the expert witness's testimony which are in dispute;
- to undermine the credibility of the expert witness in the eyes of the jury;
- to elicit facts from the expert witness which may advance the cross-examiner's own case;
- to clarify which facts are in dispute and which are not (in order to assist the court).

Counsel is not obliged to cross-examine a witness except on those matters which are in dispute. In that event, counsel must cross-examine on any disputed matters in order that the Court will have all the available information in order to come to a decision. Cross-examination is a skilled art on the part of the lawyer, and success depends far more on thorough preparation than on inspiration on the day. An expert witness should assume that the opposing counsel will be fully briefed on the technical issues and on any weaknesses in the expert's own report. The barrister may well be a skilled questioner and will be allowed considerable latitude in the conduct of the cross-examination, especially where expert evidence is concerned. Leading questions *are* permitted in cross-examination. Common techniques used to attack the credibility of an expert witness are:

- Challenging the qualifications and experience of the expert. If the expert can be shown not to be a proper expert in the field, then their evidence may be fatally weakened and may be disallowed entirely.

  If this issue is raised, the expert will have to convince the court of his or her status as an expert. There are no prescribed qualifications for an expert, although the Council for the Registration of Forensic Practitioners has defined 'competence' in a number of specified fields (including forensic archaeology and forensic anthropology). It is more a matter of demonstration that the 'expert' has a genuine expertise in the relevant field. Evidence of formal academic qualifications, published research, experience gained in similar cases and membership of an appropriate professional body may all be relevant. Some experts may be members of the Academy of Experts or of the Expert Witness Institute. It is a matter for the judge, after hearing submissions from both sides, to decide as to whether the evidence is admissible as expert evidence.

It may be important to establish that the expert is indeed an expert in the relevant field, in order to avoid the impact of the rules preventing *hearsay* or *opinion* evidence from being submitted to the court. *Hearsay* evidence is essentially evidence presented to the court of a statement made by one person to another outside the court. Evidence of hearsay is generally not allowed. Evidence of *opinion* will be based on the experience and information obtained in practice from extraneous sources such as text books, articles and journals. The testimony of an expert witness is likely to include both *hearsay* and *opinion* evidence, given that the entire purpose of calling experts is to allow them to express opinions and to test their validity in court. Both *hearsay* and *opinion* evidence are therefore allowed in the case of an expert.

- Challenging the validity of the facts on which the expert's opinion is based. If it can be shown that the expert's investigation ignores relevant facts or other evidence, then any conclusion reached by the expert will be suspect. In order to counter this, experts should ensure that they have full details of the factual background in their letter of engagement and that they are kept up to date with issues of fact as they arise.
- Challenging the reliability of procedures relating to the collection, testing, recording and handling of materials and samples. There are no legal rules as such which prescribe how the expert should deal with these matters, but expert evidence may be fatally weakened, if for example, the expert witness is unable to prove a complete 'chain of custody' in the handling of samples, or, alternatively, if it can be shown that samples may have become contaminated in transit. Failure to observe routine handling procedures is likely to be punished by a legal challenge based on allegations of possible interference with the integrity of the evidence, the inability to make such evidence available for inspection by the expert in default, and the portrayal of that expert as careless or incompetent thereby affecting the credibility of his evidence as a whole. The existence of established procedures, and the extent to which they have been complied with in particular cases should be explained in the report.
- Demonstrating that a genuine difference of opinion exists between the experts on an unresolved issue. This technique depends on showing that the current state of scientific knowledge on a relevant issue is incomplete and that there is room for a genuine and reasonable difference of opinion between experts. The defence counsel will exploit such differences by submitting that the defendant is entitled to the benefit of any reasonable doubt.

A witness who has been cross-examined may be re-examined by the party who called him or her to give evidence. The object of re-examination is to clarify matters which were raised for the first time in cross-examination. This is permitted as it is clearly impossible for the party examining the witness to anticipate every point that might be put in cross-examination. Subject to the discretion of the judge, questions may not be asked in re-examination on matters which should have been raised in the examination-in-chief. The right to re-examine cannot therefore be used to repair a defective examination-in-chief. The same rules of evidence apply to re-examination as to examination-in-chief.

To summarise, the forensic archaeologist instructed as an expert witness is more than just an expert in that field. He or she must also be an effective communicator, able to competently present evidence in the unfamiliar surroundings of the court room and be able to justify opinions under rigorous cross-examination. He or she must also possess personal qualities of integrity and independence at the highest level (see Chapter 1, Section 1.5). Although part of one side in an adversarial contest, experts have an obligation to the court to act in an unbiased and professional manner and their opinion must not be influenced by the pressures of litigation. It is likely, following the publication of the Auld Report (2002), that these rules will be reinforced in an attempt to increase the standards of professionalism integrity and independence on the part of all expert witnesses.

7.6 Human rights and the International Criminal Court

Archaeologists have been involved in the excavation of mass grave sites in a number of countries, most notably in Bosnia, following the civil war in the former Yugoslavia. Such excavations may produce evidence to support the prosecution of individuals for war crimes or genocide. Under International Law (see Kittichaisaree 2001), certain crimes including war crimes and genocide, are regarded as so destructive of the international order that any State may exercise jurisdiction to prosecute them irrespective of where the crime takes place and the nationality of the accused person.

The prosecution of war crimes dates back to the Nuremberg and Tokyo International Military Tribunals of 1945/1948 in which individuals were prosecuted for the offences of Crimes against Peace, Crimes against Humanity, and Crimes under the Laws of War. The significance of these tribunals was to affirm that individual persons could be held responsible for such crimes. According to the Nuremberg Tribunal (1945): 'Crimes against international law are committed by men, not by abstract entities, and only by punishing individuals who commit such crimes can the provisions of international law be enforced.' The view that individuals could be held directly responsible is affirmed in the *Convention on Prevention and Punishment of the Crime of Genocide 1948* (adopted by the UN General Assembly on 9 December 1948). Article 2 of the Convention defines genocide in terms of specific acts committed with intent to destroy, in whole or in part, a national ethnic, racial or religious group. Article 4 provides that persons committing genocide should be punished whether they are constitutionally responsible rulers, public officials, or private individuals. Article 6 provides that persons charged with genocide should be tried by a competent tribunal of the State in the territory in which the act was committed. In the UK the *Genocide Act 1969* gave effect to the Genocide Convention.

As a result of the atrocities committed during the mid-1990s in both the former Yugoslavia and in Rwanda, the UN took action under the Genocide Convention. Under the authority of *UN Security Council Resolution 827 (1993)* an *ad hoc* International Tribunal was set up to prosecute violation of International Humanitarian Law in the former Yugoslavia – the International Criminal Tribunal for Yugoslavia (ICTY). Similarly, under the authority of Resolution 955 (1994), the UN Security Council set up a parallel *ad hoc* Tribunal with regard to Rwanda – the International Criminal Tribunal for Rwanda (ICTR). The ICTR had the same prosecutor and appeal judges as the ICTY but had separate trial judges. Cases in these two war crimes tribunals are heard before international judges sitting in The Hague. Evidence is being collected under the auspices of a Commission of Experts appointed by the Security Council, although there are considerable difficulties in bringing individuals to trial.

The latest development in this field is the establishment in July 1998 of a permanent war crimes tribunal (the International Criminal Court). The ICC emerged from an International Conference which took place in Rome in 1998 where there was overwhelming support for the adoption of a Statute (the Rome Statute) for an International Criminal Court (ICC) by votes in favour of 120, with 21 abstentions, and 7 states (including the USA) voting against. By April 2002, the necessary ratifications had taken place and the court came into existence in July that year. The ICC is a permanent body, thereby avoiding the necessity in future of setting up *ad hoc* tribunals such as those dealing with Yugoslavia and Rwanda. Also based in The Hague, the ICC has an independent prosecutor able to investigate war crimes, genocide, and crimes against humanity with the power to question witnesses, and seek the co-operation of state authorities. The court can impose up to 30 years imprisonment, fines, and forfeiture orders (seizing the property of the convicted defendant) but has no power to impose the death penalty.

The court will operate under *Rules of Procedure and Evidence* (ICC 2002). Those rules which may be of particular significance to the forensic archaeologist are:

> *Rule 10*: The responsibility of the prosecutor for the retention, storage and security of information and physical evidence obtained in the course of the investigations by his office.
> *Rule 17*: The establishment of a Victims and Witnesses Unit to provide security, training, a code of conduct, and assistance and support.
> *Rule 76*: The obligation on the prosecutor to provide the defence with the names of witnesses whom the prosecutor intends to call to testify and copies of any prior statements made by those witnesses.
> *Rule 77*: The disclosure by the prosecutor to the defence of any books, documents, photographs and any other tangible objects in the possession or control of the prosecutor which are material to the preparation of the defence.
> *Rule 87*: Protective measures to protect a witness at risk on account of their testimony.

Inter-state negotiations may lead to the kind of curious arrangements made in the Lockerbie case to prosecute the Libyan defendants in a court situated in The Hague but applying the principles of Scottish law. Forensic archaeologists cannot possibly acquire a detailed expertise in the rules and procedures of every state's legal system. They should, however, be able to rely on the advice of those instructing them on the procedural intricacies of the case.

The investigation and prosecution of such matters – war crimes, genocide and crimes against humanity – have been given a recent boost on the domestic front by the *Human Rights Act 1998* which focuses attention on these issues and may lead to a change of culture by the UK courts, and on the international front by the ratification of the new International Criminal Court. Further, international public opinion, particularly in these days of instantaneous communication, should not be overlooked as another powerful force supporting the bringing to justice of individuals charged with appalling crimes. In all this, forensic archaeologists, as experts in their field, have an increasingly important role to play in the enforcement of human rights.

References

Auld Report. 2002. *Review of the Criminal Courts of England and Wales*. London: HMSO.

CPIA. 1996. *Criminal Procedure and Investigations Act*. C.25. London: HMSO.

DPP 2002. Department of Public Prosecutions, *Code for Crown Prosecutors*. London: Archbold.

European Convention on Human Rights 1953. Cmnd. B.969. London: HMSO.

Five Codes (Code of Practice A, 1997; Codes B–E 1995) 1997. London: HMSO.

Hunter, J. R. and Knupfer, G C. 1996. 'The police and judicial structure in Britain', in Hunter, J. R., Roberts, C.A. and Martin, A. (eds) *Studies in Crime: An Introduction to Forensic Archaeology*, London: Routledge, pp. 24–39.

ICC 2002. *International Criminal Court Rules of Procedure and Evidence 2002*, The Hague: ICC.

Kittichaisaree, K. 2001. *International Criminal Law*, Oxford: Oxford University Press.

Krawczak, M. and Schmidtke, J. 1998. *DNA Fingerprinting*, 2nd edn, Oxford: BIOS Scientific Publishers Ltd.

Royal Commission in Criminal Procedure 1978. Cmnd. 8092. London: HMSO.

Woolf 1996. Woolf Report, *Access to Justice*, London: HMSO.

Cases cited

Abbey National Mortages plc v *Key Surveyors Nationwide Ltd and Others* [1996], 3 All ER 184.

Autospin (Oil Seals) Ltd v *Beehive Spinning (A Firm)*, TLR 9 August 1995.

Bonisch v *Austria* (1987), 9 EHRR 191.

Brandstetter v *Austria* (1993), 15 EHRR 378.

Davie v *Edinburgh Magistrates* (1953), SC 34.

Loveday v *Renton and another* [1992], 3 All ER 184.

R v *Adams* (1996), 2 Cr App Rep 467.

R v *Keane* (1994), 2 All ER 478.

R v *Maguire* (1992), 2 All ER 433.

R v *Ward* (1993), 2 All ER 577.

R v *Doheny* [1997], 1 Cr App Rep 369.

Stevens v *Gullis* TLR 6 October 1999.

Whitehouse v *Jordan* [1981], 1 All ER 267.

8

SOCIAL AND INTELLECTUAL FRAMEWORKS

[P]ursuing science also involves moral considerations . . . a good result may be badly used, as it is well known that even good ends pursued with good will may have bad consequences . . . if we want science to be harmoniously integrated with all other dimensions of our life, and be responsible men (and women) and not slaves of our own creation, then we have to supervise science.

(Petra 1989: 67)

This final chapter considers some underlying reasons why forensic archaeology and anthropology are such popular subjects within the UK and internationally, and how they sit within a wider social and ethical framework (see also Cox 2001). Neither is simple to define. Popularity is ostensibly a result of archaeologists and anthropologists responding to a need to deploy familiar principles and techniques within the judicial system; it allows them to enhance criminal investigation procedures and provides some satisfaction in contributing to society. Conversely, the perceived lack of support for, and interest in, forensic archaeology from within the traditional discipline of archaeology, suggests that the readiness of increasing numbers of archaeologists to participate in this new discipline has a more fundamental basis (see, for example, the recent establishment of 'Archaeologists for Human Rights'; http 1). With respect to ethics, there is no lesser difficulty in establishing, within an existing context of ethics and codes, a framework for these new disciplines. These are challenging and complex areas for a profession accustomed to dealing with anonymous human remains without living relatives. Further, they present particular challenges to those used to operating under a relatively minimum of legal constraints, with no particular implication regarding their findings or the manner by which results are achieved.

8.1 The social framework

There are four main issues of possible relevance and these are discussed in full elsewhere (Cox 2001). This section repeats and expands aspects of these and summarises others in order to place them within the broader context of the volume. All four are interlinked and reflect the fact that archaeologists are products of, and are defined by, their place and time. As such, they all share concerns and preconceptions common to the general public in an arena of increasing globalisation. The first two consider the role of media reporting and popular culture respectively in biasing and defining perceptions of forensic reality (McNeely 1995), and the third questions the extent to which forensic archaeologists have a responsibility to empower the present through their work. The final issue examines the viewpoint that, in an environment of sanitised developer-led processes, traditional archaeology no longer presents opportunities for making a significant social or intellectual contribution.

Between them, these underlying themes have caused forensic archaeology and anthropology to become focal points of interest in both the UK and elsewhere. More and more archaeologists and anthropologists now call themselves 'forensic' practitioners, possibly attracted by an image that engenders (to the uninitiated) a *frisson* of immediacy, importance and risk. This interest is matched by a burgeoning number of programmes bearing the label 'forensic' at different levels within UK universities and the high demand for places on such courses from students of all nationalities. However, few of these present or future practitioners are likely to have any real understanding of the full implications of working within the criminal justice system (Cox 1998) or of becoming involved in the investigation of war crimes. Nor can they initially understand the full responsibilities inherent in such a role. Further to that is that some individuals seem to persist in the use of the term 'forensic' when applied to archaeology when they simply mean 'scientific'.

Like a new craze, forensic archaeology and forensic anthropology progress through certain phases of growth (Penrose 1952), developing in harness with law enforcement agencies and providing mutual opportunities. This process continues until such time as a resolution is achieved and archaeology and anthropology find their natural level and status in the investigative process. This point has yet to be achieved. A common psychological response to being involved in this type of development, even in a professional environment, is a feeling of power (ibid.) and control. Furthermore, given that participation in this new arena can also play a significant, if limited role in solving crime, the participants are likely to achieve a sense of heightened self-esteem as well as a significant measure of personal satisfaction.

Examination of statistics demonstrates that the incidence of reported crime is increasing in Western society. This is particularly the case for the crime that most often engages the forensic archaeologist: murder (an emotive term used to describe homicide and illegal killing) and the associated concealment of evidence. Similarly, with global communications and the effective activity and reporting of human rights by agencies such as Human Rights Watch, incidents of mass-murder, war crimes and genocides are increasingly and more widely reported. The terms 'murder' and 'genocide' invoke contradictory impulses in most people. They conflate evil and innocence, frenzy and restraint, passion and deliberation (Taylor 1998); they also reinforce ideas about so-called civil societies where reason and law underline essential stability. The past century saw the unlawful killing of over 200 million civilians by governments (Rummel 1997) and in this new millennium civilians continue to die. In such places as Liberia, Côte D'Ivoire, Ethiopia, the Democratic Republic of the Congo (DRC), the Darfur region of Sudan and in politically inspired 'disappearances' elsewhere, the unchecked slaughter of civilians appears to evoke very little response from the international community at large (see http 2–6).

In a shift of international perspectives and values, major states are now becoming forced into awareness of their humanitarian responsibilities, partly through increased globalisation, but equally through the growing threat of international terrorism marked by successful attacks on New York and Washington in 2001, Madrid in 2004 and

London in 2005. While this awareness might also reflect high levels of strategic or economic self-interest (and cause intervention in some countries, for example, Afghanistan and Iraq, but not others), it at least demonstrates the creation of a climate in which genocide and war crimes are being recognised and solutions actively being sought. One positive outcome of this new climate, and which is manifest in the creation of the ICC (see Chapter 7, Section 7.6), is the growing consensus that applying a rigorous legal process can act in the interest of justice and can serve as a deterrent against future atrocities. That archaeologists and anthropologists want to play a role in this movement is evidenced by the burgeoning number of teams now involved, for example, the Guatamalan Forensic Anthropology Team, the Argentinian Forensic Anthropology Team, Physicians for Human Rights, the International Commission for Missing Persons, the Centre for International Forensic Assistance and the Inforce Foundation.

8.1.1 The reporting of crime

Fortunately, most individuals and most traditional archaeologists and biological anthropologists never have to confront the reality or consequences of murder or genocide at first hand. Nor are they likely to have any real appreciation of the processes of criminal investigation and the trial of alleged perpetrators in the courts. Consequently, their perception of homicide and mass murder is inevitably influenced, biased and to some extent defined, by media reporting of incidents. In the case of homicide, this is extended through the depiction of crime in popular culture, although the investigation of genocide has yet to be exposed to the pen of the crime writer or TV/film producer as a significant component of a literary or cinematic genre.

Forensic journalism is as close as many archaeologists and anthropologists come to understanding the social- and media-constructed context of the types of serious crime that they might be asked to engage with. Although most individuals exercise selectivity in their reading and viewing, what they are exposed to is processed within the context of their own perspectives, opinions and experiences (Sanders and Lyon 1995), and the wider picture is not always apparent. In June 2003, for example, UK television viewers were presented with images of chaos as Iraqis were shown exhuming their dead from mass graves, and this evoked much reaction from international forensic organisations. However, the reality of this situation was extremely short-lived and became rapidly replaced by a more dignified and highly organised process undertaken by the same communities (Figure 8.1). One of the authors who was present (MC), identified a disinterest by the media in screening a different perspective than that of 'unrestrained chaos'. Presumably this was either 'not newsworthy' or failed to conform to the story which had been commissioned. In such circumstances there is a real danger that the media can effectively impose western nationalist values of process and justice on a community whose right to determine their own process is paramount and which may be disregarded for media purposes. Media messages are undoubtedly an important factor in the determination of public perception of criminal behaviour and the investigation of crime, and can have an extensive impact. The same messages provide stereotypical images which may be used for political purpose: they can cultivate a belief that the larger social environment is dangerous, unrestrained and frightening (ibid.: 25).

Although forensic journalism reports the details of crime and its resolution, it often fails to place such descriptions within adequate and objective discussion of the socially

Figure 8.1 Remains collected and wrapped in 'shroud bundles' near Musayib, in Iraq. These were then removed to a community hall in the town. Bereaved individuals examine clothing and other materials within the bundle and if recognised, their missing relative's details are checked against what is assumed biologically i.e. sex and approximate age. The Iraqi communities met in 2003 by one of us (MC) had worked out basic sexing and ageing methods by collating obvious skeletal differences with clothing and by reference to such generally known facts as third molars erupting around the age of 20 years.

Source: courtesy of Ed Burley.

constructed contexts in which they are embedded (Bailey and Hale 1998). Consequently, many consumers of such reporting fail to fully appreciate, or even consider, the wider social context of such crime. Further to this, there is little awareness of the differing processes and significance not only of the processes of the resolution of crime, but also of the meanings of the word 'justice' itself. Justice means different things to different peoples: the meaning of justice varies culturally, and can be multi-faceted and complex. It is difficult for Westerners to understand the effectiveness of processes of justice that differ from their own. The Gacaca system in Rwanda, for example, sits within the control of communities rather than any formally trained judiciary and is, by western standards, unscientific. It does, however, bring with it a traditional understanding of justice and is based upon a process embedded in national culture. By contrast, the International Criminal Tribunal for Rwanda is organised, expensive and more rigorous in process, but to the Rwandese is an expensive use of resources as it brings with it no sense of 'justice' to most Rwandese while the traditional and local Gacaca system does.

Another factor to consider is that the tone and content of some reporting dwell on the horror of crimes and process of resolution, without addressing why such crimes

207

take place, or why resolution takes the form it does. This trend is both complicated and compounded by the increasing tendency for such journalism to be peppered with forensic detail and mention of scientific analysis. Detail of this nature arguably gives reporting an extra edge of legitimacy (ibid.: 126) but it also overemphasises the importance of forensic application, as if such an importance was universal. Reporting and representation of this nature should be a matter of concern to a profession (i.e. archaeology), which by the very nature of its discipline seeks to identify the social context and socio-cultural significance of the material it studies. For example, in homicide cases trends in perpetrator–victim relationships such as sexual asymmetry, or familial ties, are generally ignored.[1] Furthermore, the murder of non-British people is considered to be dealt with indifferently by the UK media when compared to that of British people (Taylor 1998), thus imbuing compassion for humanity with a nationalistic bias.[2] By default, forensic journalists play a role in shaping the parameters within which many of their readers, including archaeologists and anthropologists, actively make sense of the world of civil and war crimes, crimes against humanity, and their investigation and resolution. Their power and influence reflect their place within their socio-political context. There are obviously exceptions, and some investigative journalists present largely unbiased and objective reports of the global events with which this volume is concerned. Their work, however, tends to be exposed to a more limited readership and as such has less influence and power in shaping responses.

Although there are regulatory bodies monitoring the output of the press, it is generally perceived that journalism works within largely self-defined and self-imposed limits that exclude the most horrific detail. It is, however, questionable as to what extent this still pertains given some of the media reporting from recent conflicts. Such censorship as exists inevitably evokes a responsibility that accompanies the 'moral sleep and historical amnesia' that exists when such verbal or pictorial imagery goes unseen (Taylor 1998: 6). Bell (1997: 16) reinforces this with regard to war crimes: 'in a world where genocide has returned in three [now four] continents we should remind ourselves that this crime against humanity requires accomplices – not only the hatred that makes it happen, but the indifference that lets it happen'. Journalism that provides a visual 'architecture of death' (Bailey and Hale 1998: 134) outside of a clearly defined social context is fostering the consequences of social indifference to power politics. The question remains as to where this leaves archaeologists and anthropologists involving themselves in criminal and war-crimes investigations? What moral responsibility does such involvement in criminal investigation bring?

8.1.2 Popular culture

Popular culture carries with it various expressions of this dilemma. In 1996, Arthur wrote 'As subtly as the tide, forensic science has come to pervade our culture. Go to a film, turn on the television, pick up a book, and you will almost surely come across an example of the craft.' Since the 1970s, such programmes as *The Expert* and the long-running *Quincy* have been gracing television screens with images of eccentric but case-solving forensic scientists. McCrery, creator of *Silent Witness*, observed that as the methods used to solve crimes become more sophisticated, forensic science is becoming the new detective, that consumers 'follow the experts like a favourite football team' (1996: 50), often seeking the comfort and reassurance discussed above. Fiction based on crime and punishment captures the imagination where, according to Bailey and Hale (1998), social reality is argued to have its basis. Beliefs about crime are mediated by the social context of diffusion that emanates, not only from the media and popular culture, but also from such organisations as the police, central government and the Church.

There can be no doubt that the current obsession with the forensic sciences reflected in popular culture is a real and interesting phenomenon. Despite an extensive literature in the 1980s on crime fiction and popular culture, there is currently surprisingly little discussion in the sociological and popular culture literature on the current fascination with forensic science. Nevertheless, in the UK, the 1990s witnessed the advent and immense popularity of such television programmes as *Cracker* (forensic psychiatry) and *Silent Witness* (forensic pathology). At the same time, both traditional and new genres of police-based dramas are including an increasing forensic science content (e.g. *The Bill* and *Waking the Dead*). McNeely (1995: 6) reported that in the USA, crime and law enforcement programmes on prime-time television are extremely popular with high ratings. The trend in the UK is similar and the new millennium has seen a burgeoning popularity in fly-on-the-wall crime series (e.g. *Blues and Twos* and *Cops*) and non-fiction series on forensic science (e.g. *Forensic Files*). Cinema films that include comment about the relationship between forensic scientists, society and serial killers also abound, notably Anthony Hopkins' role as cannibal Hannibal Lector in Thomas Harris's *Silence of the Lambs* and *Hannibal*.

Crime writing itself probably has its origins with the biblical story of Cain and Abel, and the use of forensic anthropology with the account of Jezebel whose remains were identified from a few surviving skeletal elements. A fascination with murder and its resolution is evident in all early folklore, in fairy tales and ballads (Bailey and Hale 1998: 5), even in the story of Little Red Riding Hood. The nineteenth century saw an explosion of crime-related genres, exemplified by such masters as Dickens and Wilkie Collins, which has continued into the twentieth century with the strong male protector of social order taking over in the 1960s in a context of unemployment and escalating violence. That the sub-genre of 'woman in jeopardy' permeated much twentieth-century crime literature (ibid.: 11) and persists is an unfortunate reflection of socially constructed gender values, as is that of the *femme fatale*. The 'vigilante cop' made *his* first appearance in the 1970s and the increased involvement of forensic science in solving crime is, perhaps ironically, exemplified in the work of such authors as P.D. James and Ruth Rendell. The creations of such authors as Patricia Cornwell represent a change of emphasis and genre away from traditional policing to increased reliance on forensic science and forensic scientists. Kathy Reich (a forensic anthropologist), writes about a heroine (also a forensic anthropologist), and marks an increased acceptance of less frequently used forensic sciences. Interestingly, one of the first fictional forensic archaeologists is also female (Cameron 2002). Discussion of the extent to which popular culture reflects changes in society and to what extent it might shape society has been explored elsewhere, Cawelti, for example (1976: 77, cited in Bailey and Hale, 1998: 6), considers that literary crime can serve as 'an ambiguous mirror of social values'.

8.1.3 Empowering the present

In practice, archaeologists must be unbiased participants, operating within an ordered and structured legal process. Consequently, they must adhere to certain regulations, ideals and standards, which effectively inhibit any expression of concern or voicing of opinion. Such constraints are generally based on the law (*sub judice*), or issues of safety or mandate and most are well-founded. To flout them would be illegal, inappropriate and unprofessional. However, Tilley reminds us that living in contemporary society is 'to be involved with, and in part, responsible for prevailing social conditions' (1998: 306). Should archaeologists and anthropologists therefore have a responsibility to use their disciplines to empower the present? Should they have a voice and opinion(s) in the debate concerning the political, religious, economic, socially structured and gendered context of crime against both society and humanity, and therefore its investigation too? Moreover, how acceptable is it, for example, for largely white, middle-class, educated Westerners to 'parachute' into less-developed post-conflict scenarios, investigate a crime – to their ideal of justice, and then bale out leaving their garbage, in all its various forms, behind? There is an argument to suggest that involvement without recognition of the impact that such involvement may have on communities could be construed as remnant imperialist intervention and arrogance. By contrast, aid agencies operating internationally undertake impact assessments both before and after participating in projects in the developing world or in post-conflict areas.

Forensic archaeologists and anthropologists investigating crimes against humanity generally do little more than participate in what is perceived as 'international justice' without contributing in any significant way to what the affected survivors perceive of as 'justice' on their terms, and in a way that might be socially constructive. To accept the sense of glamour, risk, excitement and importance that are perceived as accompanying forensic archaeology and anthropology without commenting on the background to the crimes themselves, and their mode of investigation and resolution, at an appropriate time (i.e. respecting issues of *sub judice* and security) is arguably immoral. Equally, commenting adversely on the activities of those currently involved in specific missions without appropriate understanding of context and brief is irresponsible and potentially puts at risk both lives and the processes of justice. As stated at the outset of this chapter, the ethical issues are challenging and complex, and are often difficult to disentangle without a form of 'code of conduct' or 'ethical code' to provide guidance.

Relevant here is the fact that forensic archaeologists and anthropologists rarely participate in criminal investigation without knowledge of at least some of the facts of a case. Such scenarios inevitably move them from a limited and mediated context for crime into actuality and engagement at often unexpected levels. Unlike many aspects of law enforcement and the forensic sciences, non-forensic archaeological and anthropological education and professional development do not provide training designed to remove practitioners from the context of engagement with the past. Consequently, it is difficult, if not impossible, *not* to engage with the perceived context and implications of both the crime and the investigation. Although it is easy to suggest that professionals should disassociate themselves from such matters, it is far harder to put into practice, particularly without appropriate educational and professional support. Furthermore, archaeologists might seek to ask whether they would want the indifference that such objectivity might engender. This objectivity is usually considered the hallmark of the forensic scientist, whose training and sole purpose is to provide data and evidence for the courts. Archaeology, by contrast, conflicts with this view, being seen as a 'system of social relationships in the present within which the production of meanings takes place' (Tilley 1998: 308). Forensic archaeologists and anthropologists have, thus far, largely restrained from engagement with analysis of the wider context within which they are employed. To some extent the dilemma faced is akin to that facing the photojournalist when deciding which images of horror to publish or repress. Taylor's comment on this dilemma is well expressed: 'If prurience is ugly, what then is discretion in the face of barbarism?' (1998: 196).

In the UK there are about 800 homicides annually, yet few attract the attention of the media, and hence the public, in any detail. Those that do reflect as much about social values as those that are largely ignored. Society is generally more concerned with the abduction of the white, middle-class fair-haired and blue-eyed girl than it is with the murder of a white boy of a similar age, or of a child of different ancestry, or indeed of a prostitute or drug addict of any ethnic group. In the UK, reporting of missing girls outstrips that of boys of similar ancestry and age, and both outstrip that of the child of those seeking asylum (D. Lamplugh, pers. comm.). The same can be said of genocide with the unlawful killing of an estimated 200 million people during the twentieth century (Rummel 1997). To most people genocide is synonymous with 'The Holocaust' and the massacre of six million Jews, to the almost total exclusion of any other historical genocide. Few, if any, know or care about the slaughter of Sinti, Roma and Slavs by the Nazi regime that was on a similar scale and part of the same act of barbarism (Brearley 2001). Is this perhaps because the Jewish victims are remembered because they symbolise a component of a 'victors' justice' with many white middle-class victims, while the slaughter of the disempowered and ethnically different Roma and Sinti has been ignored? Reporting of more recent genocides also shows the application of similar value-laden responses.

There can be no doubt that exposure to the scale and extent of aspects of homicide, sub-cultures and 'life' outside those delivered via the press and personal experience, is extremely difficult to engage with. By choosing not to expose the inhumanity of such crimes and the immorality of indifference to many others, particularly in the case of war-crimes and genocides, the archaeologist is arguably culpable of collaborating in the artifice created by the mass media and the apathy of the international community at large. If archaeologists and anthropologists have a responsibility to empower the past, should they not do the same for the present? Should their role in commodifying the recent past, in forensic contexts, be different from those of traditional archaeologists examining the more distant past? Alternatively, should they deny their social consciences and simply deliver data for the processes of criminal investigation? Put more simply, to whose tune should forensic archaeologists be dancing?

8.1.4 Social contribution

The social relevance of forensic archaeology has been explored in depth (Cox 2001) and has considered the development of the discipline in the UK as partly reflecting current fascination with all things forensic, including a growing literary genre and its concurrent expression on both the small and large screen. It is relevant to ask if, in the

211

application of forensic archaeology and anthropology, practitioners are part of a wider socially constructed phenomenon. Are they a sub-group seeking comfort from the legitimacy, and illusionary safety, of applying scientific principles and methods (i.e. supposedly objective knowledge), to acts against humanity? If so, it would be prudent to remember that science itself cannot give evidence in court. It relies upon a third party, the expert, to decide which method to employ, how to apply that methodology, how to interpret the results and give them voice. Archaeology and anthropology may employ science, but most archaeologists became involved in the subject because they wanted to become part of, and contribute to, a developing humanistic discipline. The need for such engagement may itself, in part, underlie their involvement in the judicial process.

Forensic archaeology and anthropology is only ever likely to approximate to a full-time career for a few. For most UK practitioners, it is only ever going to be an adjunct to other employment. This reflects the fact that, fortunately, the UK has lower homicide rates than many other countries. Here, few murder victims end their days in clandestine graves, reflecting a combination of urbanisation, rural topography and climate. Most employment opportunities relate to the investigation of war crimes, crimes against humanity and genocide outside the UK where such work is usually free-lance, contract-based and interspersed with period of unemployment. Yet, despite the minimal career opportunities, large numbers of graduates and archaeological practitioners continue to enrol on forensic archaeology and anthropology programmes at post-graduate level. This is unlikely to simply reflect traditional career aspiration, and may have a significance beyond the influence of the media.

The 1990s saw a change of balance in the rationale underlying assessment, evaluation and excavation in UK archaeology. This has also impacted upon anthropology, and reflects a number of factors discussed in more detail elsewhere (Cox 2001: 154–156). Consequently, the privilege of engaging with archaeology on a traditional intellectual level is one shared by a decreasing proportion of practising archaeologists. For many of those practising within the UK, job descriptions focus on curation, desk-based assessment and field evaluations, and lack fulfilment on many levels. Furthermore, this is coupled with a perceived level of dissatisfaction with the fact that most archaeologists are members of a society with increasing and highly visible socio-economic deprivation and challenges. It is in this context, that the meaning and social significance of a career in archaeology become increasingly challenged. Few of those engaging with developer-led archaeology have the opportunity to become involved in what they perceive as socially immediate and valuable archaeology. Forensic archaeology and anthropology meet this need especially in the context of crimes against humanity, such as genocide, where there are challenges, defined archaeological and anthropological roles, social involvement and job satisfaction.

It is suggested (Cox 2001: 156), that just as the perception by archaeologists of both serious crime and crimes against humanity, and their investigation, are mediated by journalism and popular culture, and by government policy and their responses to contemporary crises, so too is the archaeologist's need to be involved in a socially relevant area of employment. Equally, as architects of, and commentators on, social processes and relationships in the past, archaeologists cannot be impervious to social inequalities, injustices and problems confronting the present. Archaeologists who find that their chosen career is not providing a sense of social relevance, or empowering the present in a significant and valuable way, may leave the profession (indeed many do) or seek their satisfaction in less traditional applications. Increasingly, many archaeologists wish to engage with society and socially divisive problems within society at first hand; contributing to the process of justice offers a mechanism for doing precisely this. It has obvious social relevance, and a sense of control and satisfaction in dealing with threats against both the individual and a wider society. Involvement with criminal investigation undoubtedly brings multifaceted rewards. However, it is also argued (ibid.: 156) that such involvement may bring with it responsibilities that extend far beyond the requirements of the criminal justice system. At present, most forensic archaeologists and anthropologists are largely passive, unquestioning players contributing to the institutionalised silence that surrounds public perception of the social and political context of serious crime, injustice and crimes against humanity. As academics accustomed to discerning the social and cultural significance of material culture, if they decline to apply their broader intellectual skills in this context, the extent of their commitment to humanity might be questionable.

8.2 Ethics in forensic archaeology

The discussion above highlights the complexity and uncertainty of areas of responsibility that accompany engagement in the forensic arena – particularly when investigating crimes against humanity, war crimes and genocide. Further analysis of archaeological motivation and decision-making requires a greater comprehension and engagement with professional ethics. Ethics is an understanding of the science of morals in human conduct delineating standards of conduct and moral judgement. Ethics are also a system of values that have implications for all aspects of our lives, whether professional or personal. In all human cultures some, but not all, aspects of what might be deemed to be ethical issues are enshrined within legal systems, regulatory codes and religious doctrine. While many professional organisations have a code of ethics or 'conduct' for their members, an evolving subject such as forensic archaeology has yet to enshrine such concepts. Archaeologists work according to agreed 'best practice' (e.g. IFA 2002) which may implicitly contain ethical values in terms of behaviour or professional conduct, or they may conform to protocols (a description of what should be done) or standard operating procedures (SOPs – the detail of how the protocols should be carried out) established for practical purpose but which contain underlying moral reasoning (e.g. IFA 2001). Inevitably, the presence of human remains in archaeology has caused the ethical dimension to become highlighted, albeit timidly in some policy documents (e.g. HS 1997), but more openly in the wider-ranging *Vermillion Accord* of 1989 based specifically on ethics and the treatment of the dead in archaeological contexts.

8.2.1 The necessity and context of ethical codes

Forensic work concerns a different type of archaeological context. The question to be asked here is whether forensic archaeologists need to establish a specific code of conduct which addresses the complexity and sensitivity of the work they are likely to be undertaking with regard to contemporary human remains in a medico-legal environment. In providing evidence for the courts, forensic archaeologists (and anthropologists) are contributing to matters of justice and criminality as well as to human rights and humanitarian issues. They increasingly feature in the arena of crimes against humanity

213

such as war crimes and genocide, as well as in domestic murder, and their professional careers bring them into aspects of judicial processes and systems, as well as into areas of experience that involve interaction with human beings at their most vulnerable. Forensic archaeologists will come into contact not only with the recent dead, but also with the bereaved whose rights and needs, as well as their religious and cultural norms, should be considered. The victims themselves will be recovered in a manner which may need to balance practical difficulties, evidential requirements and the dignity of the individual – both dead and survivor. Most will have lost their lives unlawfully, in many cases in a manner that is abhorrent, often following periods of incarceration and torture. In political killings, particularly in mass graves, injustice may be exacerbated by denial of basic human rights or torture according to definitions of the *Geneva Convention* (1949). Archaeologists and anthropologists must learn to recognise evidence of such violations during processes of recovery and analysis. The requirements of justice and judicial processes provide fundamental operating frameworks within which these various issues are constrained, according to country or political climate. This makes it all the more imperative to develop a wide-reaching empirical code of conduct and ethical standards for forensic archaeology and anthropology, both in terms of practice and research. Any such code will need to encompass not only aspects of field practice, laboratory work, report writing and expert witness testimony, but also interaction with the public and the media, teaching, research and publication.

In the UK, the Forensic Search Advisory Group (FSAG), currently one of very few formal UK organisations within which forensic archaeologists play a key role, has the embryo of such a code. As with that of the UK's Forensic Science Society, it is presently short and generic. An initial attempt to contextualise ethical and legal aspects of research in forensic *anthropology* has been published (Thompson 2001) and this recognises and demonstrates the complexity of the situation and the need to give serious consideration to establishing an ethical code. Much of what Thompson discusses also pertains to forensic archaeology which can incorporate, and almost always interacts with, anthropology, hence the two disciplines are discussed here as one. The production of this book in a sense marks a step forward in the maturation of forensic archaeology and it is opportune to consider establishing the outline and adoption of an ethical code. Discussion here is not about general ethical thought or the philosophical source of ethics; it attempts to identify the place of ethics in forensic archaeology and thus predict potential areas of concern, or those which are particularly challenging, that may occur in an operational environment.

It is, perhaps, prudent to review the development of ethics *per se* in this context. Since the abuses of human rights recognised as a consequence of the genocide carried out by the Nazi regime against millions of Jews, Roma, Sinti and Slavs (Brearley 2001), and revealed to the world at the end of the Second World War, a moral imperative has developed to work within acceptable codes of ethics (as well as legal frameworks). This pertains to professional activity or research that involves people, animals, and other life forms, latterly including the environment. As a consequence, such directives as the *Nuremberg Code* were developed in 1947 (modified 1968, 1983) and in 1964 the *Declaration of Helsinki* (modified in 1975, 1983, 1989, 2000). These provided the benchmark for later guidance developed by organisations such as the United Nations *International Covenant on Civil and Political Rights* (Article 7, 1966). Other notable developments included the World Health Organisation's *International Ethical*

Guidelines for Biomedical Research Involving Human Subjects (1993). Individual countries have also responded in developing national initiatives in areas such as medical research. In the UK, these include the Medical Research Council's *Responsibility in Investigations on Human Subjects* (revised 1992) and the British Medical Association's Code (1993). Currently in the UK, regional responsibility for ethical issues has passed from National Health Service (NHS) local research ethics committees to a national system (2004). More recently, and following exposés of scandals involving human remains such as at Alder Hey Children's Hospital,[3] many UK universities, including both those with and without teaching hospitals, have drawn up their own ethical guidelines and regulations particularly in respect of research and teaching. Forensic anthropology has, in a sense, recently experienced its own Alder Hey with the recent exposé of the alleged unethical collection and retention of body parts for research purposes by a member of a UN team working in a mortuary in the Balkans (*The Sydney Morning Herald*, 31 October 2001; *The Age*, 31 October 2001).[4] This exercise is alleged to have been undertaken without the consent of victims or relatives and falls outside any of the guidelines for research as set out in the codes listed above. Fluehr-Lobban's comment regarding the fact that anthropology has tended to react to events 'rather than anticipating the need for dialogue' has been shown to be an unfortunate truth (1991: 15). Anthropologists working through the British Association for Human Identification (BAHID) are now setting codes of conduct and ethics, and archaeologists (if only by virtue of this chapter) are following a similar route. The Inforce Foundation has adopted an ethical code (http 7) that is similar to that described in this chapter.

As forensic archaeology and anthropology develop as disciplines, they would do well to learn from these various experiences and, consequently, standards such as those enshrined within the *Declaration of Helsinki* (whereby all research should be carried out within an ethic of respect for persons and living beings in general, as well as knowledge, justice and quality) should apply to the interaction with, and treatment of, the dead and the bereaved. Furthermore, these standards should extend from professional practice in the field and laboratory into research and education in forensic archaeology and anthropology. This may entail little more than making 'practical adjustments' in order to achieve 'ethical and moral resolutions through a balancing of experience and reason' (Schroeder 1984: 985).

Unfortunately, archaeologists and anthropologists have an unimpressive track record in this arena, not least by virtue of the 'cultural practice' of some individuals in the long-term collection and retention of human remains both archaeological and modern. The legislation here is complex and appears to be governed by the *Anatomy Act* (1984) which specifies that individuals or institutions holding human remains require a Home Office licence, while the *Human Tissue Act* (1961) governs the removal of remains for research. Irrespective of the legal position, the issue of whether individuals' long-term retention of such material is ethical also merits consideration. Ethical values and legal requirements are not necessarily the same (below). Issues of consent and beneficence are also relevant, and local ethical committees offer guidance in this area.

As the new millennium commences, UK forensic archaeologists and anthropologists have now had sufficient experience in their field to apply moral reasoning and develop a code of ethics that clarifies areas of uncertainty, informs the unwary, and can guide the intern. Challenges in undertaking this task include the fundamental truth that ethics are culturally defined (White and Folkens 2000) which is particularly relevant when working in multinational groups, in various geographical and cultural regions, and when involved in the investigation of sites relating to crimes against humanity. Another key requirement of any code is that exemplified by Frankel (1996) whereby the ideal professional community encourages an environment of group and social obligation while still respecting individual freedom. An effective and moral professional community requires the ability to operate within a moral vision and by defining the ethical prescriptions of practice. Lucas (1989) points out that practitioners must function within constraints, but must also accept ultimate responsibility for their conduct. The existence of a code not only supports the scientist but importantly, also provides guidelines by which the outsider judges conduct and ultimately the credibility of the profession.

The *Declaration of Helsinki* specifically sets standards of good practice in research that includes the concepts and guiding principles listed below:

- beneficence – to do positive good.
- non-maleficence – to do no harm.
- informed consent.
- confidentiality/anonymity.
- veracity – to tell the truth.

All these should apply to professional practice and research in forensic archaeology and anthropology, and many are enshrined within legal and regulatory codes (see Chapter 7). However, it has to be recognised that while the law dictates what is legally allowed by the society within which it operates, ethics are concerned with what is permissible from a moral stance (Thompson 2001: 262). It is a mistake (and is naïve) to assume that what the law and ethics consider to be permissible always agree; they do not. Neither is the law the basis of ethics (ibid.).

Without dissecting the ramifications of each of the Helsinki principles, it is clear that on occasions, both in professional practice and in research, these criteria may be in conflict. When this is so then it becomes necessary to apply moral reasoning. Most archaeologists are aware of what is 'right' or 'proper' but for each this will vary according to their background. What remains questionable is whether reliance upon individual integrity, in all its diversity, is adequate for the more complex environment of forensics, and whether the ability to apply moral reasoning is something that is required to be taught?

Most education in relevant forensic sciences involves no explicit teaching on ethics (Galloway and Simmons 1997; Rosner 1997; Congram 2000). Most of the published forensic literature dealing with ethics concentrates on ethics and expert testimony, with texts on forensic anthropology generally only providing a cursory summary (e.g. Ramey Burns 1999: 201–202; Byers 2002: 410–413). However, as the subject areas of forensic archaeology and anthropology mature, it is behoven on those practicing in the educational sphere to extend the context of the advice of Swazey *et al.* (1993). They consider that students should not only learn scientific methods and techniques but also what is and is not acceptable behaviour and the application of value judgement. These values must be highlighted during the educational process if they are to be applied in professional practice (Resnik 1998). There is also an argument to suggest that this should to be extended into research in forensic sciences, that research ethics provide the necessary framework for 'examining the ends and goals that research serves' (Schrader-Frechette 1994: 9).

8.2.2 Areas of ethical guidance

Ethical considerations permeate all aspects of the theory, practice and reporting of forensic archaeology, as do all aspects of work undertaken for either judicial or human rights purposes. Having considered this matter in much depth, we consider that ethical guidance can be broken down into several broad areas, including overriding concerns that govern the component parts. Current experience identifies several themes and sub-elements, and these also underlie the *Code of Ethics* developed by the authors for the Inforce Foundation (http 7):

1. Code of conduct

    - to at all times uphold respect for human life;
    - to act with integrity and honesty in all circumstances;
    - to provide confidential, informed and impartial advice;
    - to practice within relevant current legal and regulatory frameworks;
    - to respect the cultural and religious values of the host country when working overseas;
    - to uphold rules of confidentiality and, where appropriate, of *sub-judice*;
    - to promote the improvement of standards and services through professional bodies, education, research and best practice, particularly in overseas environments;
    - to keep up-to-date with developments in field and/or laboratory techniques;
    - to refrain from issuing statements which appear to represent the position of the profession as a whole without the specific authority to do so;
    - to prevent and outlaw malpractice.

2. Contractual and operational involvement

    - to provide services to the highest standards of excellence within the practitioner's field of competence;
    - to uphold the terms of service agreed at the outset of any contract;
    - to work within defined resource constraints (time, personnel, financial);
    - to set 'reasonable' fees consistent with those charged by other forensic scientists;
    - to refrain from undertaking work on a contingency fee basis;
    - to refrain from taking instructions from any party that are legally or morally unacceptable, or which preclude good scientific practice;
    - to recognise and advise on techniques from an informed basis only;
    - to maintain the highest level of objectivity in all cases and to accurately present the facts involved based on the limitations of the evidence itself;
    - to accept the need to adapt methodology when warranted by particular circumstances;
    - to ensure appropriate reporting and archiving of findings and data;
    - to refrain from working with non-police or other formal investigative agencies or to jeopardise on-going police enquiries.

3. Human materials in the field and in research

    - to accord human remains the utmost decency, dignity and respect under all circumstances;
    - to accord survivors and relatives the utmost respect and have due regard to their emotional, religious and cultural needs;
    - to refrain from removing samples from human remains for forensic or research purposes without appropriate permission from relatives or next of kin;
    - to refrain from removing samples from human remains for forensic or research purposes unless commensurate with legal, religious and cultural dictates;
    - to ensure, wherever possible, that all human material taken for sampling, or removed in the process of sampling, is ultimately interred with the remains;
    - to avoid undertaking research using material or data derived from unethical contexts;
    - to undertake research based only upon sound scientific principles;
    - to disseminate, where possible, the results of research and fieldwork which may increase knowledge or provide beneficial information for future work;
    - to respect the fieldwork, research, and intellectual property of others;
    - to refrain from undertaking research using animal remains outside of current legislation and regulation and without due regard to the environment and public health.

4. Acting as an expert witness

    - to offer opinions only on matters within one's own area of specialism and competence;
    - to explicitly state the limitations of the evidence itself;
    - to explicitly state the limitations of the methodologies employed;
    - to make every effort to use language and terminology that can be understood by the court;
    - to clearly differentiate between scientific results and expert opinion;
    - to disclose all findings, irrespective of their implications;
    - to advise on the work of another expert in good faith, objectively and not maliciously.

5. Education and public liaison

    - only to use human remains in teaching if their provenance is acceptable both legally and ethically;
    - to avoid using human remains in education in any way that might detract from the value of human life and dignity;
    - only to use illustrative material of human remains when necessary in publication or lecture irrespective of the level of the intended readership or audience;
    - to make efforts to ensure that illustrative material will not be offensive from any legal, political, cultural or religious point of view;
    - only to use shocking, explicit or gruesome illustrations where such is beneficial, and only to professional audiences;
    - to make every effort to include tuition on ethics in forensic practice in programmes at all levels of education.

In most respects, these are straightforward issues that would not be out of place in more traditional archaeological or anthropological environments dealing with ancient material. The conflicts begin to surface, however, when they become applied within a contemporary setting, with forensic implications, or perhaps in overseas situations where standards, values and working practices may differ substantially. At first sight, some of the aspects listed above may appear unnecessarily restrictive. For example, it might be argued that the 'end justifies the means' in such cases as the sampling of human remains from multiple graves for research purposes. An opposing view, however, might argue that the victims excavated have already been subject to sufficient violation of their human rights on a multiplicity of levels. Thompson (2001: 263) argues that when dealing with 'modern' dead subjects the four generally recognised principles upheld by researchers (Gillon 1986) should apply. These are: *autonomy* (the right of self-determination); *non-maleficence* (not to cause harm); *justice* (fair access to all), and *beneficence* (the obligation to further the interest of others). These principles can all be upheld when informed consent is given but, by implication, when it is not, they cannot. The use of unclaimed or unidentified bodies, body parts or samples of human tissue entails a lack of consent of the individual and of relatives and as such, no-matter what the potential net gains to science and ultimately to society, cannot be justified.

A further consideration is that such individuals or groups of people often come from vulnerable, disenfranchised or traumatised sectors of society. As such, further abuse of their fundamental human rights (such as those as set out in the *Geneva Convention* and the *Declaration of Helsinki*) is unacceptable even although in the UK and USA it may be within the law (Thompson 2001: 266). UK legislation does not presently cover all areas where remains might be collected for research in forensic anthropology (Thompson 2001) and, as they are not medical practitioners, forensic anthropologists are not, at the time of writing, strictly covered by such legislation as is available. As a result, the need for a professional code of ethics and compliance with medical ethics committees is all the more pressing. However, anthropologists must comply with local and/or national ethics committees (above), which presently exist for specifying protocols for handling human remains (and data pertaining to living subjects) in the UK, even where material is imported from another country.

8.2.3 *Forensic complexities*

It is when the forensic parameter is introduced that a second level of complexity arises, and there is a fundamental difference between the altruisms of research and the practicalities of forensic purpose. Human remains may require recovery, handling and sampling for very different and more immediate reasons than research – for identification, investigation of human rights violations, or forensic evidence – thus introducing potential conflict with ethical *mores*. But which is more important, strict adherence to a code of ethics, or is the forensic context so important that the end really can justify the means? Recovery of forensic evidence is a matter of balance and of weighing up respective values. Collection of some types of evidence may negate the value of other types, and knowing how to evaluate the problems in any given situation should come with confidence borne through experience. A 'mature' and experienced forensic archaeologist should have learned how to discriminate, and can then make decisions on the basis of experience and knowledge. This sounds relatively straightforward but it is not. The wider one's experience, the greater one's realisation of the complexity of the issues that arise. As with all areas of experience, the more one knows the more one realises how little one understands. Consider, for example, whether or not it is more important to achieve accurate identification and a successful conviction, or to preserve the rights of the individual and perhaps achieve neither. Does the archaeologist, the anthropologist or the investigator have the right to make that decision, and what does the archaeologist do if he or she feels unable to accept an imposed judgement?

Although ostensibly clinical, archaeological recovery in forensic cases is rarely straightforward, partly through the state of the remains which may be putrifying, saponified and/or maggot-infested, or simply for practical reasons. For example, some bodies need to be disarticulated in order to understand their depositional sequence in a mass grave, separation of fleshed body parts may be necessary for measurement, DNA requires sampling, and the rigours of the autopsy process itself to establish cause/manner of death may also require intrusive practice for specific purposes. While it is relatively easy to propose a set of codes that might cover these actions (e.g. UN 1995), it is not always so easy to adhere to them in practice. In reality, can a code be written that can enshrine these issues, or is it just better to let the archaeologist or anthropologist work to their conscience on the principle of 'best judgement'?

The third level of complexity is where the archaeologist or anthropologist is confronted with work overseas in an environment where they are not in charge of operations, are required to 'assist' or 'observe', or find themselves in an operation which is under-funded, lacks experienced support and adheres to different laws and values. Whose standards should apply then? Should the archaeologists seek refuge in moral and professional purism and decline to operate in such circumstances, or should they argue that to provide some professional input is better than having no input at all? This dilemma confronted anthropologists working with communities in Iraq (Figure 8.2). In this case, they assisted the local people who were recovering their dead in an 'unscientific' manner; to decline to do so would have achieved nothing while to assist helped to reconcile a few families with their dead relatives and provided comfort and some measure of closure. The archaeologist may be asked to respond to requests which might be illegal under UK law, but which are legal within the country of operation. He or she may be involved in an investigation that, as it develops, requires participation beyond his or her humanitarian and moral terms of reference. Once started, how should this be dealt with, and how could it be concluded satisfactorily? How are we expected to respond?

It is possible to become involved in investigations where the management of the operation may be beyond the archaeologists' control. For example, work undertaken by local exhumation groups without recourse to formal (Western) standards, perhaps without a secure chain of custody or adherence to ethical codes, and with ignorance of stratigraphic importance, grave edges or depositional events. There may be an absence of systematic sampling strategies. Human remains may be left exposed seemingly unnecessarily for any number of reasons – some more valid and excusable than others. Bodies may be walked upon because no other access is possible with the facilities available, the stacking of unlabelled dislocated body parts in bags may be seen as perfectly proper, and isolated bones trodden into the ground may be ignored. How should we react to such situations? Ultimately, the mission mandate should provide

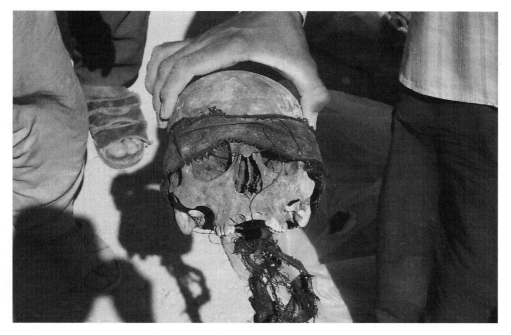

Figure 8.2 The skull of an individual from Al Hilla, Iraq, who would appear to have been blindfolded before being killed and deposited in a grave.

Source: courtesy of Ed Burley.

some guidance as to what to expect and in any event should define to some extent the terms of reference before commencement.

Other challenging areas are, for example, where local people might be employed as labourers to 'excavate' graves for the investigating team. Who are these local labourers? At best, they may be part of the survivor community and will have lost family members; at worst, they will be collaborators in the criminal processes under investigation. In either case, they are unlikely to be impartial witnesses to fact – essential criteria in providing evidence for serious crime such as genocide – by Western standards. Either way, they will be inexperienced forensic practitioners with no significant contribution to the practicalities of a forensic investigation but the potential to destroy evidence. In some contexts local communities may exhume their dead unaided by experts, their main concern being to obtain the return of their loved ones. In such a context, what moral authority has the archaeologist to deny them that basic right? They might consider that they only have a very limited window of opportunity to do so, witness Iraq where many feared the return of the former regime and the subsequent denial of further opportunities. To exacerbate this dilemma, in some less than satisfactory circumstances,[5] there may be pressure on the observer to say nothing but to effectively 'collude' with the general impression that such work is making a significant contribution and is worthy in every sense. This raises another ethical issue discussed above. Should all teams of archaeologists and other forensic practitioners working in post-conflict contexts, consider undertaking how their work has impacted on local survivor communities, a

221

process undertaken as a matter of course by human rights organisations contributing aid to developing world contexts? Should archaeologists consider issues of interaction, and effects of such interactions, between groups with cultural and religious differences and divergent life-styles and life-goals? Perhaps there should also be transparent audits of field and laboratory procedures, i.e. a technical and scientific audit that will also have judicial value in terms of transparency of process.

The sheer quantity of victims and availability of staff or political and financial constraints may have turned the excavation of a mass grave into one of bulk body processing towards an end of mere 'recovery'. Does the archaeologist just walk out, or are there minimum standards to which he or she can turn or endeavour to implement in order to support identification or acquire evidence (Hunter *et al.* 2001)? Is it possible to engage in such work cognisant of the human rights of the deceased and survivors and not behave in a manner that might be deemed to be patronising or neo-colonial in attitude? We should consider to what extent archaeological involvement requires the archaeologist or anthropologist to encourage other cultures to undertake their own forensic investigations? But, if they do, to what standard should these be aimed? In any event it would seem appropriate that the goal should be to empower survivor communities to own and manage their own process of justice, and truth and recon- ciliation programmes through a process of education.[6] Such education may also act as a deterrent and help prevent further abuses of human rights. What should be offered are *opportunities* for training, if required by survivor communities, with a dialogue of net gains and losses so that informed decisions can be made by those presently lacking forensic skills.[7]

What stance should an archaeologist take if asked to undertake investigations for a judicial authority in full knowledge that anyone found guilty on the basis of the case against them would be subject to a death sentence (assuming that culturally and legally this would be unacceptable to the practitioner)? Such could happen all too easily, for example, within the Rwandan Gacaca and national court systems (36 convicted genocidaires were executed in Kigali in 2002). Should a personal or cultural objection to the death sentence prevent an archaeologist or anthropologist from contributing or should they be overruled by a moral duty to help the Rwandese achieve a measure of local justice? This is a difficult dilemma to resolve and one that can set personal morality against professional ethics. However, there is no excuse for not being aware of this particular issue prior to undertaking such work. Is it is beholden upon the practitioner to enquire about contextual information prior to undertaking any mission.

Similar conundrums exist at all levels. Consider too that investigations as carried out by organisations such as the International Criminal Tribunal for the Former Yugoslavia (ICTY; see Chapter 7, Section 7.6) contribute to a process where the Prosecution and the Court are effectively the same organ of 'justice' (a situation which the UK has now avoided by the creation of an independent Crown Prosecution Service). This position continues with the newly established International Criminal Court (ICC) in its present form. Should UK archaeologists and anthropologists feel comfortable contributing to a system of justice which differs from UK or US standards?

The code of conduct and ethical standards listed above is contextualised by reference to the socio-intellectual framework discussed earlier in this chapter. Within the overall structure as presented above, it outlines the broad themes relevant to forensic work which will, to a greater or lesser extent, influence practitioners. They may be deemed by some to be too detailed and too complicated to operate within, but in essence most of what is discussed is about the basic human traits of honesty, decency and respect for others. Undertaking what is usually taxing work, operating within what can be complicated structures of power and command, often in unusual and difficult cultural and geographical terrains, can lead practitioners to lose sight of over-riding basic tenets of humanity while adapting to challenging working environments. The development and adoption of this code, or one along similar lines, is intended to help define and maintain clarity of intent and professionalism, or, as stated above, articulate a moral vision by defining the ethical prescriptions of practice within the context in which we seek to engage.

Notes

1 A recent US study has shown that most (93 per cent) of homicides are carried out by males (Bailey and Hale 1998: 129) and most (79.1 per cent) by a familial relation (ibid.: 127). The same trend exists in the UK.
2 At the time of writing it is less than two weeks since 20 illegal immigrants lost their lives in an avoidable accident in the UK. To our shame, 'jokes' about this incident already abound.
3 Alder Hey Children's Hospital (Liverpool, UK) was the subject of an official enquiry the results of which were published in January 2001 (http://news.bbc.co.uk/hi/english/health/newsid_ 1144000/1144129.stm accessed 22/04/02). Here a specialist was allowed to systematically take organs from children (including foetuses) without the consent of parents and subsequently falsified records. The organs were taken for research purposes but never used for such. This case led to another report, which highlighted the scale of organ 'harvesting' in other parts of the NHS; it revealed that more than 10,000 body parts had been stockpiled, mostly without any consent.
4 It is alleged in these reports that bone and tooth samples have been taken from thousands of the victims of the genocidal massacres taking place in the 1990s in the former Yugoslavia when they were subject to examination in the mortuary. The samples were allegedly collected over several years as part of a research project without consent of the relatives. There may also be legal implications with regard to a verifiable chain of custody if the material ever needs to be re-evaluated.
5 These may arise for various reasons including mismanagement by so-called forensic practitioners.
6 The Inforce Foundation has undertaken three forensic training programmes for Iraq (funded by the UKFCO). It trained scientists and police officers (5 months), lawyers (2 weeks) and scientists and police to be trainers (3 months).
7 Such a feasibility study is being undertaken in Rwanda by the Inforce Foundation in conjunction with local communities, education authorities and the government.

References

Arthur, C. 1996. 'The fall of forensic science?', *The Independent*, 16 May 1996.
Bailey, F. Y. and Hale, D. C. 1998. *Popular Culture, Crime and Justice*, New York: West/Wadsworth Publishing Company.
BBC News. 30 January 2001. Police to probe Alder Hey. http://news.bbc.co.uk/hi/english/health/ newsid_1144000/1144129.stm Accessed 22 April 2002.
Bell, M. 1997. 'TV News: how far should we go?', *British Journalism Review* 8: 1, 7–6.
Brearley, M. 2001. 'The persecution of Gypsies in Europe', *American Behavioral Scientist*, 45: 588–599.
Burn, G. 1998. *Happy Like Murderers*, London: Faber and Faber Ltd.

Byers, S. N. 2002. *Introduction to Forensic Anthropology: A Textbook*, Boston, MA: Allyn & Bacon.

Cameron, D. 2002. *Grave Consequences: An Emma Fielding Mystery*, New York: Avon Press.

Congram, D. 2000. 'Ethics in forensic archaeology', unpublished MSc dissertation, Bournemouth University.

Cox, M.J. 1998. 'Criminal concerns: a plethora of forensic archaeologists', *The Archaeologist* 33: 21–22.

Cox, M.J. 2001. 'Forensic archaeology in the UK: questions of socio-intellectual context and socio-political responsibility', in V. Buchli and G. Lucas (eds) *Archaeologies of the Contemporary Past*, London: Routledge, pp. 145–157.

Fluehr-Lobban, C. 1991. *Ethics and the Profession of Anthropology*, Philadelphia, PA, University of Pennsylvania Press.

Frankel, M.S. 1996. 'Guidelines/codes of ethics: merging process and content', *The Science of the Total Environment* 184, 13–16.

Galloway, A and Simmons, T.L. 1997. 'Education in forensic anthropology: appraise and outlook', *Journal of Forensic Sciences* 42, 796–801.

Gillon, R. 1986. *Philosophical Medical Ethics*, Chichester: John Wiley and Sons.

Hunter, J.R., Brickley, M.B., Bourgeois, J., Bouts, W., Bourguignon, L., Hubrecht, F., De Winne, J., Van Haster, H., Hakbijl, T., De Jong, H., Smits, L., Van Winjngaarden, L. and Luschen, M. 2001. 'Forensic archaeology, forensic anthropology and human rights in Europe', *Science and Justice*, 41: 3, 173–178.

HS 1997. *The Treatment of Human Remains in Archaeology*, Historic Scotland Operational Policy Paper 5, Edinburgh: Historic Scotland.

IFA 2001. *Standard and Guidance for the Collection, Documentation, Conservation and Research of Archaeological Materials*, Reading: IFA.

IFA 2002. *Code of Conduct*, revised, Reading: IFA.

Lucas, D.M. 1989. 'The ethical responsibilities of the forensic scientist: exploring the limits', *Journal of Forensic Sciences* 34, 719–729.

McCrery, N. 1996. 'Murder most fascinating', *New Scientist* 151, 2040: 50.

McNeely, C.L. 1995. 'Perceptions of the criminal justice system: television imagery and public knowledge in the United States', *Journal of Criminal Justice and Popular Culture* 3: 1, 1–20.

Melvern, L. 2001, *A People Betrayed: The Role of the West in Rwanda's Genocide*. London: Zed Books.

Penrose, L.S. 1952. *On the Objective Study of Crowd Behaviour*, London: H. K. Lewis & Co. Ltd.

Petra, M. 1989. 'Should science be supervised, and if so, by whom?' in Shea, W.R. and Sittler, B. (eds) *Scientists and their Responsibility*. Canton, MA: Watson Publishing International, pp. 58–71.

Ramey Burns, K. 1999. *Forensic Anthropology Training Manual*, Englewood Cliffs, NJ: Prentice Hall.

Resnik, D.B. 1998. *The Ethics of Science*, London: Routledge.

Rosner, R. 1997. 'Ethical practice in the forensic sciences to justification of ethical codes', *Journal of Forensic Sciences* 42, 913–915.

Rummel, R.J. 1997. *Statistics of Democide: Genocide and Mass Murder since 1900*. Charlottesville, VA: Center for National Security Law, School of Law, University of Virginia.

Sanders, C.R. and Lyon, E. 1995. 'Repetitive retribution: media images and the cultural construction of criminal justice', in Ferrell, J. and Sanders, C.R. (eds) *Cultural Criminology*, Boston: Northeastern University Press, pp. 25–44.

Schrader-Frechette, K. 1994. *Ethics of Scientific Research*, Lanham, MD: Rowman and Littlefield Inc.

Schroeder, O.C. 1984. 'Ethical and moral dilemmas confronting forensic scientists', *Journal of Forensic Sciences* 29, 966–986.

Swazey, J.P, Anderson, M.S. and Lewis, K.S. 1993. 'Ethical problems in scientific research', *American Scientist* 81, 542–553.

Taylor, J. (1998) *Body Horror: Photojournalism, Catastrophe and War*, Manchester: Manchester University Press.

Thompson, T. 2001. 'Legal and ethical considerations of forensic anthropology research', *Science and Justice* 41: 261–270.

Tilley, C. (1998) 'Archaeology as socio-economic action in the present', in D.S. Whitley (ed.) *Reader in Archaeological Theory: Post-processual and Cognitive Approaches*, London: Routledge. pp. 301–314.

UN 1995. *Guidelines for the Conduct of United Nations Enquiries into Allegations of Massacre.* New York: United Nations.

Weiner, S. (1993) 'True crime: fact, fiction and law', *The Legal Studies Forum* XVII: 3, 275–290.

White, T.D. and Folkens, P.A. 2000. *Human Osteology*, 2nd edn, San Diego: Academic Press.

Websites

http 1   www.afhr.org
http 2   www.web.amnesty.org/library/index/engafr310122003
http 3   www.hrw.org/africa/liberia.php
http 4   www.hrw.org/africa/cotedivoire.php
http 5   www.hrw.org/africa/congo.php
http 6   www.endgenocide.org/warnings/congo.htm
http 7   www.inforce.org.uk

INDEX

Note: page numbers in italics refer to figures or illustrations.

Related titles from Routledge

Archaeology
The Basics
Clive Gamble

'Gamble's book provides an excellent introduction to the aims and methods of archaeology, which is by no means easy within the confines of one book. But to do so in a manner which is intellectually engaged with the subject matter and which evokes the excitement and interest of archaeological work is a considerable achievement. The best short introduction to the subject I know and one which will become a standard text for any teacher of archaeology or related subject.' - *Chris Gosden, Pitt Rivers Museum, University of Oxford, UK*

'The digger boasting the worn stub of a trowel in their right back trouser pocket should feel incomplete without a copy of *Archaeology: The Basics* in the other.' - *Current Archaeology*

From archaeological jargon to interpretation, *Archaeology: the Basics* provides an invaluable overview of a fascinating subject and probes the depths of this increasingly popular discipline, presenting critical approaches to the understanding of our past.

Lively and engaging, *Archaeology: The Basics* fires the archaeological imagination whilst tackling such questions as:

- What are the basic concepts of archaeology?
- How and what do we know about people and objects from the past?
- What makes a good explanation in archaeology?
- Why dig here?

This ultimate guide for all new and would-be archaeologists, whether they are students or interested amateurs, will prove an invaluable introduction to this wonderfully infectious discipline.

Hb: 0-415-22803-4
Pb: 0-415-22153-6

Available at all good bookshops
For ordering and further information please visit:
www.routledge.com

Related titles from Routledge

Archaeology: An Introduction
Fourth Edition
Kevin Greene

'The best one-stop introduction to archaeology.'
Mick Aston, University of Bristol, Time Team

This substantially updated fourth edition of the highly popular, and comprehensive *Archaeology: An Introduction* is aimed at all beginners in the subject. In a lucid and accessible style Kevin Greene takes the reader on a journey which covers history, techniques and the latest theories. He explains the discovery and excavation of sites, outlines major dating methods, gives clear explanations of scientific techniques, and examines current theories and controversies. This fourth edition constitutes the most extensive reshaping of the text to date. New features include:

- A completely new user-friendly text design with initial chapter overviews and final conclusions, key references for each chapter section, an annotated guide to further reading, a glossary, refreshed illustrations, case studies and examples, bibliography and full index

- A new companion website built for this edition providing hyperlinks from contents list to individual chapter summaries which in turn link to key websites and other material

- An important new chapter on current theory emphasizing the richness of sources of analogy or interpretation available today.

Archaeology: An Introduction will interest students and teachers at pre-university and undergraduate level as well as enthusiastic general readers of archaeology. The stimulating coverage of the history, methods, science and theory of archaeology make this a book which has a life both within and beyond the academy.

Hb: 0-415-23354-2
Pb: 0-415-23355-0

Available at all good bookshops
For ordering and further information please visit:
www.routledge.com